Series Editors:
Dario Castiglione (University of Exeter) and
Vincent Hoffmann-Martinot (Sciences Po Bordeaux)

# causes of war

the struggle for recognition

Thomas Lindemann

© Thomas Lindemann 2010

First published by the ECPR Press in 2010

The ECPR Press is the publishing imprint of the European Consortium for Political Research (ECPR), a scholarly association, which supports and encourages the training, research and cross-national cooperation of political scientists in institutions throughout Europe and beyond. The ECPR Press located at the University of Essex, Wivenhoe Park, Colchester, CO4 3SQ, UK

All rights reserved. No part of this book may be reprinted or reproduced or utilised in any form or by any electronic, mechanical, or other means, now known or hereafter invented, including photocopying and recording, or in any information storage or retrieval system, without permission in writing from the publishers.

Typeset by the ECPR Press
Printed and bound by Lightning Source

British Library Cataloguing in Publication Data
A catalogue record for this book is available from the British Library

Paperback ISBN: 978-1-9073010-1-8

www.ecprnet.eu/ecprpress

# Publications from the ECPR Press

**ECPR Monographs:**

*Citizenship: The History of an Idea* (ISBN: 9780954796655) Paul Magnette

*Deliberation Behind Closed Doors: Transparency and Lobbying in the European Union* (ISBN: 9780955248849) Daniel Naurin

*European Integration and its Limits: Intergovernmental Conflicts and their Domestic Origins* (ISBN: 9780955820373) Daniel Finke

*Gender and Vote in Britain: Beyond the Gender Gap?* (ISBN: 9780954796693) Rosie Campbell

*Globalisation: An Overview* (ISBN: 9780955248825) Danilo Zolo

*Joining Political Organisations: Institutions, Mobilisation and Participation in Western Democracies* (ISBN: 9780955248894) Laura Morales

*Paying for Democracy: Political Finance and State Funding for Parties* (ISBN: 9780954796631) Kevin Casas-Zamora

*Political Conflict and Political Preferences: Communicative Interaction Between Facts, Norms and Interests* (ISBN: 9780955820304) Claudia Landwehr

*Political Parties and Interest Groups in Norway* (ISBN: 9780955820366) Elin Haugsgjerd Allern

*Representing Women?: Female Legislators in West European Parliaments* (ISBN: 9780954796648) Mercedes Mateo Diaz

*The Personalisation of Politics: A Study of Parliamentary Democracies* (ISBN: 9781907301032) Lauri Karvonen

*The Politics of Income Taxation: A Comparative Analysis* (ISBN: 9780954796686) Steffen Ganghof

*The Return of the State of War: A Theoretical Analysis of Operation Iraqi Freedom* (ISBN: 9780955248856) Dario Battistella

*Widen the Market, Narrow the Competition: Banker Interests and the Making of a European Capital Market* (ISBN: 9781907301087) Daniel Mügge

**General Interest Books:**

*Parties and Elections in New European Democracies* (ISBN: 978-0-9558203-2-8) Richard Rose and Neil Munro

*Masters of Political Science* (ISBN: 978-0-9558203-3-5) Edited by Donatella Campus and Gianfranco Pasquino

*Please visit www.ecprnet.eu/ecprpress for up-to-date information about new publications.*

## ACKNOWLEDGEMENTS

I owe significant intellectual debt to my 'political scientist' colleagues and friends. Some of them read drafts on several chapters or provide me with helpful comments. I thank especially Pierre Allan, Fabrice Argounes, Elena Aoun, Bertrand Badie, Dario Battistella, Didier Bigo, Daniel Bourmaud, Philippe Braud, Tobias ten Brink, Yves Buchet de Neuilly, Jean-Gabriel Contamin, Jérémie Cornut, Guillaume Devin, Michel Dobry, Charles Doran, Sophie Djigo, Olivier Dubos, Elisabeth Etienne, Christina Ehlers, Jacques Faget, Eddy Fougier, Virginie Guiraudon, Volker Heins, Axel Honneth, Alexandre Hummel, Jean Joana, Jean Klein, Peter Koeings, Josepha Laroche, Richard Ned Lebow, Rémi Lefebvre, Jean-Pierre Marichy, Vincent Hoffman-Martinot, Slobodan Milacic, Rémy Martinot-Leroy, Pierre Muller, Christian Olsson, Franck Petiteville, Patrick Le Bihan, Erik Ringmar, Paul Saurette, Frédéric Sawicki, Claude Sorbets, Vincent Touze, Pascal Vennesson, Alexander Wendt and Reinhard Wolf.

I also thank my students in Lille 2-CERAPS, Paris 1-Sorbonne, Sciences Po Paris and Sciences Po Aix.

Thanks to Vincent Hoffmann-Martinot who encouraged my editorial projects. Special thanks to Pierre Allan.

I am particularly grateful to Ildi Clarke from ECPR Press and Coline Trautmann-Gabin for their able assistance in the formatting and the correction of the chapters.

Several brilliant young political scientists translated chapters from French to English. My most profound thanks go to Michael Ahmed, Matthieu Chillaud, Justin Cook, Stephen Humphreys and Peter Koenigs. Financial assistance for my 'English research projects' came from the CERAPS – Lille.

I owe an enormous debt to Cécile Foulquier, who has contributed with outstanding patience, affection and humour to the maintenance of this project and the 'mental balance' of its author.

Finally this book is dedicated to my son Charles-Louis.

# CONTENTS

Acknowledgements ... iv

List of Tables ... vi

Introduction ... 1

## PART I 'SYMBOLIC' APPROACHES TO WAR

Chapter One: The Struggle for Recognition in Social Relations ... 9
    Utilitarian logics ... 10
    'Psycho-logics' in the quest for recognition ... 12

Chapter Two: The Struggle for Recognition in International Relations ... 15
    The recognition problematic in international relations theory ... 17
    Hypotheses on the link between non-recognition and war ... 27

## PART II: CASE STUDIES

Chapter Three: Losing the War, but Winning Respect? ... 47
    The pacification between great powers by respect ... 52
    War to avoid shame? ... 64

Chapter Four: Saving Face and Peace; the Politics of Recognition in International Crises ... 87
    The Politics of Recognition in International Crises ... 88
    Crises with a Bellicose Outcome (losing face) ... 97
    Crises with a Pacific Outcome (saving face) ... 112

Index ... 159

# list of tables

## Tables

| | |
|---|---|
| Table 2.1: The struggle for recognition as a cause of war | 43 |
| Table 3.1: Recognition, non-recognition and Great power conflicts | 83 |
| Table 4.1: The different aspects of a policy of recognition | 94 |
| Table 4.2: The effects of a policy of recognition, a mixed policy and a purely deterrent policy on the preservation of peace as a function of the motivation of the instigator | 95 |
| Table 4.3: Approaches to War and Peace | 133 |

# 1 introduction

The majority of theories on the origins of war are based on the premise of a rational actor in pursuit of material satisfaction, whether for the quest for power (the *homo politicus*[1]) or wealth (the *homo economicus*[2]). Realist explanations of interstate war insist on the struggle for power and the importance of deterrent postures. These approaches staunchly maintain that actors always seek 'to maximize their share of world power' (Mearsheimer 2001:2), and advocate that actors systematically weigh the costs and benefits when resorting to armed force (Fearon 1995). Furthermore, such explanations share the conviction that actors avoid war when the adversary is likely to inflict on them disproportionate costs as compared to anticipated profits. Thus the principal assumption of this camp of thought is that it is 'deterrence' which impels actors to initiate or renounce war.

Such thinking has evolved into two primary schools of thought. The first, the 'theory of preponderance', asserts that wars are prevented when there exists an unequal distribution of power between actors. As such, the weakest party, knowing that it will lose the war, will make the necessary concessions to avoid conflict. An extension of this reasoning (Blainey 1973), 'transition theory', notes the effect when there is a shifting of power between the *hegemon* and the challenger (Gilpin 1981; Organski and Kugler 1980). The second, the theory on the balance of power (Waltz 1979: 123–8; Mearsheimer 2001), focuses on the calculus of the strongest actor. Thus, when a situation of approximate equilibrium exists, even the slightly stronger and victorious party will endure large losses during an armed confrontation. The precepts concerning the 'pacifying' virtues of deterrence have been clarified in mainly 'abstract' studies on international crises. Issues of engagement, communication, proportionality of threats, and credibility are addressed in perspective to assure 'efficient' deterrence in international crises management.[3]

Assumptions on deterrence have been found to be suspect when viewed through the lens of psychological approaches that espouse the limits of rationality. It is true that the imperfect nature of information, the existence of misperceptions, and/or the tendency of actors to take great risks to avoid losses have been consistently

---

1. For internal political interests see Eberwein, Hubner-Dick, Jagodzinski, Rattinger and Weede (1979), Geller, Singer (1998 : ch 3); De Mesquita (1981); Battistella (2006); Mansfield, Snyder (2007); Cashman and Robinson (2007: 9–12). For external political interests see Gilpin (1981); Doran (1991); Vasquez (1993); Van Evera (1999); Copeland (2000); Sindjoun and Vennesson (2000). The approach in terms of recognition is not completely incompatible with the rational actor model if we presuppose that rationality is solely the conformity of means in relation to a given preference (*Zweckrationalität*). A more open rationalism could admit the existence of 'ideals' and not only material objectives. On this subject, see Shepsle and Bonchek (1997: ch 2); Varian (2005). I owe this discovery to Patrick Le Bihan.
2. For a good summary see Levy and Thompson (2010); Caplow and Venesson (2000); Cashman (1993); Levy (1996: 3–24). For an approach in terms of *homo economicus* see Mueller (1989); Moravcsik (1997).
3. See in connection to this Huth, P. and Russett, B. (1993) and for a synthetic presentation Cashman, G. (1993).

observed.[4] However, even these approaches seldom question the belief that actors will resort to war to obtain power or wealth. But it is precisely this assumption held by *homo politicus or homo economicus* which seems to be contestable. Neorealist and liberal approaches propose that actors exploit not only the choice of means in relation to obtaining objectives ('thin rationality'), but also have fixed preferences in their objectives, such as the maximisation of power or of well-being ('thick rationality').

Accordingly, there are at least two inherent weaknesses in those approaches that assume actors' 'thick' rationality. First, they neglect the need for *homo symbolicus*, which relates to the preservation of a positive self-image for both emotional and instrumental reasons. A good reputation ensures authority and procures material resources. From this point of view, threats may ultimately serve to accelerate the outbreak of hostilities instead of deterring them, because such threats are not compatible with the maintenance of the positive self-image held by the 'intimidated' party. 'Thick' rationality explanations ignore the role of emotions in the development of international crises; as illustrated by the conditions between the United States and the Taliban state after the attacks of the 11th September.

Second, 'thick' rationality underestimates the difficulty that political decision makers have in justifying and legitimatising wars carried out for purely material motives. Even when a war is started mainly for profit, political decision makers must consider moral domestic and international opinion if they want to avoid losing face. It would be illusory to suppose that political actors can conduct calculated displays of power without taking into account demands for 'rightness' and 'recognition' by those being governed. The truncated view of human motivation often propounded by liberal and realist approaches[5] runs counter to the identification of multiple motivational logics in other disciplines. Studies in philosophy (Honneth 1991), social psychology (Mead 1963), sociology (Weber 1971; Mauss 1991; Goffman 1973; Pizzorno 1990; Bourdieu 1979; Boltanski and Thévenot 1991; Wieviorka 2005; Caillé 1989), history,[6] and in political science (Braud 1996, 2003) have demonstrated the importance of symbolic issues in social relations. The quest for recognition is closely linked to man's nonmaterial needs. Contrary to the objective to possess tangible objects, A. Kojève considers the desire for recognition to be the decisive criterion that distinguishes man from the animals.[7] Without the need for recognition, the fight for dignity in relatively prosperous dictatorships does not occur, as was the case during Pinochet's reign over Chile.

Recognition is crucial for emotional reasons – not only for increasing an actor's self-esteem, but especially for avoiding shame (dishonour) and humiliation. Recognition is also necessary for cognitive reasons. One's identity is reinforced through its confirmation by significant others: *I cannot consider myself without*

---

4. See for example, Kahneman and Tversky (1979) and Jervis (1976).
5. This interpretative focus on material interests is not only valid for war studies. See Hassner and Vaïsse (2003).
6. Becker (2004) notion of 'political culture'.
7. Modern biology no longer reinforces this assertion. On this topic, see also Rosen (2005).

*these others and they cannot consider themselves without me.*[8] Furthermore, the quest for recognition involves a strategic dimension: in that a good reputation is essential to obtaining advantages in terms of material resources.[9] The political man is by definition particularly preoccupied with his self-image. His electoral survival depends, for a large part, on the opinions expressed by other 'important' people and, as a consequence, on his symbolic capital. The political man is also a public man whose image is often of greater value for his career than his real persona.

Whilst in everyday disputes it is accepted that issues of prestige, honour and image matter, in studies on the origins of war these concerns are nearly ignored.[10] The purpose of this book is to empirically address this 'recognition *problématique*' by integrating 'constructivist' Kratochwil 1989; Wendt 1999; Guzzini and Leander 2006; Bertrand 1995) literature to the identity-based dimension of security interests. The consideration of recognition allows us to question ourselves with regard to the symbolic dimension of war. For example, a civil power such as the Federal Republic of Germany does not have the same symbolic interest in resorting to armed force as a power that projects a virile self-image – as did national-socialist Germany. Thus, why can't war be a means of preserving actors' self-images instead of being the simple expression of the will for enrichment or power? Do political decision-makers not also take into account the symbolic gains and losses (in terms of personal and collective self-image) that result from armed force? Aside from economics and power-based motivations, what role do symbolic motivations play in the outbreak of war, such as when the United States resorted to armed force against the protectorate state of Bin Laden (the Taliban State) and against those who 'celebrated' the attacks of the 11th September (Saddam Hussein)? Is it possible to ignore such recognition-based motivations when certain actors risk their lives (i.e., suicide bombers in the Arab-Israeli conflict[11]) in the name of 'dignity'? After all, in democracies, the desire of political decision makers to preserve a positive image can dissuade them from declaring a war that may be difficult to justify in the face of domestic opinion, as may be in a case of armed conflict against another democratic state.

According to my general thesis, non-recognition can be as much as an explanation of war (and peace!) as that of other explicative 'variables', such as threats, power, or wealth. I proceed from the idea that far from being an international relations epiphenomenon, non-recognition, as defined by attacks (real or imaginary) on an actor's self-image, can have very real effects on the fuelling and legitimising of

---

8. For Hegel, the actual starting point is not the singular Self, but that which begins with the relation of two self-consciences and their reciprocal recognition, see Rosen (2005).

9. See for example, Plato, *La République*, Book II, 357–83: 'it is not for itself that they (the parents) praise justice, it is because of the consideration that justice procures'.

10. For some exceptions but for studies more 'focalised' on the quest for prestige than 'recognition': Lebow (2008); Markey (1999); O'Neil (1999); Ringmar (2006). For some very stimulating studies on the origins of war: Millner (2007); Davis (2001); Ikenberry G. C. (2001); Welsh (1995); Doran (1991); Holsti (1991); Jervis (1976). For recognition, emotions and international relations: Wolf (2008); Greenhill (2008); Heins (2008); Allan and Keller (eds.) (2006); Mitzen (2006; Wendt (2003); Finnemore (2003); Crawford (2000). See also Lindemann and Ringmar (eds.) (2010).

11. Such a logic would also shed light on the motivation of those responsible for the September 11th attacks.

physical violence.

Non-recognition in international relations is both identifiable and even 'quantifiable' and can be affirmed by examining the self-presentation of great powers in government architecture, the number of great powers excluded from international decision-making bodies, the 'hard' or 'soft' character of peace treaties or the multilateral or unilateral exercise of hegemony. Unequal structures in international politics constitute another tangible and material reality. If all inequalities develop into potential sources of non-recognition, then political inequalities are especially considered as injurious because they threaten the sacred principle of national sovereignty. Case in point, the United States' powerful military coupled with its unilateral hold on power is often perceived as humiliating to weaker states. It thus follows that U.S. efforts to combat nuclear proliferation are interpreted by Iran and North Korea as a policy of contempt and not as one of peace.[12]

Because the quest for prestige and honour is generally associated with older conflicts (i.e., those which opposed the 'glory' of the great European coalitions – France under Louis XIV or Napoleon, or the first half of the twentieth century under Wilhelm's II Empire and national-socialist Germany), sceptics could realistically question the application of such a thesis to modern war. We know that wars for prestige and honour are typical of aristocratic societies, such as Rome. Even so, can we say that symbolic logic is still a part of consumerist modern societies where material satisfaction is more important than the question of honour? In contemporary international relations, the use of antiquated notions of 'honour' can easily mislead us on the importance of self-image. The symbolic logic of war has not vanished, but the concept and vocabulary of what creates a 'good reputation' and 'dignity' of a state or a social group in international and national politics has changed. The desire for prestige persists, but in a modified form, in that there are still superpowers that are concerned with a reputation of firmness, as the US in Vietnam in 1965 or Russia against Georgia in 2008. In the same way, does not the aspiration for glory persist today in the form of diverse messianisms, for example, when the US engaged itself in Kosovo in 1999 as 'defender' of the free world and of human rights (Badie 1999:14)? In addition, even states and social groups of more modest means, such as postcolonial Algeria, desire to be treated with 'dignity' by others.

Discriminatory behaviour is likely to provoke aggressive reactions especially when common standards of dignity, such as the principle of sovereignty in international society, are violated. The classic retaliation-grudge-vengeance-grudge-retaliation, etc., cycle that nourishes a large number of contemporary conflicts is an example that supports this thesis, insofar as it illustrates the quest to regain self-esteem by punishing those who project a negative image of us. Globally, we now see the rise of recognition claims on the international scene. This is due, in part at least, to the increasing fluctuation of social relationships in a modern context when traditional social hierarchy is questioned. Globalisation facilitates a cross-society comparison, which brings attention to unequal living standards and minority discrimination. Following the diffusion of both egalitarian values and comparative criteria, discrimination has become progressively more identifiable, thus resulting

---

12. On this subject of discriminatory presuppositions in the nuclear non-proliferation treaty see Klein (1999).

in greater provocation of actors than previously. If economic and strategic rivalries persist, an ever larger number of actors will revolt against the arrogance and lack of respect, not to mention the mistrust, displayed on the international scene.

The last spontaneous objection that could be made against the recognition-thesis is that such an approach presents a naïve, idealist vision on the origins of war, and that it misunderstands, not to say obscures, economic and strategic interests which have often been critical issues in wars from the Roman Empire's predation to the invasion of Kuwait by Saddam Hussein in 1990. It should be quickly pointed out that the link between war and the quest for recognition is *probabilist*. This study aims to complete rather than totally replace, existing materialist theories. The quest for recognition and the search for material goods often go hand in hand. A discredited state, such as Libya between 1986 and 2004, will find it difficult to integrate itself into international society and to gain allies to strengthen its security. Conversely, the accumulation of wealth and power generally improves a state's reputation, at least in terms of prestige and *soft power* (Laroche 2005: 77f). The quest for recognition can therefore be purely instrumental, assuring a state's reputation for firmness, as was the case when the United States entered the Vietnam War.

In the weakest causal sense, the symbolic imperative to preserve a positive self-image impels political decision-makers to justify the initiation of armed conflict. Even a war for oil or for territorial conquest is only possible against a 'rogue state' and not against a 'friendly' one. In this respect, would the Bush administration have been able to go to war in 2003 if Saddam Hussein had fully cooperated with IAEA authorities and 'showed his hand' during the weapons of mass destruction fiasco?

In the strongest causal sense, the quest for recognition can be the determinant factor in armed confrontation, above all when 'narcissistic wounds' (such as the destruction of the World Trade Centre on the 11th September) are associated with *hubristic* self-images (inflated self-descriptions i.e., a large number of American political leaders feel that their nation represents a beacon of world freedom). Thus, the American war against the Taliban state that was openly protecting Bin Laden in 2001 was highly probable if we consider the situation using 'symbolic'[13] logic.

Utilising research from social and political philosophy, I will first and foremost try to formulate a theoretical framework for the study of social conflict in general; a framework which takes into account the recognition problematic. Then, I will clarify how this analytical tool can be transposed to analyse international relations and I will then formulate some hypotheses on the origins of inter-state war. These working hypotheses will be used concurrently as a guide for an empirical study on great power conflicts in four international systems and as an explanation of the peaceful and bellicose outcomes of four international crises. The main objective of this book is to empirically explore the link between non-recognition and the causes of inter-state war.[14]

The first empirical study will examine how non-recognition figures meaning within the organisational principles that regulate interaction between great powers (Holsti 1991; Ikenberry 2001; Battistella 2006: 400; Girard 1993). The link

---

13. Erik Ringmar's stimulating work Identity, Interest, Action (1996) is close to an interpretation of war in terms of recognition.

14. This limitation of armed conflict does not presume anything about the pertinence of the proposed hypotheses in the explanation of more diffused violence.

between structural non-recognition and the use of force will be outlined through an examination of great power conflicts in four international systems. Some of these, such as the Treaty of Versailles (1919–1939) and the start of the Cold War (1945–1953), can be considered as unstable as they were short in length and the great powers were frequently implicated in *'militarised disputes'*,[15] not to mention fully fledged war. On the other hand, two other international (sub)systems, the first period of the Congress of Vienna (1815–1853) and the relationship between great democratic powers during 1945–1991 are characterised by a remarkable longevity and by weakness, not to mention the absence of militarised disputes between great powers. According to the principal thesis presented in this chapter, stability does not solely rely on the balance of power, but also on the compatibility of states' identities, on peace treaties, on the integration of all the great powers in international institutions, and on the existence of a benevolent hegemony that avoids humiliation. In other words, the style and legitimacy of hegemonic power – its 'tact' towards others' self-images – sometimes counts more than its material reality.

Recognition and non-recognition (Honneth 1992: 212–26) are also reflected by what actors do, that is, in their interactions. Goffman (1974) has revealed the importance of 'tact' to avoid difficulties in social relations, such as a simple *hello* to express to others to acknowledge that they exist. This 'fluid' dimension of recognition will be treated in the fourth chapter studying four international crises. The term 'crisis' is used here to describe inter-state tensions that can lead to war.[16] According to the general hypothesis presented in this chapter, war is not always born out of premeditation, but sometimes waged in a context of interaction in which there has been a veritable 'symbolic' escalation. I defend the thesis that peaceful management of international crises depends heavily on the ability of actors to engage in a kind of politics of recognition which confirms universal and more specific identity claims. The offered analysis is inspired by sociological and philosophical studies on 'recognition' (Taylor 1992; Honneth 1991) and attempts to apply them to the study of international crises.

I have chosen four international crises to demonstrate: two of the crises resulted in war (the Israeli-Egyptian crisis which preceded the Six Days War of 1967, the crisis between the United States and Iraq 2001–2003), while the other two crises have been peacefully resolved (the Cuban missile crisis of 1962 and the crisis between Libya and the United States from 1986–2004). The first of these two crises was also not inevitably 'programmed' for war, at least not in its initial phase. The war option against Iraq favoured by American neo-conservatives had little support in September 2001. In the interpretation of the crisis, I will assess if this variation of outcome is associated with the variation of the independent variable: the politics of recognition. The politics of recognition has to conform to accepted 'Westphalian' norms of a state's 'dignity', such as diplomatic recognition ('visibility'), equal sovereignty ('respect'), internal autonomy (tolerance of state's 'identity') and even some consideration for historical traumas ('empathy'). While not previously fully respected, these standards shape a state's normative expectations and their violation can fuel aggressive reactions.

---

15. Crises where military resources are 'mobilised' (Stuart Bremer).
16. For an introductory bibliography see Lebow (1981); Dobry (1986); Gelpi (2003).

# PART I 'SYMBOLIC' APPROACHES TO WAR

# chapter one | the struggle for recognition in social relations

This book defends a differential and interactionist conception of non-recognition that comprises of the offended actors' self-images as well as their confirmation or non-confirmation by others. Drawing inspiration from sociological theory (Goffman 1996; Braud 1996; Honneth 1992), we can surmise that 'denials of recognition' are the difference between a claimed self-image and the image we perceive others to give us. If there is a rough equivalence between our asserted self-image and how we are treated; meaning that if others treat us according to what we consider ourselves to be, our self-image is recognised. If, on the other hand, we have a greater positive image of ourselves than the image of us projected by others, we are not recognised (Wolf 2008). The greater the disparity between these two images, the stronger the feelings of humiliation. The perception of non-recognition is inevitably the product of an interaction between the offended actor and the offender. Moreover, the reflected image is not only translated through words, but through material actions, too. Thus, torture constitutes, as well as physical harm, a denial of a person's moral value. In this sense, non-recognition takes into consideration all of the 'wounds inflicted on identity, associated or not with material acts (Braud 2004). The recognition of an actor does not necessarily imply that the other completely shares their self-images, but solely that they *treat* them according to the way they understand themselves. For instance, it is quite possible that states treat other states as equals and respect their internal legitimacy without having a positive image of them. More than 'real' recognition, what matters to the actors is to be able to preserve their face in social interaction.

We should ideally distinguish between two aspects of non-recognition. In the first case, actors do not feel recognised because their self-image (which is possibly very inflated, e.g., nationalism) is not confirmed by other actors. The difficulty in satisfying these inflated self-images is brought to attention in studies on Sweden's intervention in the Thirty Years War (Ringmar 1996), on the sacred character of Israeli self-descriptions (Aoun 2003) and on the 'virile' self-images attributed to the Bush Administration (Saurette 2006). This identity-related 'denial of recognition' is traditionally described as a struggle for prestige and glory and more linked to the subject's identity than to disrespectful behaviour from others (Lebow 2008; O'Neill 2009). In the second case, actors may feel as if they have not been recognised because social norms have been violated (Doran 1991). These kinds of struggles are best defined as a fight for dignity because they are driven by the quest to be considered as *equal* members of a community more than as *special* with a superior identity. The struggle for identity and dignity are related to each other. For example, self-glorification and *hubris,* such as that in Nazi Germany, were often the result of a process of *stigmatisation* by which excluded actors transposed their negative difference as something particularly positive; transforming a 'pariah people' into an 'elected people'.

One may challenge the 'ethical' difficulty in defining non-recognition as a negative difference between an asserted self-image and a returned image, conflating sources of non-recognition such as grossly inflated self-images and the denial of equal dignity. Indeed, ethically it would not be justified to recognise actors with inflated self-images. In this book, however, recognition is not a normative concept, but an 'independent variable': what matters is an actor's subjective feeling that he is not recognised, which in turn, can provoke 'symbolic frustration' that can be used as motivation to engage in international conflict.

## UTILITARIAN LOGICS

From intuition, we know the impact of recognition in social relations, whether it is the beggars who position themselves in front of churches or a husband who, in front of his wife, abstains from lusting at the sight of a young attractive lady. We also know that non-recognition can provoke a powerful emotional reaction when, for example, someone deliberately ignores us or insults us in public. Lastly, there are many situations where we feel that our attachment to certain values and to an identity (being an honest citizen) prevents us from capitalising on a situation of chance, such as finding a wallet full of notes that does not belong to us. Sociological analysis retains, in variable proportion, the instrumental, emotional and cognitive aspects of the link between social conflict and the quest for recognition.

Schematically, one can identify two perspectives for understanding the *need* for recognition. The first is that recognition is above all instrumental when it permits material gains. However, even this interpretation bases itself on the idea that the quest for recognition has a certain causal weight. It presumes at least that manipulated others have a symbolic interest in preserving a positive self-image. The beggar's symbolic strategy would not work if certain people were not concerned with their generous image. Other perspectives put the psychological costs of 'the denials of recognition' into the foreground. They emphasise the emotional dimensions of non-recognition or the possibility of an attachment to certain values that they defend with honour.

### Material interests in the quest for recognition

Some authors consider that the quest for recognition is above all a way to obtain economic resources or a dominant position in a social hierarchy. However, most authors admit the existence of psychological gratification in this desire. Published for the first time in 1899, the *Theory of the Leisure Class* by Thorstein Veblen is one of the first works to address this theme of sociological issues. Veblen demonstrates how the conspicuous consumption of the American middle-class corresponds to the concern 'of being distinguished' from other social classes and thereby having a worthwhile image of itself. The quest for prestige *via* the possession of wealth is instrumental: it facilitates domination as an end in itself. However, wealth also provides narcissistic gratification

> In order to stand well in the eyes of the community, it is necessary to come up to a certain, somewhat indefinite, conventional standard of wealth […] Those members of the community who fall short of this, somewhat indefinite, normal degree of prowess or of property suffer also in their own esteem, since the usual basis of self-respect is the respect accorded by one's neighbours. (Veblen 1953: 38)

This idea is continued in Marcel Mauss' *Essai sur le don* (1924), which interprets ostentatious practices, such as the 'potlach', in Northwest American tribes as a 'struggle of the nobles to ensure the hierarchy between them' (Mauss 2007). However, beyond the utilitarian aspect in the quest for hierarchical positions and material advantages, Mauss, like Veblen, speaks about the 'emotional' satisfaction of those who obtain recognition from their superiors. Referring to the Trobriander tribe of the Western Pacific he notes

> In their gifts and expenditure, there is not the cold reasoning of the shopkeeper, the banker or the capitalist. In these civilisations, people take a share of profits, but in another manner than we do today. Money is hoarded to be spent, to 'oblige', to have 'human lieges' […] to give back more than what was given is a display of superiority […] and not only to reimburse. (Mauss 2007: 270)

Pierre Bourdieu also asserts that the quest for prestige (distinction) constitutes a means to assert oneself in the battle for domination. Thus, in his studies on Kabyle societies, Pierre Bourdieu shows how festivals, ceremonies or gifts aim to prolong domination. The quest for distinction exists as *doxa*. Distinction manifests itself in practices without the actors necessarily being conscious of the fact that their practices comfort their domination

> In fact, the central idea is that to exist in space, to be a point, an individual in a place, one has to differ, to be different; however, according to the Benveniste's formula about language, "being distinctive and being significant is the same thing". (Bourdieu 2003: 24)

Pierre Bourdieu, more than Veblen, accentuates the strategic dimension in the quest for 'distinction' or the accumulation of what he calls 'symbolic capital'. Numerous studies on symbolic strategies prove the extent to which obtaining a 'positive image' is crucial in order to maximise influence in the political arena (Lefèbvre and Sawicki 2006). Pierre Bourdieu also suggests that claimed identity brings positive emotions into play. Contrary to La Rochefoucauld, he believes that the honour and generosity of the so-called Lord of the Manor are not the supreme form of cynical calculation (an attempt to prove superiority), but that they are subjectively experienced as altruists in 'well to do' (Bourdieu 2003: 163) aristocratic societies. In his analysis on gift exchange, he insists on the 'temporal interval that distinguishes the exchange of goods from giver-giver'. This dissimulation is incomprehensible if one ignores the need to keep a positive self-image by supporting a system of 'free, generous gifts, for which payback is not necessary…'. (Bourdieu 2003: 171)

## 'PSYCHO-LOGICS' IN THE QUEST FOR RECOGNITION

The quest for recognition as an end in itself is explicitly present in Philippe Braud's writings. He puts emphasis on emotional 'psycho-logics', which are at the foundation of this quest. The lack of recognition has a distinctive significance – it is a threat to our self-image and self-esteem (Braud 2004). The extreme character in physical violence is difficult to explain if we concentrate solely on material gains. It becomes clearer when we consider the mobilisation of powerful emotions such as fear for one's survival or hate culture (Wieviorka 2005).

These types of extreme violence often aim to make those who are judged to be responsible for humiliation appear as inferior. Thus, torture also constitutes a denial of the individual's moral value. This implicitly valorises the 'executioner'. Deplorable violence, such as the butchering of babies with machetes in Rwanda, is more about destroying the victim morally rather than physically through a symbolic removal of the victim's human character via corporal mutilation. The emotional aspect does not suggest that the reaction to an insult must be immediate, spontaneous and rash. John Galtung believes deep humiliation leaves deep wounds in an actor's psychology.[1] Resentments are usually enduring, as is shown with premeditated murder and jealousy.

Another emotional need in the quest for recognition is uncertainty and even existential anguish, which is born from the 'fragilisation' of an identity. The loss of borders through a transformation or weakening of the state, migratory flux, cultural fragmentation and new forms of social inequality can lead to, in certain cases, actors becoming uncertain of their identity. Cultural homogenisation dialectically engenders the 'narcissism of small differences' (S. Freud) (Hassner 1995). Another possible answer to this loss of individuality is the eruption of violence which re-establishes borders between 'them' and 'us'

> Violence [...] is used here when collective identity exists no more [...] Violence is the terrifying expression of a person removed of all identity, or on the point of becoming such. (Wieviorka 2005)

*Cognitive and moral needs in the quest for recognition*
Recognition also brings actors' moral judgements into play. The dichotomy between rationality and emotion is somewhat artificial since that which provokes powerful emotions is often perceived as an attack on 'moral reason' (Kant's practical reason). Thus, constantly putting a student down will have emotional consequences of particular importance if the student believes that his professor bases his judgement on personal sympathy and that this is contradictory to the universal principal of non-discriminatory treatment.

Axel Honneth has clarified the perspective of a 'moral grammar' of conflicts that is in opposition with utilitarian theories, asserting that individuals make a

---

1. In a 1999 letter on humiliation Johan Galtung, writes that it 'is not physical, but a deep wound in the psyche', quoted by Lindner (2001). For a good analysis of the role of emotions in international politics: Rosen (2005).

calculation in terms of maximisation of their pleasure (the 'satisfaction' of individual desires). Honneth puts emphasis on an 'expressive' dimension in terms of values and moral sentiments in social struggles. A strong argument that one can propose against the simplistic vision of social struggles for the allocation of material resources is the enduring damaging effect on an identity as a consequence of the denial of recognition. The passivity *vis-à-vis* an experience of 'social humiliation' leads to the diminution of one's self-esteem (Honneth 1991). Unlike Sorel or Sartre, A. Honneth points to the 'rational' dimension of experiences of non-recognition. Thus, discrimination becomes a catalyst for contestation when it is perceived as contrary to socially accepted standards of dignity. This cognitive ability to link personal grievances to 'global' norms of justice is at the origin of social mobilisation.

Luc Boltanski and Laurent Thévenot demonstrate similarly that actions against universal principles and practical reason are both prone to provoking strong feelings of injustice. In *De la justification; Les économies de la grandeur* (1991), Boltanski and Thévenot maintain that human behaviour is not only guided by utilitarian interest and cynicism, but also by superior common principles that regulate different segments of society. They examine the importance attributed to six different judgement methods in the resolution of social conflicts. For these authors, such judgement plays an authentic role in resolving disputes. The feeling of injustice therefore emerges when social conventions inside of these judgement methods are violated. They believe that the starting point for conflicts resides less in their material dimension and more in 'the denunciation of a scandal'.

**The indirect effects from the denials of recognition in social conflicts**
Non-recognition is capable of influencing our identities, which, if transformed, can also become a cause of conflict. Authors attentive to 'symbolic' interactions insist to a variable degree on the sentiment of exclusion and marginality, which often presides over the forming of 'deviating' behaviours and of violent acts. As a result, social conflicts are nourished by an operation of labelling during which individuals are deprived of the incentive to behave in conformity with social norms. In a study on a group of outsiders in a Leicester suburb, Norbert Elias noted that the most rebellious minority of young people felt rejected

> They strived to take their revenge by behaving badly. Knowing that by being rowdy, causing damage and being aggressive, they could annoy those who rejected them and treated them as outcasts, this was a supplementary encouragement to misbehave [...] taking vengeance on those who condemn them (Elias 1997: 52f)

With exclusion, moral barriers fall. A. Pizzorno maintains that

> when one is isolated, when one has left one's homeland, when one "floats" through other places, then there is a strong probability that the moral cost is weak. (Pizzorno 2005)

E. Goffman has demonstrated how self-mortification in asylums – for example, through isolation from the external world – favours a transgression of norms.

Confronted with a general atmosphere of de-humanisation, and having suffered numerous relocations the interned come to consider that the images that others have of them are inconsistent, labile and that at the end of the day they are able to live without too much concern for these images (Goffman 1969). Apart from these calculated 'resistances', exclusion also generates feelings of revulsion and injustice which, too, are determinant in the outbreak of physical violence.

Each of these perspectives recognises the importance of 'symbolic interests' in the explanation of social conflicts. As A. Caillé rightly underlines, the recognition issue is opposed to the view that man wants to maximise *only* his assets and contrarily states that the 'primary question for (man) is to be, or in other words to seem to be achieving symbolic existence – a question of meaning' (Caillé 2004). The quest for recognition can be compatible with rational choice theory when it is instrumental; for example, in the pursuit of material gains. It can also be rational in terms of value (*Wertrationalität*, so dear to M. Weber). This is when individuals feel that defending certain values associated with an identity is worth even self-sacrifice, as for example, the captain of the Titanic who went down with his ship in order to save his identity as a gentleman and a responsible captain. However, the quest for recognition can also correspond to more emotional dynamics when individuals, believing to have been offended and under the influence of anger, resort to violence. In this debate between supporters of either a rational choice or a psycho-logical approach, the recognition problematic does not have a determined position and can easily be adapted into both of these perspectives.

chapter two | the struggle for recognition in international relations
---|---

A consideration of symbolic interests as causes of war constitutes a rediscovery of an old tradition more attentive to the non-utilitarian aspects of human motivations.[1] Thucydides' account of the Peloponnesian War (431–404 B.C.) had stressed that fear and honour were the causes of war. The Spartans' values and self-esteem were inextricably related to the questions of glory and prestige. Accordingly, they considered their honour ridiculed by Athenian actions and even more so by the reproach that was addressed to them from their allies to surrender to the Athenians, Potidaea and Megara without resistance. Finally, the Corinthian leaders' strategically appealed to Spartan honour and to feelings of guilt, which produced the desired effect. Thucydides also demonstrates that for weaker actors, honour can take precedence over physical survival. During the Peloponnesian War, Melians preferred extermination to capitulation. Up against the Athenians laying claim to the law of the strongest, the Melians opposed the force of 'justice':

> Thus, for we who are still free, what spinelessness, what cowardice to not at all to attempt to avoid the servitude […] We as well, we believe it difficult, do not doubt it, to fight at the same time, with unequal forces, against your power and against riches; but, on the side of fortune, we have strong hope, with the protection of the gods, to be not inferior to you, in defending sacred rights against injustice. (Thucydides 2000)

This resistance cost them dearly because the Athenians

> put to death all those Melians that they captured and which were of military age; as for the children and the women they made slaves of them'.

Thomas Hobbes, considered as a precursor to realism, had quoted in his *Leviathan* three reasons for war: profit, which corresponds to the liberal perspective, security, which is at the crux of realistic reasoning, and *reputation*.[2] The Italian philosopher G. Vico accordingly identifies 'wild pride' as a major reason for war and for mankind's destructive forces in his work entitled *Principi di una scienza nuova*, published in 1725 (Boltanski, Thévenot 1991: 18).

*Precursor*

Among the precursors to the study of the symbolic aspects of war, it is especially appropriate to quote Carl von Clausewitz. His work, *On War* (1832) is often interpreted as a model of 'controlled and limited war' (Clausewitz 1955; Aron 1976). According to Raymond Aron or more recently, Martin van Creveld, Clausewitz perceives war only as a means to political ends. War is portrayed as an *object* that

---

1.  For a presentation on international relations 'philosophers': Battistella (2003).
2.  See on this subject: Battistella (2006).

is interrelated through political decision makers' intelligence. Considering that a war's finality is more often or not limited – the possession of an unspecified object (territory, economic resources, prestige) – they deem that wars always amount to a 'cold' violence. More recent interpretations such as those of Emmanuel Terray, Herfried Münkler, Hew Strachan or Andreas Herberg Rothe remind us of the existence of another Clausewitz more responsive to the thesis of the *war-subject*, or in other words, the 'existential war' (Terray 1999; Münkler 2002; Herberg Rothe 2007). First, Clausewitz does not exclude war that is led predominately by 'passion' and in particular hatred: 'Each battle is an expression of animosity. This instinct also manifests itself during the unfolding of the battle' (Clausewitz 1959). Hatred is inseparably related to the recognition problematic. It is often founded on the perception that others have treated me badly. Moreover, hatred has a psychological function of restoring one's self-esteem while making others responsible for any misfortunes. Lastly, hatred against the *out-group* strengthens the sentiment of identity; the *in-group* (Beck 2000).

In Clausewitz's work, hatred is a central concept. The possession of an unspecified 'material' object for him is one finality among others in armed conflicts.[3] He puts emphasis on the fact that the limitation of violence corresponds to a hostile intention (*feindliche Absicht*), but which implies the weakness of 'the hostile feeling' (*feindliches Gefühl*). He even acknowledges that the power of hostile sentiments can be such that political considerations are completely absent in the lead-up to war (Clausewitz 1959). In this eventuality, war naturally progresses towards its 'absolute' form. The objective of a war of 'passion' is to eliminate that which constitutes an 'identity threat' for the actor. The mobilisation of hostile feelings in a war is by no means an 'archaism', but it is effective to motivate armed forces to engage with ardour in armed confrontation. It is often the protagonist who is more motivated, and not necessarily the strongest, who wins the war. According to Clausewitz, even the most 'instrumental' war requires a minimal amount of animosity. On a number of occasions, Clausewitz recalls that the quest for glory (recognition of superiority) and for honour (equal dignity) are powerful motivations in armed confrontations. He also affirms that one should not underestimate 'the desire to strike back and to avenge' in combat.[4] He suggests that a war – even lost – is preferable to dishonour. Thus, in 1812 he writes in a memoir to General Scharnhorst that a lost, but 'honourable' battle, is essential for Prussia in order to preserve its identity and to save its chance of rebirth:

> One humiliates oneself and the nation when by fear one takes part in a government which is our biggest enemy [...] and who has treated us badly to the extreme. I believe and I strongly state, that nothing must be more sacred for

---

3. See on this subject Clausewitz, *Théorie du combat*, p. 25: 1. The destruction of the enemy forces, 2. The possession of an unspecified object, 3. A simple victory for the honour of arms, 4. Several or the three objectives together.

4. Clausewitz (1998) Book 8, Chapter 7.

a people than the freedom of its existence.⁵

All in all, the importance that Clausewitz places on moral forces in war contradicts a purely utilitarian interpretation of his work. For him, war for purely strategic or economic ends is far from being the rule. Such wars assume the absence of hostile feelings and the implicit mutual recognition of the protagonists as 'autonomous' actors in a 'duel', meaning that their opposition is as rivals, but not as enemies.⁶

## THE RECOGNITION PROBLEMATIC IN INTERNATIONAL RELATIONS THEORY

The 'symbolic' motivation at the start of war was also mentioned by classical realists such as Hans Morgenthau and R. Aron⁷ under the designation of 'prestige' or 'glory'. However, traditional analyses of war made 'prestige' a constant variable in political officials' behaviour without really taking into account the historical variation of the values associated with prestige and glory. Thus, a 'civilised' society such as the ex-FRG does not value 'violent' behaviour *vis-à-vis* minor provocations, contrary to martial societies like that of Prussia.

### Can the state be 'offended'?

The transposition of the concept of recognition to interstate relations can appear problematic. Does not such an approach result from an abusive 'personalisation' of the state?⁸ Why should state decision makers feel 'offended' when non-recognition is directed at the political entity and not at the person? Only people and not states have a 'need for affection' or for self-esteem.⁹ Behaviour of contempt towards a state, such as the refusal to let the state be integrated into the international community as well as stigmatisation, rhetorical depreciation or severe punishment within the framework of a peace treaty against the state are not comparable to insults against particular people. Is it really conceivable that political decision makers are outraged by the 'humiliation' of an abstract entity to such a point that they resort to armed force? Moreover, is it not true that 'bureaucratic' and decisional logics inside democratic political entities obligate political decision makers to contend with a multitude of political forces? Such a pluralist configuration of power channels the 'anger' provoked by insults.

---

5. Quoted by Einsel (2006), 'Man würdigt sich und die Nation herab, indem man aus Furchtsamkeit für eine Regierung streitet, die unser ärgster Feind ist, uns unsere Grösse beraubt und misshandelt hat aufs Äusserste. Ich glaube und bekenne, dass ein Volk nicht für höher zu achten hat, als die Würde und Frieheit seines Daseins'.

6. Rothe (2007) p. 106: 'This symmetry brings with it a tendency to justify wars, but it has other consequences as well. It includes a recognition in principle that one's opponent is *iustus hostis* – an equal – so the enemy is no longer considered a criminal'.

7. See on this subject: Aron (1984: 81–103). Also see: Roche (2005:110 sq).

8. I owe this objection to Heins, V. and to A. Honneth during a discussion of my presentation of 'War for Recognition' at the *l'Institut für Sozialforschung* in Frankfurt A.M., July 9, 2007.

9. I owe this observation to a suggestion made by Heins, V.

A strong argument against this objection is the 'affective' and even the 'identity' value that an abstract institutional entity – even if it is highly 'fictitious' – can possess for officials of such an institution. Emotional dynamics initiated by an act of contempt against a state are far from being negligible. The founding references of groups, such as religious beliefs – constitute an 'emotionally invested commodity' (Braud 2007). The image of the nation (the national symbol) can be of extraordinary importance for an individual and can even become the object 'of a totemic cult' (Boulding 1965: 110 $f$.). Whether it is the issue of 'patriotic' suicides following the Franco-German war (1871), the 'humiliation of Versailles' for German nationalists after the First World War, the collapse of the *World Trade Centre* (11th September, 2001) or the 'blasphemy' of the caricatures of Mohammed (2006), the indignation generated by the disrespect of identity references is often very real. The growing individualisation of Western societies does not make them completely indifferent to attacks on their collective symbols as American patriotism illustrated after the 11th September.

The 'affective' burden associated with the symbols of collective identity is particularly important for political officials of a state entity. In order for an individual to be able to embrace a role such as that of Minister of Defence or even that of government leader, it is necessary for him to be identified, at least partially, with the institution which confers this role to him. The identification of a political official with his 'state' is all the more probable given that the prestige associated with the institution strongly influences his personal prestige. When the President of the French Republic defends France's standing in the world, he fights at the same time for personal respect that other heads of state convey to him. The loss of a nation's prestige – which was the case for France after the Second World War – involves the depreciation of its leaders. Thus, General de Gaulle had trouble being accepted as an official spokesperson during the Yalta and Potsdam conferences in 1945. Furthermore, organisational studies – for example, those on armed forces – have for a long time recognised that not only 'autonomy' and 'resources' are at stake in 'corporatist' warfare, but also 'organisational prestige'.

Undoubtedly, the 'transposition' of the recognition problematic into international relations on ethical questions[10] poses the most problems. State recognition can imply the contempt of its populations when they are exposed to political, cultural and economic discrimination on behalf of the central power. Such *dilemmas of recognition* are frequent in an international community where only a small minority of states grant 'equal dignity' to the whole of their populations. Despite this, one cannot reasonably push aside the 'ethical' duty to respect the symbols of the collective identity of a population.

### The state and the role of emotions in the quest for recognition

Another objection asserts that political decision makers in 'modern' democracies should be too strongly inserted in a bureaucratic process to succumb to emotional dynamics and to be concerned with attacks on the symbolic integrity of their

---

10. See on this subject: Heins, V. (2006).

state.[11] Are there not impersonal administrative procedures taking action against a decision governed by a head of state's emotions? Accordingly, only dictators like Adolf Hitler, Saddam Hussein or Kim Jong-Il can make their resentments and wounds to their self-esteem an object of contention, being able to lead to a war. Is it not 'naive' to believe that a head of state that is confronted with multiple forces and is accustomed to controlling his emotions in the struggle for power could have to act according to an attack on his 'personal dignity' or on that of the state which he represents? Consequently, even if President Bush felt offended by the attack against his father which was attributed to Saddam Hussein, he could not easily formulate a sufficient enough reason to go to war against Iraq. Before considering resorting to armed force, he had to garner support from the members of his party, Congress, military officials, as well as 'published' and public opinion.

This argument conceals the fact that emotions are not necessarily 'individual', but instead can be collective, especially if the offence does not attack the head of state on a personal level, but as a national symbol. Thus, taking a compatriot hostage, or massacres inside another state (see Serbia in 1999 in Kosovo), stimulate emotions in the formation of internal opinion, making it difficult for political decision makers to remain inactive if they want to save face. Public and organised 'offences' by different entities render political decision makers vulnerable to losing face in the arena of political support and public opinion. Regarding the difference from the nineteenth century in which cabinets could implement a secret policy, today's officials from differentiated entities are constantly subjected to the media's spotlight and to their compatriots' scrutiny. This leaky character in their foreign policy makes 'complex' states more sensitive to the influence of the emotions coming from 'the bottom'. Thus, at the time of the crisis in 1967, both Egyptian and Israeli decision makers were entrenched in a heated rhetorical exchange which became militarised because of their 'flammable' internal opinions.

Paul Saurette asserts that the 11th September attacks incited such emotional energy – the desire for revenge – that it became difficult for political decision makers not to undertake any 'punitive action' (Saurette 2006). It is not only internal opinion that is likely to be 'ruffled' by these 'offences', but also other administrative units like the armed forces who experience the same collective emotions. All the members of an institution who wish to belong to an entity that benefits from a positive social identity are consequently implicated when that entity is a victim of depreciation. According to J. Snyder and B. Posen, the quest for prestige explains for example, that armed forces encourage military doctrines due to the fact that a 'true' victory naturally increases the military institution's prestige more so than a peaceful compromise negotiated by the civil power (Snyder 1984; Posen 1984). The military institution's loss of prestige encourages military officials to work openly for armed confrontation, as was the case of the Russian soldiers during the second Chechen war.

---

11. See however Rosen (2005). The author defends the thesis according to which even decision makers controlling complex democracies often act in accordance with traumatising 'formative experiences' (see for example, the ever present analogy of 1938 Munich) and to their positive or negative emotions associated with an event.

Furthermore, even in a democracy, the *leader* of the executive branch, such as the president of the United States, enjoys considerable autonomy compared to his entourage. He can choose his advisers and can monopolise critical information. In the same way, administrations are infrequently completely homogeneous. The executive *leader* can as a result, exploit internal divisions in an '*administrative unit*' to obtain information and the necessary support.[12] Thus during the Cuban Missile Crisis, President Kennedy – *via* his brother Robert – secretly negotiated with the Soviet Union for the withdrawal of Jupiter rockets from Turkey. Almost nobody was informed of this affair. The president's relative autonomy supports the assumption that he is sometimes able to politically assert his personal 'resentment'. Thus, S. Rosen defends the thesis according to which President Kennedy had without any preliminary discussion made the decision to take a firm stance with regard to Khrushchev after the discovery of the missiles on the Cuban island in October 1962 because he felt personally mislead and offended by the Soviet leader (Rosen 2005).

All in all, dictatorships as well as democratic regimes should be sensitive to 'offences of the state'. The essential difference between the two regimes lies in the fact that dictatorial regimes are irritated by 'personalised' offences (the crimes of lèse-majesté) whereas 'bureaucratic' and 'democratic' regimes are more sensitive to offences against symbols of the collective identity.

**The state and instrumental motivations in the quest for recognition**

It would be a misconception to believe that the desire for recognition *necessarily* goes hand in hand with emotional impulses. Even for an emotionally insensitive decision maker[13] it would be risky not to take note of emotions expressed in connection with an offence (real or presumed) by the community because he would likely risk losing the support of internal opinion and its entourage. More generally, officials in 'authoritarian' states rely heavily on a 'virile' form of legitimacy, which will have difficulty ignoring such provocations. Democracies are in theory less vulnerable to these provocations because their identities are more 'open', 'harmonious' and accustomed to compromise than those in non-democratic regimes. The latter often believe that policy is reduced to force and to 'the struggle for power'. They are all the more inclined to accept the virtues of force that their regimes rely on (a problem of a lack of popular legitimacy), such as a military apparatus and an impressive 'security' force. A dictator who displays himself as a 'virile' man on the domestic scene is not able to permit an admission of weakness and subordination before the international community without weakening his political legitimacy. However, the same can occur for a democratic head of state, elected on the promise to assert himself against external enemies or the 'forces of the evil' (see President Bush).

A second difficulty associated with a wait and see policy *vis-à-vis* provoca-

---

12. See on this subject concerning France: Cohen (1986) and (1994).
13. I owe this suggestion from a discussion with Axel Honneth (9.7.2007).

tions against 'symbolic integrity' lies in the fact that a humiliated and 'weak' state risks losing its 'authority' in the international scene (Mercer 1996). Reputation and 'credibility' are at the crux of realist reasoning when it comes to measuring the state's ability to deter an aggression on behalf of another (Schelling 1960). For the sake of credibility alone, certain decision makers even voluntarily bind their hands in order to render their engagement irrevocable. The issue of credibility leads decision makers to consider that a conciliatory policy could question their 'reputation'. Thus, the growing commitment of American power in Vietnam from 1965 along with its difficulty to withdraw from Iraq after 2004 are explained mainly by the fear of losing 'face' and thereby leadership in the international community. However, in a 'Kantian' anarchy (A. Wendt), founded on the rule of non violence and mutual aid instead of military honor, this same 'strategic' interest in preserving a 'good reputation' can also play in favor of advocating moderate policies. Furthermore, having a reputation for being 'weak' or for being 'steadfast' is not only due to concessions, but also to the interpretation of these concessions: are they 'imposed' or are they the expression of a lack of character (Mercer 1996)? Accordingly, there exists a quite 'cold' symbolic interest on the behalf of state decision makers to defend their political entity's good image against 'offences'. Moreover, rational choice theorists have partially integrated symbolic issues when they make reference to the actor's identity role by his preferred definition[14] or to the importance of having a positive self-image.[15]

However, this same 'internal' and 'strategic' interest in preserving a 'good reputation' can also play in favour of advocating moderate policies when a state 'is not directly offended'. Decision makers of a discredited political entity who are perceived as aggressive, will have more difficulty in obtaining material resources such as security (*via* allies) or even in preserving their economic resources (the risk of *boycott* is high for a state perceived to be as *rogue*). Libyan state decision makers seem to have understood such material costs of a state being banished by the international community. Their policy of taking into consideration the victims of the Lockerbie attacks, as well as the release of the Bulgarian nurses in July 2007, certainly does not represent just a show of compassion towards the victims, but rather represents their cold interest in rehabilitation, in order to be reinstated into the international concert.

Hence, expressions of empathy towards a population or a state struck by a catastrophe are not inevitably the expression of a 'romantic' attitude, but that of the desire to obtain political or economic profit. The instrumental force of empathetic testimony does not hinder any less than an absence of compassion, coldly displayed, is likely to be perceived as the expression of supreme contempt by concerned state decision makers. Thus, the only state which openly celebrated the events of the 11th September found itself two years later implicated in a war against the American power.

---

14. For example, Boudon (1976) and Coleman (1973).
15. See Drazen (2001).

## The constructivist approach on recognition

In the discipline of International Relations, constructivists have been especially known to debate issues of recognition. Consequently, they put emphasis on 'appropriate behaviours' for a given identity (Jepperson, Wendt and Katzenstein 1996; Waever 1995). This means, for example, that it is important to know if state actors perceive themselves as representatives of a traditional military power or as that of a 'civil power' in order to understand their interest or their hesitation in sending their soldiers into battle; such as during the debate on the participation of the German army in the ex-Yugoslavian conflict between 1992 and 1995. The originality of the constructivist approach really does not reside in the 'idealist' postulate according to which the structures of the international system would be normative, rather than material in nature (the standard of sovereignty 'would protect', for example, Luxembourg from any annexation by the bigger states, like France or Germany) or in the supposition of a co-constitution of agents and structures. These premises were already explored by the 'idealist' school and its axiom of peace by law or liberal interdependence theories.

Rather, the core of the constructivist paradigm resides in its opposition to 'fixed' theories of rational choice according to which actors' preferences would be stable. Constructivists point out the fact that the choice between military force (i.e., North Korea), economic well-being (i.e., Switzerland) or the defence of humanitarian rights (i.e., Sweden and Canada) is variable and depends in particular upon the identity reference framework within the international community (for example, what constitutes a great power according to era). Such a framework within national elites (which roles do state decision makers aspire to play in the international scene: 'civil' power, military power, world power or continental, etc?) is also important. Erik Ringmar's study on Sweden's entrance in the Thirty Years War in 1630 illustrates how role identities are often formed within states and as a result, are likely to encounter the realities of international politics. From the start, the author explains his hostility with a confined vision of human rationality by pointing out the importance of obtaining recognition from others for the 'self's constitutive stories' (Ringmar 1996). Ringmar's investigation is enthralling and he takes a special interest in identities in crisis, that is to say identities in their 'formative moment' like that of Sweden's Gustavo Adolphus II, anxious to put forth his identity (not recognised) as a great Protestant power while intervening on the side of the Protestant German princes. In other words, asserted identities do not always correspond to the returned images by other actors. This discrepancy is a source of conflict.

Other constructivist studies concentrate on the intersubjective aspects of recognition; that is to say actors' shared norms and identities (Kratochwil 1989; Katzenstein 1996; Richard Price 1997; Adler 1998, Tannenwald 1999; Janice Bially Mattern 2004). The absence of a shared identity morally facilitates – as I have observed – the resort to armed force. Accordingly, A. Wendt showed that even anarchy in international politics, costly to 'realists', assumes consent and above all the recognition of other states' sovereignty. This intersubjective structure explains why the ex-USSR was not easily able to incorporate its Eastern European buffer zone because such an undertaking would have delegitimised it in the eyes of 'progressive' opinion (Wendt and Friedheim 1995).

For constructivists, the interests of states and of actors are justly variable because of the corresponding variability of the identities and the norms that evolve more or less quickly.[16] From this perspective, 'identities' have a firm place in negotiations without being completely malleable. Thus in 1991, united Germany did not have the same identity and normative reference as that of Nazi Germany, but this change did not occur in a sudden and random way.

Changes in identity are likely to occur in economic or security situations of crisis (for example, after the 11th September, 2001) or following normative changes within the international system (for example, the end of the bipolar system in 1991) or, on the contrary, by internal evolutions (for example, the Soviet Union's transition into Russia in 1991). Moreover, it would not be advisable to dispatch power dynamics and elites which are often at the origin of identity changes. This aspect was discussed by so-called 'critical' approaches of international security. These approaches which were resumed in France by D. Bigo (Bigo 1997), assert, for example, that the 'speech act' of 'securitization' (B. Buzan, O. Waever *et al.*), the fact in constituting a problem regarding national security (such as immigration), corresponds to the interests of an elite (Cadier 2006). However, elites acting from the constructivist perspective will do so according to their perceived interest which depends in their turn on their identities as opposed to that of their 'real interests'. Hence, the political elites of the European great powers at the beginning of the twentieth century all believed that it was in their interest to acquire colonies (considering their values of 'military grandeur'), whereas those in the mid twentieth century gradually realised that colonial possessions were not only costly, economically speaking, but also incompatible with their aspiration to represent democratic powers (Lindemann 2001). Such changes in internal actors' identity also lead to a change in standards and rules which, in turn, constitutes new practical policies[17]. An actor whose identity has evolved – for example, somebody who no longer dedicates oneself to an Arnold Schwarzenegger model, but to that of Albert Einstein – will inevitably have other standards of reference (for example, less likely to cultivate 'virility' than 'reflexivity') and from this fact another interest (for example, attending courses at the university instead of going to the gym).

The evolutionary character of interests is only conceivable if one postulates implicitly that actors seek to confirm identities (as well as the norms which constitute them), which are precisely variable[18]. The recognition problematic clarifies the central postulate of constructivism according to which norms and identities constitute interests. Any opposition to the theories of traditional rational choice

---

16. Some reproach to Alexander Wendt for treating identities as 'data' and by estimating that they evolve more quickly than he imagines, Zehfuss (2002) and Guzzini and Leander (2005).

17. Koslowski and Kratochwil (1994: 216) 'What is important is the way in which changed practices arising from new conceptions of identity and political community are adopted by individuals, and the way in which the interactions among states are thereby altered or vice versa'.

18. I owe this idea from a conversation with D. Battistella.

would be futile if one did not replace the motive in the conquest for material profits with that of the confirmation of an identity.

This premise of identity[19] and moral motivation in social interactions is subjacent in the majority of constructivist work. Thus, Friedrich Kratochwil affirms that human beings appeal to moral categories in their interpretation of the world. He maintains that rationality also implies our behaviour's compatibility with moral norms and feelings (Kratochwil 1987). In the context of international politics, one could wonder why national interest must consist of the quest for an 'abstract' good such as power and not, for example, the preservation of an identity reference within particular communities (Kratochwil and Lapid 1996). Thus, was it not more important for Gorbachev and his team to try to make the Soviet Union more transparent, economically competitive and 'Western', than to preserve the satellite countries in Central and Eastern Europe? The Soviet threat was seen in the beginning not as a military threat, but 'as a threat to the American society and its representation as free community'.

However, unlike the work which I have cited in sociology and philosophy, constructivist authors have been relatively unconcerned as to why the confirmation of an identity is of important significance to actors. Certain authors cite the emotional dynamics identified in the works of Axel Honneth and Philippe Braud. Thus, in contrast to the belief according to which only the preservation of physical integrity should 'count' in defining national interest, Janice Bially Mattern supports the concept of the psychological power of damaged 'identities': 'threats to the psychic integrity are certainly as real as the threats to the integrity of the body' (Bially Mattern 2001). From an explicitly 'psychological' perspective, this emotional aspect of identities is particularly raised by Paul Saurette (Saurette 2006). According to Goffmanian terminology, if our face is rejected, we are not able to measure up to our perception of our own self-image. We feel humiliated, ashamed or blush.

### Constructed needs and 'vital' needs for recognition

In contrast to 'thick' constructivists, I maintain that not all quests for recognition are constructed and from this fact, relative. The stability of certain requirements for recognition is founded on elementary psychological needs identified by Axel Honneth, such as respect (a social status), social self-esteem – the need to have a distinct and developed identity (Giddens 1990) – and self-confidence (affection). Philosophers (Axel Honneth), psychologists (Abraham Maslow 1973; H. Tajfel; J. C. Turner) as well as specialists on international conflicts – Pierre Allan, John W. Burton (Burton 1990; Kehlman 1990) and Jennifer Mitzen (Burton 2007) – affirm that such needs are almost universal motivations in human behaviour. One's self-esteem brings affective benefits (Braud 1996) whereas a negative image of oneself can paralyse the individual by condemning them to 'social shame' (Honneth 1992). The loss of 'self-respect' for a member of a community equal in rights can,

---

19. For an introduction concerning the 'identity'-motivations in foreign policy, Vennesson (2006).

in extreme cases, produce self-mutilating behaviour.[20] Recognition of the others status and autonomy can be described as *thin* or *minimal* recognition (Allan and Keller 2006). Alexander Wendt also admits that certain desires for recognition are stable such as the preservation of actor's autonomy.[21] He observes that the creation of an identity depends on the other's recognition of it. Subjectivity (=identity) presupposes intersubjectivity (= recognition). Moreover, the majority of constructivists implicitly admit the fundamental need for self-respect when they assert for example, that an actor's '*subjectivity*' would be threatened by stories about 'good and evil'.

As for social self-esteem, which relies on the continuity of a *particular identity*,[22] questioning it triggers both emotional and cognitive problems. First, recognition 'of an original identity'[23] is the condition to cultivate an authentic self-esteem. A developed self-image is not based solely on what one shares with others (Honneth 1991: 203). This is also true for social identities. A positive social identity is founded, to a large extent, on favourable comparisons which can be made between a group of affiliation and other 'relevant' groups (Tajfel and Turner 1986). Then, a 'distinct' identity (Glen Gabbard 1993) brings individuals an ontological security, meaning a group of stabilised and routine relations with *significant others* (G. H. Mead). It marks the borders between 'them' and 'us' and enables us to better direct ourselves in, and to interpret, the world (Burton 1998). Jennifer Mitzen has more recently highlighted the need for ontological security, meaning the desire for standardised relations with significant others that are capable of conferring a stable sense of one's self to social identities and communities (Mitzen 2006). It also gives a sense of existence by providing a story which binds the present, the past and the future of *me*. On the other hand, the 'wobbling of identity reference marks' causes fears because of the insecurity produced by the loss of a routine mental system. Inconclusive identities expose the individual to existential uncertainty and bring them face to face with their completeness. It follows that individuals whose fundamental beliefs are questioned will have difficulty in understanding the world and will quickly be confronted with a 'chaos' which prevents them from setting objectives and making decisions.

Lastly, the need of 'affective' recognition relies partly on empirical discoveries such as those of Donald W. Winnicott. He shows that even newborns require affection if they want to develop self-confidence and later to escape psychological disturbances, such as 'borderline' or 'narcissistic' personality disorders (Honneth 1991). The child's 'social' existence is due to a certain demonstration of empathy:

---

20. See on this subject Renault, E. (2004).
21. Wendt (2003: 491–542) 'Only through recognition can people acquire and maintain a distinct identity. One becomes a Self, in short, via the Other, subjectively depends on intersubjectivity'need exact pg no. for quote.
22. See Honneth (1991:197): 'Im Unterschied zur rechtlichen Anerkennung...gilt die soziale Wertschätzung den besonderen Eigenschaften, durch die Menschen in ihren persönlichen Unterschieden charakterisiert werde'.
23. Also see on this subject Taylor (1992:53f).

the smile and empathy constitute the pre-linguistic gestures with the means of which infants learn how to appear socially by indicating for the first time their eagerness to interact with reactive smiles (Honneth 2006).

From an approach that is attentive to human needs, conflict settlement assumes the satisfaction of the elementary needs for identity and recognition. Thus, John Burton affirms 'that there exist objectives' which do not lead 'to compromises' and which are among 'shared human aspirations'. He considers that the desire for recognition is a 'human need' and that its violation can bring about aggressive behaviour (Burton 1990; 1996). Hence, the resolution of the Israeli-Arab conflict is not only a question of the distribution of territory or water between the two communities. It only becomes possible when actors recognise their right to existence and the expression of their national aspirations as a precondition.[24]

But if such recognition needs characterise individuals, can they characterise social organisations such as states? The answer could acknowledge that once created, an institution normally aspires to survive and from this fact has some fundamental interests. There are several arguments in favour of the existence of fundamental aspirations for recognition, such as self-esteem. A state despised by a majority of others, such as the regime of Saddam Hussein, is therefore threatened in its survival. Accordingly:

> Actors that are not recognised, like a slave or an enemy in the state of nature, have no such social production, and so may be killed or violated as one sees fit. (Wendt 2003)

Moreover, when a state's social identity is inadequate, its citizens can be tempted to leave it in order to join or to establish a more developed political entity (see the citizens of ex-GDR).

The preservation of a community's positive image is also an emotional need. In effect, it would be difficult to find actors who are not upset by disparaging remarks with regard to their institution by such labels as *Great Satan* and *Rogue State*. The depreciation of an institution naturally touches those which personify it, as I have already observed. In addition, a 'distinct identity' is also crucial for state decision makers. It gives them a sense of ontological security (the continuity of oneself) by defining their relations with others and by helping them to establish political objectives (Mitzen 2006). Political decision makers must have a relatively stable comprehension of their identity role and the history of their nation in order to act in an extremely complex international environment.

A distinct identity *via* the attachment of historical or cultural references is a security imperative. A state from which specificity is not recognised is in danger of disappearing, such as that of Austria in 1938, the GDR in 1990 or ex-Yugoslavia in 1991. Finally, the need for '*minimal* empathy' is to be taken into account by others in order to ensure state survival. Such a need does not constitute a 'luxury'

---

24. Burton (1985) and Touvaal (1996: 403–18). The author attributes the failure of Western diplomacy in the prevention of the war in ex-Yugoslavia to the negligence of fundamental human needs for identity and security.

because it is a part of any social organisation's interest. A state towards which others show themselves to be completely indifferent will not be able to defend its most vital interests of survival (such as Czechoslovakia in 1938). The analogy of fundamental human needs with those of a social organisation is certainly imperfect. The individual can survive with the disappearance of his institution. An institution's will to survive depends on its members will to be positively identified with it. However, once created, constructed and consolidated, an institution will have a vital need for recognition. In other words, non-recognition is not entirely the product of a social construction whose existence would depend only on the perception of 'offended' actors.

Beside 'corporatist' and minimal demands for recognition, there exist those which are socially constructed. In order to understand non-recognition, it is important to study actors' concrete identities and normative expectations about dignity. More often than not social identities confer upon behaviour the significance of an act of contempt or an act of respect. Janice Bially Mattern rightly states that intentional symbolic violence presupposes a strong knowledge of others' identity vulnerabilities such as the Israeli sensitivity *vis-à-vis* the Holocaust (Bially Mattern 2007). The majority of asserted identities are by no means functional requirements for survival. As in the economic life, the satisfaction of the most elementary material need does not always prevent individuals from consuming more and from seeking to acquire luxury goods. Empirically, we know that political entities are not always satisfied with 'equal dignity', but instead they often seek a superior recognition. Thus, the mission to which a political entity aspires (role identity) is by no means determined by a material infrastructure, but it is variable in space and in time. For example, with a potential of power relatively identical to the Clinton administration, the Bush II presidency aspired to a more unilateral and 'military' *leadership* on the international scene as its engagement against Iraq since 2003 has illustrated. In addition, political identity (*identity type*, Alexander Wendt) and states' collective identities are subjected to constant variations. Historically, dominant 'vital' powers conveyed the most varied political identities. Moreover, a state political identity cannot exist without being recognised by others. A democratic state exists really only when the other significant entities perceive it as such.

All in all, *human need* approaches and the constructivist approach are far from being incompatible. The first clarifies the vital interests of recognition; the second makes it possible to understand the large variety of recognition requirements beyond survival and its normative content in a given international society.

HYPOTHESES ON THE LINK BETWEEN NON-RECOGNITION AND WAR

*How non-recognition causes war*
According to the general thesis presented in this book, non-recognition can be as much a cause of war as that of security concerns or profits in terms of power or wealth.[25]

---

25. For a good summary: Neumann (1998).

A first argument in support of the link between non-recognition and war is the strong 'emotional' dynamics which is jump started following identity depreciations. If the actors have the means, they will often react to such an affront to their symbolic unity with a 'muscular' response. In a more strategic manner, it is very difficult for state decision makers claiming a 'great power identity' to remain inactive *vis-à-vis* a 'terrorist attack' such as that of Sarajevo 1914, as it constituted a 'narcissistic' injury.

A second argument in favour of the link between recognition and the dynamics of peace and war is the need for decision makers to morally justify the entry into an armed conflict. This justification is facilitated when 'others' question the positive image of a community. It was definitely easier for the United States to carry out a 'war for oil' against Iraq, who routinely defied the American authority, than against Saudi Arabia or Libya. The latter avoided carefully from 2001 any provocation that would justify a war on Washington's behalf.

Finally, the 'objective' result of a war is generally the defeat of one of the belligerents, procuring 'symbolic' benefits to the winner. The victors will to draw symbolic benefits from a war is apparent through peace treaties such as that of Versailles (1919) or the judgement of war criminals in courts of justice like Slobodan Milosevic. The international media have largely diffused the image of Saddam Hussein, deliberately humiliated by American officials in 2003 during his arrest, by showing him bearded, dirty and open mouthed while being subjected to a medical examination, like an ordinary prisoner. On the other hand, the economic and diplomatic benefits from winning a war are often uncertain, as the two world wars illustrate by accelerating the decline of Europe.[26] More positively, the armed struggle against domination is a means for the oppressed actors to (re)construct an identity (such as colonised people) and to experience their freedom and equality with others. Such positive moral experience in the social struggle have already been underlined by various authors like R. Luxemburg and H. Arendt (Blätler and Marti 2000). However, apart from the recognition benefits, war is admittedly, even for the winner, often a very expensive affair.

### The 'force' of causal links between non-recognition and wars

This study does not affirm that any refusal to recognise a state is likely to be transformed into war. Other factors must *often* intervene to incite a 'humiliated' state to defend its 'reputation' with arms: identification of 'offences' by the offended actor, power resources allowing the 'humiliated victim' to effectively resist undergone offences[27] and the impossibility of obtaining 'satisfaction' through peaceful means (for example, 'official' excuses).

---

26. It is of course possible that decision makers subjectively assert power in order to benefit from a war without their calculations being founded on an objective reality.

27. See on this subject Braud (2007). The author distinguishes, 'two ideal-type opposite scenarios: when the victim has the means to carry out retaliation because it is ultimately, the strongest and when it remains in an irremediable state of inferiority. In the first case, the symbolic violence that is endured exacerbates a desire to wash away the insult, to exorcize the feeling of vulnerability and helplessness [...]. One sees this in the way in which the United States reacts to the attacks of the 11th September, 2001, or Israel with harassing of the armed Palestinian organisations'.

The existence of a causal relation between non-recognition and armed conflict is probabilistic and not deterministic. Thus, the fact that proud decision makers of a stigmatised state, such as Ahmadinejad in Iran (2007), are still not implicated in a war does not invalidate the principal recognition hypothesis. It would only be refuted if 'stigmatised' states (for example, those excluded from international organisations like Germany of Weimar or Soviet-Russia) and hubristic states (for example, political decision makers having conceived a 'superior mission' for their nation, like Nazi Germany, Iraq under Saddam Hussein and Serbia under Milosevic) did not have a proportionally higher engagement in wars than the 'integrated' states (for example, European Union member states). The latter should also display more modest identities (for example, the Federal Republic of Germany).

This study will thus amply employ formulas such as 'can', 'encourage' or 'probably' to indicate causal relations between wars and the quest for recognition. There will always exist 'minimal variations' (Favre 2006) or *frictions* (C. v. Clausewitz) which are concealed within any systematic and deterministic explanation attempt. The denial of recognition increases the *risk* of war without making it inevitable. No theory on the origins of war affirms that only one factor would be likely to start wars. Even the name of one of the most well known research projects on the origins of war, the *Correlates of War Project* (Small and Singer 1981), is rather revealing of the necessarily limited character in explanatory claim of the warrior phenomenon. War is both rare and exposed to the influence of a multitude of actors and variables coming from international and internal environments. It is possible to compare the thesis' explanatory facts ambition with the preventive measures for highway accidents. Although certain accidents on highways are caused by sober people and travelling at low speed, it is obvious that a speed limit or a more strict control of the blood alcohol content of motorists, decreases the risk of an accident.

The claim is not that all wars must only be explained in reference to the recognition problematic. This factor's weight is variable from one conflict to another. In certain situations where actors dispute tangible properties such as diamonds or oil (see the war in Sierra Leone or the action of the oil *lobby* in the American war against Iraq) and where they fear for their physical survival (see Western nations' political decision makers *vis-à-vis* Nazi Germany in 1939), the desire to preserve or to defend a positive self-image will play a rather subordinate part. Thus, the motivation to defend America's reputation (Mercer 1996) was certainly stronger in the war against the Taliban state (2001) protecting one of the presumed authors behind the attacks of the 11th September than at the time of the war against Iraq (Batistella 2006). However, even in situations where actors seek the acquisition of material goods above all, one will not be able to systematically exclude the quest for symbolic gratification especially when social prestige is inseparably related to the possession of richness.

Schematically, one can identify three situations where the desire for recognition affects the outbreak of war. Firstly, *the quest for recognition* is subjected to the quest for political or economic profits. Thus, some wars like the Falkland war

(1982) seem to be owed to the will of contested elites – threatened by a process of democratisation – to remain in power *via* the diversion of internal tensions towards a scapegoat. However, even in such wars, political entrepreneurs must worry about making their aggressive policy compatible with the moral expectations of their public. Any predatory war must be legitimated and as a result justifiable if the decision makers want to preserve a good self-image within internal opinion. This requirement limits the range of bellicose options for 'profit'.

In a second possibility, the desire for recognition is a co-factor (*flankierende Erklärung*) in the decision to resort to armed force.[28] Such a situation arises when there are different groups within an administration – those who desire material profits and others who stand for honour and prestige. Thus, it is probable that *vis-à-vis* the oil lobby, a non-conservative group in 2002/3 was very anxious to carry out the 'democratic mission' in Iraq led by the American power. In the same way, it is possible that a crisis initially started for political profit, like that between Egypt and Israel in 1967, gradually escapes its initiators, who are suddenly forced to engage in armed confrontation so as not 'disappoint' a galvanised internal opinion.

Lastly, there are cases in which the desire for recognition is certainly the primordial factor in the explanation of armed confrontation. This possibility arises for example, when two factors combine in a particularly explosive way: on the one hand, *hubristic* images of the political decision makers of their own selves or from their community and on the other hand, a refusal of recognition on behalf of an actor likely to be overcome. The war of the American 'democratic superpower' against the Taliban state, refusing to deliver Bin Laden, is an illustration of the difficulty found in avoiding war from a symbolic point of view.

*Hypotheses*
My study defends four major hypotheses on the origins of inter-state war. Unlike contemporary theses on the origins of war,[29] the four hypotheses share the simple premise that non-recognition is, in analysing the start of war, at least as important as purely utilitarian motivations (within the meaning of the satisfaction of a material desire).

The first two hypotheses put emphasis on the constitution of security interests by political units' identities. The first hypothesis relates to the impact of *role identity* (Wendt 1999: 226) in armed conflicts, meaning the way in which a state defines the nature of its relations with other states (for example, a hegemonic power or a neutral state). A state's role identity can exist without its recognition by other political entities[30] and instead obtains its confirmation by actors on the domestic level. The decision makers in Nazi Germany claimed to represent a 'chosen race'

---

28. I owe these nuances to a discussion with A. Honneth (09.07.07).
29. For example, the thesis 'war for security' (realist logic) or that of war for 'profit' (liberal logic).
30. See Wendt (1999: 227): "…role identities are not based on intrinsic properties and as much exists only in relation to Others […] one can have these identities only by occupying a position in a social situation and following behavioural norms toward others possessing relevant counter-identities'.

in spite of a lack of actions in line with this identity by states acknowledging themselves 'slaves',[17] such as the United States. Thus, the first hypothesis postulates that *hubristic* identities are a possible cause of war. The second hypothesis asserts that it is the absence of a collective identity which lowers recognition costs of the recourse to armed force.

These hypotheses consider that shared ideas on identities confer significance to non-recognition. Recognition and non-recognition also depend on the 'offended' actor's self-image. Thus, the transformation of Eastern Europe into satellite countries by the Soviet Union after the Second World War did not constitute in itself a form of contempt against American power. It was only because American decision makers perceived their nation as a *beacon of world freedom*, and so did not share any common identity with the Soviet Union, that they could interpret Soviet behaviour as an insult to their nation.

Subsequently, these hypotheses are constructivist insofar as they consider that identities are at the foundation of interests (Ruggie 1998). They constitute, to some extent, the interests of states and other actors and consequently influence their behaviour. This is the holistic postulate of the constructivist approach which affirms that an actor's interests consist of shared ideas about identity and its associated norms. A change in identity generally involves a change of interest. The 'American' interest to counteract the Soviet Union's influence in Eastern Europe after the Second World War was partly conditioned by the will to reproduce its identity of a democratic superpower opposed to 'totalitarian' regimes.[18]

Lastly, these two hypotheses are also constructivist because they assess that *hubristic* and 'negative' identities are not natural or engraved in 'cultural' history, but rather they are due to social interaction. In fact, it is precisely recognition or non-recognition by significant others that explains identity formation. The formation of 'unpretentious' and collective identities would be difficult to comprehend if there was no notion of '*good behaviour*' corresponding to the concerned actors' satisfaction of the elementary needs for recognition.[19] In the same way stigmatisation such as that of post-communist Russia fuels 'idealised' identities and therefore armed violence such as Russia's Georgian war (2008).

Hypotheses three and four are based on the premise that non-recognition of the accepted norms of a state's 'dignity' such as rhetorical depreciations, stigmatisation, the exclusion of international organisations or inference in internal affairs cannot be easily ignored if one supposes that political units aspire to survive.

## War for prestige

*Hubristic identities are a possible cause of war. Hubristic identities* are defined by the aspiration for recognition on the part of other actors on the international scene of one's superiority, which is not recognised by other major international actors. For instance, National-Socialist pretension of 'racial superiority' over other nations is an extreme expression of such *hubristic identity* because this pretention is very different from great power ambitions to participate in international leadership by virtue of international norms which are formalised. In the first case, superiority is totally subjective and hence disconnected from any international norm of recognition. In the second case, superiority is recognised by others on the basis of well established norms. The desire for *hubristic* superiority is translated above all into terms of image.[20] The image which states give to others accounts for more than 'real' material power. The objective of such actors is thus to induce others' admiration (Fukuyama 1992). This claim to superiority can be manifested in many forms. State authorities can declare to be superior as a race (nationalist-socialist Germany), as a nation (nationalism), as a culture (the idea to 'civilise' other countries), as a religion (theocratic states) and as a political regime (by propagating democracy's superiority over authoritarian regimes). Authorities from the same nation can simultaneously aspire to be recognised as equals (such as the relationship between European powers after the Congress of Vienna in 1815), and as superiors, when interacting with their colonies. Hubristic identities are characterised by a typically charismatic domination based on the leaders or the community's imagined exceptional qualities.

Empirically identifying the existence of hubristic identities to study interstate war is not an easy task. However, traces of such claims to superiority can be found in multiple domains. Speeches by political decision makers that presuppose a leadership role or a special international mission may be a valuable indicator of such an ambition. Another is the architectural, musical, and theatrical staging of power, as characterised by the Versailles palace, Hitler's love for Wagner's powerful music, or the immense statues and military parades in 'totalitarian' states. It is clearly impossible to analyse each individual manifestation of these claims to superiority. In the next chapter, I will focus on the architectural characteristics of governmental buildings. The more grandiose and costly governmental buildings are in comparison to those of other powers, and the more rigid and overbearing their form (for example, those built in a neo-classical style), the more likely it is that state power is idealised. Thus, the numerous statues and portraits of Stalin, Hitler, Ceausescu, and Saddam Hussein, as well as their 'pharaonic' buildings, promulgate claims for a nearly 'divine' power. Taking the historical antiquity of most of these buildings into account (in countries like Spain, France and Russia), we should be aware that even a modest and democratic power could be 'housed' in such grandiose buildings. For this reason, I will concentrate on examining architectural works commissioned by the ruling powers for the periods that correspond with our analysis on the origins of inter-state war.

The links between hubristic identities and the outbreak of war are multiple. Actors who lay claim to an idealised and virile *role identity* for themselves and their community are particularly vulnerable to 'narcissistic wounds' (particularly in the case of both Wilhelminian and Hitlerian Germany). This thesis is buttressed by recent psychological research undertaken by Roy F. Baumeister which reveals that violent personalities are characterised by an imposing self-image and often even by narcissistic features. The author notes in accordance with the logic of the quest for recognition that megalomaniac actors are not in themselves aggressive. They only become aggressive if their hubristic self-image is called into question. They tend 'to explode' even if the provocations and the incidents were considered minor by 'normal' people (Bushman 1998; Baumeister 2006).

This relation between hubristic sensitivities, on the one hand, and aggressiveness on the other hand, is also pointed out by B. Steinberg (Steinberg 1996). The notion of perceiving the action of others as an insult initially depends on the image that we have of ourselves. To paraphrase Alexander Wendt, *I cannot know what insults me, if I do not know who I am* (Wendt 1999: Ch.3). Decision makers in a laic state will not have the same reaction *vis-à-vis* 'blasphemies' as decision makers in a theocratic state, such as Ahmadinejad's Iran. Actors conveying hubristic identities will have every opportunity to feel humiliated, even by minor provocations.

A more systematic confirmation of this thesis appears in Erik Ringmar's investigation of Sweden's involvement in the Thirty Year War. He demonstrates how the 1630 Swedish Monarchy's self-representation as a descendant of Noah and of the Goths, and as the oldest country in the world, involved the risk of being contradicted by other powers (Ringmar 1996: 159). The king was even afraid to open his mail because the other sovereigns often refused to acknowledge him as even the *King of Sweden*. This same fear of humiliation pushed the Swedish Monarchy to enter the Thirty Year War in order to affirm its role of protector of the Protestants. Accordingly, Daniel Chirot asserts that leaders who are proud of themselves and of their nation such as Adolf Hitler or Saddam Hussein, are more likely to go to war for reasons of honour (Chirot 1994).

Secondly, leaders encouraged by *hubris* are more inclined to take risks, even at the price of their security and that of their nation. In theory, any '*perilous*' occasion to force the admiration of others should be exploited by this type of legitimacy. Hegel underlines the determining role of the *Todesverachtung* (contempt of the dead) in the assertion of the Master's superiority over the slave's attachment to biological life.[21] A person committed to making his superiority recognised will not hesitate to take risks, even if it means putting his life in danger – as in the film *Rebel Without a Cause*, starring James Dean where two motorists race towards the edge of a cliff in the hope that the other will stop in first. In *Politics Among Nations*, Hans Morgenthau acknowledges the existence of *risk-taking* by revisionist powers like Nazi Germany (Morgenthau 1948). Contrary to the materialist theories of rational choice, officials whose legitimacy rests on glory can prefer risk to physical survival. The attempts to conquer Russia by Napoleonic France, and then by national-socialist Germany, are typical examples of such taste for unwise risks, for the promotion of the quest for glory. Raymond Aron notes accordingly:

> Concerned only about living in peace, neither Pyrrhus neither Napoleon, nor Hitler would have consented to so many unquestionable sacrifices in the hope of a contingent profit. (Aron 1984)

Admittedly, there are 'megalomaniac' officials such as Stalin, who have shown more concern for their physical survival than for the security of their state. However, their 'charisma' was founded less on a superior role on the international scene (for example, as an elected person) than on their domestic pre-eminence. Moreover, Stalin, just like Saddam Hussein or Slobodan Milosevic, had a foreign policy that was incredibly more risky than that of their predecessors. Thus, Lenin decided in December 1917 to sign the hardly 'glorious' armistice of Brest-Litovsk with Germany. Nonetheless, who would have claimed that Stalin, *vis-à-vis* the nuclear monopoly of the United States until 1949, would have carried out a sagacious foreign policy in Central and Eastern Europe (for example, in Poland), in Germany (blockade of Berlin of 1948) or in Korea (1950)? Actors committed to making their superiority recognised will not hesitate to take risks.

Thirdly, actors driven by a feeling of superiority will have little reservation to engage in violent acts against states considered to be inferior. The costs of resorting to armed force in terms of recognition will be in such an event a weak possibility. The perception of superiority is not necessarily 'racial', but it can be of political nature. The belief in the superiority of the democratic regime over the authoritarian regime is likely to legitimise democratic crusades such as, for example, the American war against the Taliban state in 2001 and Iraq in 2003.

Lastly, in a situation where several states lay claim to superiority over another, an identity dilemma emerges – one's identity assertion implies the non-recognition of the other. The other side of the coin of this presentation of superiority is the depreciation of others. An armed conflict ensues when the state confronted by others' identity pretensions is not satisfied with its 'slave identity'. The fragility of imperial dominations – every 'Empire will perish' – is also due to the fact that subjected and humiliated populations remain only submissive as long as their power resources are weak.[22] Recognition dilemmas between two powers that claim superiority are quite frequent in international politics. Such was the case between the United States and the Soviet Union after the Second World War, in the confrontation between nationalisms in ex-Yugoslavia, in East Asia between China and Taiwan, and between Israel and the Arab states. Nonetheless, when a state settling for an equal identity must face a state asserting its superiority, we then speak about a war for honour – an event that will be raised further.

Aspiration to symbolic superiority encourages the quest for material power. It is easier to force others to recognise one's superiority when one possesses a means of retaliation. In the same way, the demonstration of superiority may be a source of material power. S. Guzzini affirms that American domination is based above all on the *belief* in its superiority; any form of effective power requires an intersubjective agreement on its reality.[23] So, how can one analytically distinguish between the quest for power, put forth by realists, from the quest for prestige? Such a task will always be difficult. Nevertheless, this distinction between power and prestige becomes possible whenever a state asserts its superiority while losing objectively power in trying to display a 'manly' identity. Thus, the Soviet Union engaged itself in the costly war against Afghanistan (1979) *also* in order to preserve its prestige, which precipitated its collapse.

Mlada Bukovansky alluded to the possible prevalence of an idealised self-image over strategic interests in her enthralling study on America's defence to preserve the right of neutral countries in the maritime trade in times of war (1787–1812). This 'right' gradually became a principle, even a founding part of American identity (Bukovansky 1997). The author demonstrates that the assertion of this principle on the international scene consisted of many disadvantages. It led the United States to war with Great Britain in 1812. Even the Jay Treaty in 1794, when the United States subjected itself to British demands, does not contradict this analysis because Mlada Bukovansky reveals how much this treaty was resented as a national source of 'shame' and for this reason 'was quickly declared null and void'.[24]

### War facilitated by the absence of norms and shared identities

According to the second hypothesis,[25] *the propensity for armed aggression between political actors is higher when there is no positive identity link between them.*[26]

A collective identity presumes a conscience that others belong to one's same community, even if our similarity is reduced merely to the affiliation of mankind. According to E. Adler and Mr. Barnett (Adler and Barnett 1996), a collective identity also requires identification with others and it relies even sometimes on a 'magnetic pull'. A security community[27] thus implies a minimal emotional participation in terms of distress and the needs of others. Identification rests on the perception that others' lives must be protected (Finnermore 1996). The Kantian anarchy of NATO is partly founded on shared identity. For Thomas Risse, American solidarity with the ex-FRG during the Berlin Crises (1948, 1961) did not express only strategic interest, but also a feeling of responsibility towards an ally who shared the same values. On the contrary, the complete absence of collective identity is associated with indifference, the feeling that we and the others represent noticeably distinct communities, without the least possible link (Hassner 1999).

A shared identity does not presuppose a list of objectively shared qualities between two communities. Even though the Tutsis and Hutus shared numerous physical, linguistic, cultural and social characteristics, they nevertheless perceived each other as complete opposites. The Tutsis considered themselves to be of aristocratic ethnicity while the Hutus felt oppressed. What counts in this case is the awareness of belonging to one and the same community, of creating an 'imagined community' (Anderson 1991).

Unlike religious and physical traits, the similitude in political regimes (homogeneity) is a source of shared identity, while the absence of common traits (heterogeneity) is easily a source of strong negative identity in inter-state relations. A shared world view of a group of states becomes significant when it is confronted by powers claiming a different domestic legitimacy – such a situation can be defined as ideological heterogeneity.[28] Monarchic solidarity was not existent in the eighteenth century, but developed after the French Revolution. The Congress of Vienna was founded on the knowledge that monarchic states were threatened by 'revolutionary forces'. The same identity threat logic can be applied to democratic regimes that uniquely considered themselves as 'value communities' in a confrontation with the Soviet Union from 1946–1947. The repeated evocation of 'community' in speeches by political authorities constitutes another, decisive empirical criterion to detect a shared identity.

The absence of collective identity can be found in leaders' speeches when it is expressed that there is an insurmountable difference between 'us' and 'them', when they use a dichotomous vocabulary, and when they prove to be unable to put themselves in the other's shoes. The existence of exclusive identities, which refute all ideas about common links, is particularly evident in cases of ethno-cultural nationalism and theocratic conceptions of political authority. Such identities tend to interpret otherness as an offence.

A first reason for a link between the absence of any shared identity and wars is the facility to legitimate the latter when the 'other' is demonised. The recourse to armed force has to be justified by decision makers especially if this implies, with a certain probability, a very high human loss (Wieviorka 2005). Admittedly, in order 'to justify the recourse to methods which will inevitably cause sufferings, it is necessary to limit, at least temporarily, the paralysing effect of pity' (Braud 2005). The pitiless logic of 'Hobbesian' anarchy is incomprehensible if one disregards negative reciprocal images. Because I diabolise others, I can destroy them without compromising my positive self-image. In such a context, the indispensable condition for recourse to force is assured – its legitimacy (Gurr 1970). In the absence of a positive identification with the other, an actor will not show empathy. He will thus define his own interests without taking into account those of others (Wendt 1994). The colonial European powers did not have any scruples in waging wars of extermination, whether it was of Belgian Congolese or the Hottentots. The moral costs of a bellicose engagement are relatively low when the 'other' is perceived as radically different. From this angle, it is hardly surprising to note that *the majority* of contemporary interstate conflicts oppose heterogeneous political regimes such as the United States and Iraq (1991, 2003), the United States and Taliban Afghanistan (2001) or Pakistan and India.[29]

The existence of collective identities and shared norms considerably increases the costs of symbolic aggression. The more the normative density in a social field is strong, 'the more the costs of exit are likely to be high for those who would not play the rules of the game' (Devin and Gautier 2003; Devin 2005). Thus, the internalisation of sovereignty as a norm is from now on sufficiently strong within the international community to make its most obvious violation very risky, such as the annexation of the territory of Kuwait by Iraq in 1990 (Bull 1995). Janice Bially Mattern affirms that the non-recourse to armed force between Great Britain and the United States during the Suez crisis (1956) would mainly be due to the actors' ability to threaten the other's 'identity'. British decision makers were able to silence the charge according to which their 'complicity' with Israeli authorities, at the start of the military operations against Egypt, without the knowledge of the United States, was 'imperialist' and hardly earnest. They claimed that the secret nature of these operations would be motivated by the desire to preserve President Eisenhower's image, who was eager to present himself as a candidate of peace before the presidential election. As a result, British 'secret' behaviour was not only congruous with the 'special' British-American relation, but even indispensable to this. According to Bially Mattern, American decision makers were almost forced to silence their charge of collusion if they did not want to call in question this special relation and, at the same time, their own identity as a 'reliable' and 'peaceful' leader of the free world.[30] In short, the lack of shared identities diminishes the recognition costs of war, while the recognition costs of armed conflicts are especially high in security communities. Such shared identities may also be used 'instrumentally' by decision makers to prevent war.

**War for a state's 'universal' dignity**
Hence, according to the first hypotheses non-recognition is also caused by those which deem themselves to be offended insofar as identities give often meaning to respectful or disrespectful behaviour. However, states are not only struggling for individuality, but also for dignity. In this perspective, it is not a desire to affirm one's superiority that is at the origin of rivalry between states, but 'the desire to escape from contempt and precisely from the unequal assertion of superiority' (Caillé 2004). These kinds of recognition struggles are for dignity, meaning that states are also striving to be recognised as *full* members of a community. In this case recognition is strongly linked to the problem of justice. *According to the third hypothesis presented in this study, attacks against accepted standards of a state's universal dignity, are likely to incite wars.*

State actors can feel despised because they are denied 'normal' standards of consideration in a given international system. Recognition denials have to be noted by the offended actor to trigger off violent reactions. Even actors who have been strongly discriminated against do not always consider themselves as oppressed because they have internalised their 'inferiority'. Justice and injustice (Welch 1993) are always relative to some intersubjective norms because actors only realise their condition of non-recognition when their own situation is compared to social standards of recognition. State relations are also governed by this intersubjective logic of recognition. Political leaders feel most offended when norms of accepted social interaction, such as congratulations to a newly elected president of a nation, are not respected (Honneth 1992). It is easy to show that norms of respect, tolerance and empathy are frequently violated in international relations. The impact of these norms is not so much positive, but negative: they provide states with a 'moral grammar' (A. Honneth) that allows them to distinguish which kind of acts are offensive to a state's 'honour'. The formal and informal codification of rules for a state's recognition gives meaning to disrespectful behaviour that could otherwise be perceived as 'normal', such as burning flags.

Many international norms of respect – especially more recent ones – may be open to interpretation, contestation and therefore opposite reactions and behaviours. Some actors may believe that they are struggling for justice and in conformity with accepted rules, while most others consider such claims as manifestations of arrogance. For instance, while US decision makers were feeling betrayed in 2002/2003 by Western Europe's opposition to the Iraq war, France and Germany's decision makers invoked the very same value of transatlantic solidarity to criticise American free-riding. Therefore, there may be a type of dignity-related struggle more grounded on subjective interpretation of shared norms. However, it would be a little rash to conclude that dignity is a totally malleable aspiration depending on an actor's identity and perceptions. While it is rare that an actor will feel offended by the refusal to obtain the annexation of its neighbour, such as Germany in 1939 regarding the West's defence of Poland, it is more than likely that a state actor will feel non-recognised by violations of widely accepted norms such as 'non-interference in internal affairs'. In other words, some norms of international respect are so deeply anchored in social practices and expectations of state actors that their violation universally triggers feelings of non-recognition.

Such general, accepted norms that are the basis for state dignity can be violated in two ways. In the first place, denials of a state's recognition can be directed against its 'universal status' as an equal and autonomous player in international relations. In the second place, non-recognition may hurt a state's more 'particular *status*' as an actor with specific values, historical experiences and a right to obtain special attention from other members of the international community. In both cases, even in the latter one, feelings of non-recognition are mainly triggered by violations of shared accepted norms and injustice, rather than by threats to some hubristic identity. A state's universal dignity, meaning the abstract respect of an actor as a member of a state community and not as an actor with special qualities, is protected by a great number of conventions. For instance, international legal and social norms provide states with some 'visibility'. This means that a normal state is taken into account by the international community. Normal states are recognised by others and engage in official diplomatic relations with them. This kind of thin recognition implies that each party recognises the other's right 'to exist and to continue to exist as an autonomous subject' (Allan and Keller 2008). A recognised state enjoys the right of territorial integrity.

Thick recognition implies treating other states as full members of the international community. There are certain norms which claim some respect for the hierarchical status and autonomy of states. Equal sovereignty, affirmed by the 'Westphalian Myth' (Osiander 2001), implies that each state is its own master and free from any external authority (Barterlson 1995). Treating others as equals in common institutions will not only lead others to feel recognised, but may also positively transform our image of them to the extent that they carry out duties associated with membership. On the contrary, rhetorical deprecation, 'coercive or manipulative' state behaviour is not compatible with the idea of a state's equal dignity and autonomy. In spite of strong power disparities between state actors, recognised members of the international community benefit from several rights assuring, at least formally, the fiction of equal dignity such as the rule of pre-eminence based on seniority. Even small powers will jealously protect their rights such as the immunity of their ambassadors and their pre-eminence over lower ranking diplomats of 'big' powers. International organisations have developed formal and informal procedures to guarantee a state's equality and to avoid any hierarchical discrimination. Moreover there exist more informal norms of equal dignity among states. The norm of reciprocity is probably one of the universal principal components of moral codes. Symmetry in behaviour and mutual renouncement means that nobody suffers any discrimination. It is also widely admitted that fair treatment in a dispute involves some concessions.

Moreover, since the Holy Alliance system there has been among great powers the rule to integrate all great powers into some *common institutions* (Bull 1995). The refusal to concede a place to a great power in international institutions (for example, the Soviet Union, Weimar Germany post-WWI and Mao's China until 1970) fuels resentment. International institutions are not only important to remedy problems relating to collective action dilemmas – they also permit states to save face, by reminding them that they are associated with the most important decisions in international politics.[31] The more the international system is governed by those unilateral powers which place all their hopes on military force and deterrence, the more other powers will feel their 'face' threatened.

In an international crisis, non-recognition is represented by the refusal of states to engage in face to face negotiation, as well as the proliferation of authoritarian instead of 'rational' arguments. Offences to a state's 'positive face' are manifested by the rhetorical devaluation of the hierarchical or moral standing of others, for example, by violating a protocol,[32] in the addition of racist definitions, or the non-recognition of the state with brutal demands or ultimatums. Furthermore, a decisive material condition of a politics of recognition in an international crisis, is the protagonist's willingness to propose a minimum concession that is capable of saving the other's face. The ability to maintain a positive face also depends on actions taken by states transparent to their own internal public opinion. Boastful rhetorical declarations[33] or measures taken for military mobilisation render concessions more difficult. It is thus important to examine the interactions between political elites and opinions in their temporal development. Actors can modify their initial intentions under the influence of another actor's behaviour and reaction. In the same way that non-premeditated murders exist after two actors have exchanged insults, war can also result from the same type of 'symbolic' escalation.

Many studies suggest that recognition/non-recognition of accepted standards of dignity is a possible cause of peace and war (Lebow 1981; Allan and Keller 2006; Lindemann 2001; Ringmar 1996; Schroeder 1994). For instance, states that are non-recognised and/or excluded from leading international institutions are more aggressive and war prone than more established states. Newly created state-entities, not fully recognised in the international community, such as Communist China until 1971 and the Hamas entity in 2008 often use violence to establish themselves as existing actors in international relations. Nations treated as 'parvenu powers' (R. Lebow) such as Wilhelminian Germany and excluded powers such as contemporary North Korea or Russia are more likely to engage in armed conflict or displays of military might than integrated and accepted powers. States with insecure and contested identities which do not recognise each other will easily be involved in militarised disputes to prove their real existence to others. Furthermore, punitive and discriminating peace treaties, verbal depreciation of the other's status and harsh injunctions such as ultimatums can trigger violent reactions aiming for the re-establishment of a state's threatened dignity (Schroeder 1994). A policy of non-recognition against great powers which have the means to punish the offender will especially fuel humiliation and violent reactions.

The hypothesis of war for a state's 'universal' dignity offers alternative explanations on the outbreak of war in relation to traditional approaches of either realist or liberal inspiration. Therefore, the resistance of weaker states (such as Serbia in 1999 or Iraq in 2003) against American hegemony on the international scene can be clarified when one takes into account these 'dignity' dynamics. The experience of contempt is not reserved for weaker states. It can also motivate stronger powers when they see themselves as – wrong or right – 'humiliated' by weaker states. For instance, Israeli decision makers decided in the summer of 2006 to carry out military operations in the Palestinian territories and in Lebanon probably also to restore 'national honour' after the capture of two soldiers. Attacks on a state's universal dignity can also indirectly encourage war *via* feelings of exclusion which gradually develop during the formation of irritable identities (Elias 1997). In this last case, war becomes a kind of self-fulfilling prophecy: others, by its ceaseless denigration, become indeed a *bad boy*. Identities thus are mainly constructed by the others' regard (Wendt 1992).

### War for a state's 'particular' dignity

According to my fourth hypothesis *attacks on specific identities such as a state's political or cultural references or a lack of empathy are also likely to encourage the outbreak of armed conflicts.* Attacks on specific state identities are identifiable by deprecation of its national values or by the negation of past traumas as well as an indifference towards the suffering of victims in national catastrophes. Two forms of a state's struggle for specificity can exist. In the first case, treated in the first hypothesis, states try to affirm inflated self-descriptions which produce identity dilemmas. In the second case, a state's struggle for 'specificity' is canalised by reference to general international norms that are not incompatible with the other's cultural existence. The respect for some specificity is another aspect of actor's desire to share the same rights as others, while maintaining some cultural particularities.

Many legal and moral norms have progressively been developed in the interstate system to assure the respect of a state's specific identity. The development of norms regarding mutual tolerance is linked to the traumatic experience of destructive religious and ideological wars where state actors realise that without a principle of internal sovereignty, involving the respect of political independence, there would be a permanent threat to their survival (Biersteker and Weber 1992). One of the first attempts to prevent war by political tolerance was the principle of the German Peace of Augsburg, *cujus ejo, ejus religio* ('whose realm, his religion', 1555). Political theorists further developed and extended, in the eighteenth and nineteenth centuries, corollary principles such as the rule of non-intervention in internal affairs (Bull 1995: 35). It is easy to show how often this norm of political tolerance is violated especially by great powers when they are confronted with smaller nations. However, normative expectations of internal sovereignty survived even when violated.

Thus, states proclaim their right to exercise 'their inalienable right to self-determination and national independence, which will enable them to determine their political, economic and social systems, without interference'.[34] Indirect actions such as covert actions against political independence are also against normative expectations of the state community.[35] Great powers assure the norm of 'internal independence' in relations amongst themselves by operational rules such as those of 'pacific coexistence' during the Cold War (Bull 1995: 41). Concerning the violation of a state's internal sovereignty, the link between ideological messianism and armed conflict is the most apparent. Thus, as we will see, *homogeneous* international orders are more stable than *heterogeneous* ones especially if the latter is governed by powers spreading their ideology, such as during the Religious War or the French Revolution (Aron 1984). Classical realist scholars such as Morgenthau and Kissinger consider ideological messianism as a cause of war because it neglects power realities. However, it is also worth investigating the symbolic effect of such political moralism on state leaders such as Kim Il Song or Saddam Hussein. Peaceful international crisis management involving powers of different *types* supposes the recognition of the coexistence principle, such as during the Cuban missile crisis in 1962. Furthermore, offences against national symbols such as flags are condemned and designated as *moral dommage* in international law. State populations strive for respect of their cultural and political achievements. Some norms of 'particular' recognition such as respect for traumatic historical experiences and recognition of past crimes shape, at least since the end of the Second World War, the normative expectations of state and non state actors.[36] Such issues of past history fuel conflict. More recently, the act taken by Iranian authorities to deny genocide could encourage Israeli action. The denial of historical trauma in cases, such as genocide or the defacing of sacred places and national symbols, is an empirical criterion defining a violation of the other's particular dignity.

Finally, informal international norms confer states the right to receive some empathy from others and the reciprocal duty to offer some to others. The lack of empathy reveals itself, in particular, by indifference against human suffering which is especially offensive in the context of the rise of humanitarian norms. For this reason, it is particularly useful to examine state reactions when another state is hit by a natural or human disaster (such as 'terrorist' attacks). A state shows itself to be empathetic when it takes into account 'other's needs' by showing at least a minimal level of engagement when the population of another state is hit by an attack or natural catastrophe. State actors strive for some empathy (at least in words) when they are struck by human catastrophe. For instance, American leaders were deeply offended by Saddam Hussein's and the Taliban state's celebrations of the terrorist attacks of 9/11.

Other experiences of indifference by state actors can be made by formulas underlying the differences between 'us' and 'them', unilateral arguments and behaviour (Albin 2001: 26). Peace researchers underline that rhetorical practices stressing differences between the 'in-group' and the 'out-group' motivate conflicts whereas the display of some empathy toward others by stressing a shared identity is often able to pacify international conflict. The absence of empathy also reflects a difficulty in communication. One of the conditions for a valid argument is its intersubjective and justifiable character.[37] Nobody can expect another to consent to take action without relying on socially accepted norms.[38] Thus, empathy assumes 'sincerity'. In spite of the difficulty in quantifying a notion such as sincerity, a leader's subjective feeling of being mocked by others fuels conflict. Such was the case, for example, when Colin Powell believed that Iraq was not being 'honest' in not respecting the non-proliferation treaty engagements and by playing cat and mouse with the IAEA; or even when Saddam Hussein himself perceived that a cooperative attitude would not substantially hinder America's determination to go to war.

The hypothesis according to which the contempt of a state's political or historical characteristics and the experience of indifference (real or perceived) can be a source of war, is likely to be criticised, to be even ridiculed, by a tradition which asserts the prevalence of the state's reason and its 'interests' in international politics. The leading argument to justify such a link is the negative emotional experience that state actors have when they are not taken into account, if one denigrates their domestic legitimacy (Blättler 2004; Kymlicka 1997). States are far from being people or 'living beings', but they are governed by people in flesh and bones who are sensitive to emotional dynamics.[39] The assertion of a state's distinctive identity also reveals cognitive dynamics because differentiation plays a big part in our need for orientation in the social world. The more subjective and intersubjective aspects of recognition, the struggle for inflated self-descriptions (hypotheses 1 and 2) and the struggle for dignity (hypotheses 3 and 4), are related because it is often through stigmatisation, such as Germany's exclusion from the League of Nations, that actors develop hubristic and negative identities.

**Four hypotheses put to the test with two empirical studies**
The goal is to test four hypotheses by applying them to two empirical case studies. There are essentially three ways to validate the proposed hypotheses. Firstly, it is useful to establish concomitant variations between unpretentious and shared identities, politics of recognition on the one hand, and the preservation of peace on the other. Thus I will verify in Chapter 3 whether the variations observed of the stability of international systems go hand in hand with non recognition. A strong link between on one hand, the frequency of inter-state wars and militarised conflicts, and on the other hand, grandiose governmental architecture, absence of shared identities, exclusion of great powers from international institutions, and 'severe' punishment for the vanquished power in peace treaties, would confirm my main thesis. In Chapter 4, I will verify whether the variation of the outcome of four international crises goes hand in hand with a variation of the independent variable, the presence or absence of a politics of recognition. Such a politics of recognition includes the existence of minimal concessions, saving face for both involved actors, each state's rhetoric complying with the other's sovereignty, and a minimal consideration of the other's historical references and suffering. Secondly, it is possible to examine political actors' *subjective motivation.* [31] Do they express the sentiment that they must engage in a war to save face, and even their 'honour'? Thirdly, it is necessary to compare the explanations that are based on recognition with more classical interpretations in order to see if these concurrent explanations are more or less pertinent.

---

31. To examine actors' 'subjective' motivations, case studies are particularly useful. See to this end Venesson, P., 'Case studies and process tracing: theories and practices' Della Porta, D. and Keating, M. (Ed.) (2008), Approaches and Methodologies in the Social Sciences. Cambridge University Press.

In a succinct manner, the hypotheses can be summed up according to the overriding motivations that underlie a state actor's non-recognition: war for prestige (Hypothesis 1); war by antipathy (H2); war for 'universal' dignity (H3); and war for 'particular' dignity (H4). War for prestige corresponds with an absence of recognition that tends to be caused by a leader's hubristic self-images. War by antipathy is fuelled by 'anomie' traits characterised by a complete absence of shared identity. On the other hand, war for dignity (honour) is due to the violation of accepted standards of a state's 'universal' dignity such as non-recognition of its sovereignty. War for 'particular dignity' corresponds with the problem of respecting accepted standards of a state's 'specificity' such as empathy towards its traumatic historical experiences. The four motivations of 'prestige', 'antipathy', 'honour' and 'identity' often converge in wars. Thus, WWII was above all a war for nationalist-socialist Germany's quest for prestige and the expression of hatred of Russian Slavs, but for the attacked states, it was a war for honour and identity.

The hypotheses put forward about the link between non-recognition and wars can be summed up with the following table:

*Table 2.1: The struggle for recognition as a cause of war*

| Causes for non-recognition | Hubristic identities | Normative heterogeneity | Non-recognition of a state's universal dignity | Non-recognition of a state's particular dignity |
|---|---|---|---|---|
| Empirical indicators of great power's non-recognition | 'Megalomaniac' or 'modest' governmental buildings | Heterogeneous international systems | Exclusion and punishment of great powers; depreciations; refusal to make concessions in order to save the other's face | Denying traumatic historical events; lack of empathy after natural and human catastrophes |

# PART II: CASE STUDIES

# chapter three | losing the war, but winning respect?

The stability of an international system is the most frequently assessed with regard to the distribution of material capabilities, namely within great powers or the degree of institutional and economic interdependence (Dehio 1959; Waltz 1979; Aron 1984; Morgenthau 1985; Carr 2002). Certain realist analyses state that the decline of a benevolent hegemony, such as Great Britain in the nineteenth century, leads to the multiplication of armed conflict (Kugler and Zagare 1990; Gilpin 1981; 1989; Organski and Kugler 1980). Current discussions on the vices and virtues of American hegemony or American 'hyper-power' (H. Védrine) prolong this tradition, favouring the study of material forces rather than the meaning that actors themselves give to it. The theory of hegemonic stability directs our attention to the peacefully dissuasive elements of a hegemonic power (Gilpin 1981; Organski and Kugler 1980). This theory suggests that wars are avoided through strong disparities of power because weaker powers are aware that war would be fatal to them. In this respect, the nineteenth century *Pax Britannica* or the *Pax Americana* in Western Europe after the Second World War are cited as examples of pacifying hegemony.

My approach, in examining recognition, shows interest, above all, in terms of exercising hegemonic power. It investigates the role played by a hegemony's identity in relation to other powers[1], that is to say the compatibility of the exercise of power with a weaker power's self-esteem. Where a realist would estimate that interstate war should be rare within the post-Cold War order, thanks to the imposing hegemony of American military power, an analysis sensitive to recognition themes could place serious doubts on this thesis. The stability of the international order will not depend only on the material capacities held by the hegemonic power, but also on its aptitude to include other powers in the international system and to avoid humiliating them. The fact that there exist states designated as forming part of an 'Axis of Evil' (President Bush in January 2002 regarding Iran, Iraq and North Korea) and that significant decisions, such as the American war against Iraq, were taken without the United Nations Security Council's authority fuels feelings of resentment and exclusion; such is the case with Russia. The symbolic interest of maintaining a positive self-image may prevail over the search for 'physical' security. Resistance, even in suicidal forms, against the arrogant hegemonic power becomes understandable from the point of view of the desire 'to be recognised'. As far as Saddam Hussein (1991 and 2003) and Slobodan Milosevic (1999) were concerned, their 'honour' prevailed over their desire for physical security in their opposition to the American super-power's 'diktat'.

---

1. On identity and regional wars: Millner (2007: Ch.3).

The other realist variant, the theory of the balance of power, emphasises the costs for each potential belligerent and not only on those challenging hegemonic power. The balance of power does not automatically deter states headed by leaders who are more willing to give value to symbolic gains over physical security. War stemming from a balanced international system, such as the two World Wars is due to the fact that there are some powers that have hubristic identities. Equality between great powers is seen as being unbearable for the self image held by these hubristic powers. The European balance was guaranteed in 1939 however national-socialist Germany was willing to run huge risks in order to realise its ambition to become the leading nation in Europe and in the world. Likewise, it should not be forgotten that President Ahmadinejad's entourage prefers to have the prestigious status of being a nuclear power, albeit a potential one, over concrete military security.

The fact that state decision makers calculate the symbolic costs of a political option might also explain why states that have a significant superiority over their rivals do not systematically resort to armed force. From this perspective, peacekeeping at the time of the balance of terror might not only be due to the mutually assured destruction (MAD), but equally to the fact that the use of nuclear weapons was perceived after Nagasaki and Hiroshima as being morally reprehensible. The United States did not resort to using a nuclear weapon against the USSR in spite of its monopolistic situation, at least until 1951–1953 (Joxe 1990; Price 2007; Tannenwald 1999; 2008).

'Commercial liberalism' is another approach in the analysis of international orders (Rosecrance 1986; Levy 1989, Copeland 1999; Laroche 2004). Here, states do not resort to armed violence when the economic costs of armed aggression are high and when the benefits of such aggression are weak. And yet, the costs of an aggressive action are high between interdependent economies, to the extent that the destruction of the other, means the loss of investors, imports and exports. Conquests no longer pay off in economies where factors of production are increasingly mobile and disconnected from the national territory. This thesis is on the whole verified if the example of the OECD is considered, where a war between its member states is unimaginable. Against the extreme thesis that interdependency would automatically lead to peace, an approach in terms of recognition poses the question of how cross border fluxes affect identities promoted by political actors. Most trade has positive identity effects on the implied actors. Being perceived as a commercial partner is the beginning of recognition. Thus, the détente between the Soviet and the Western bloc in the 1970s was preceded by a commercial opening. Nonetheless, for authoritarian regimes (de facto 'closed' regimes) the perspective of a commercial opening is often perceived as a threat, as shown by the North-Korean, Iranian or Taliban cases. The fact remains that the unequal separation of the benefits of the globalised market and of commercial trade is a major cause of identity frustration. The differences in standards of living between nations also affect peoples' self-esteem, particularly during our era of 'rolling news' and the influxes of tourism. 'Islamist' attacks are often on luxury hotels, such as in Egypt and in Indonesia, demonstrating the frustration experienced by the worst off who consider themselves to be scorned.

Finally, the theory of institutional liberalism ('peace by institutions') corroborates the recognition argument to a certain extent (Keohane 1984; Kupchan and Kupchan 1995; Devin 2007). As John Ikenberry has underlined, an order is stronger and sparks off less opposition and counter-coalitions when the hegemonic power limits itself and exercises its domination in a multilateral way (Wolforth 1999; Ikenberry 1981; 2002).

However, from a symbolic perspective, it is not only the satisfaction of the material interests of weaker states by 'benign hegemony' that guarantees international stability. The durability of an order also is maintained if this domination is not perceived as being 'humiliating' by the weaker states. Thus, the Clinton administration, keen on multilateralism, attracted less opposition than the G.W. Bush administration because European political powers had the feeling that they were being treated as key players in world politics.

**Approaches in the analysis of international orders from the recognition point of view**

The recognition approach is without a doubt the closest of the constructivist analyses that evaluate the stability of the international system in relation to identities and shared norms (Kratochwil 1987; Wendt 1994; Hopf 1999). This intersubjective perspective may explain why states comply, more frequently than is usually assumed, as they are naturally concerned with maintaining a positive self-image within the international community. Thus, the United States refrains from using tactical nuclear weapons despite their strategic advantage in breaking down dictators' bunkers, like in 1991 in Iraq, fearing reprisals from the international community. It is illusory to think that power can be exercised without taking account of shared morale sentiments (Thomas 2001: 22–47). Going further than constructivists, I would like to highlight the 'material' existence of a 'recognition denial' (Honneth 1991) that is capable of leading to war. The stigmatisation of great powers and their exclusion from international institutions constitute, from this perspective, such denials.

*Working hypotheses, methods and plan*

This chapter is based on a comparison of four great power systems. The selection of my four cases is directed by the objective to choose cases with a great deal of variation in the dependent variable – armed and militarised conflicts – and little variation in the independent variables.[2] Thus while the four cases vary a great deal in regard to armed conflicts and militarised disputes such as the first period of the Congress of Vienna (1815–1853) and the Versailles system (1919–1939), they vary little in regard to numerous variables such as the powers involved (all of our cases involve great powers), the nature of power distribution (in nearly all systems except one – we examine multipolar systems) or the historical background (all great power conflicts are taken from the nineteenth and twentieth century).

The first method of verification is to see whether there exists a co-variation

---

2. For the selection of case studies: George and Bennett (2005); Elman and Fendius (2001).

between systems with few armed conflicts and militarised disputes and the degree of recognition in relations between great powers. For example, is it true that international systems with 'self-restraining' powers, shared political identities, non-punitive peace treaties and inclusion of all powers, are more stable than others? Secondly, I will mobilise many historical studies to detect political actors' subjective motivations. For instance, to what extent does historical research show that decisions to engage in war or militarised disputes – such as Hitler's invasion of Poland or the Berlin Blockade (1948/49) – were inspired by recognition themes such as revenge or the desire to save face? Finally, I will expose my recognition hypotheses to a congruence test, meaning that I will weigh them against alternative explanations, particularly of realist thought (Van Evera 1997). All of our cases are the 'least likely' cases (King, Keohane and Sidney 1994) for the theme of recognition. They are all related to 'great' power conflicts. Scholars expect that in such issues physical survival should easily come before vanity. Contrary to such intuitive understanding of armed conflict, evidence in this chapter suggests that the quest for recognition is as much a cause of international conflict as that of security concerns or profits in terms of power and wealth. The cases presented here show that far from being an epiphenomenon of international relations, attacks (objective or perceived) on esteem or against a state's self image can have very tangible material effects by legitimising and nourishing physical violence, manifested through war.

According to the first hypothesis, an international order in which great powers claim a superior role over the others is propitious to armed conflicts. Such a configuration easily forms an identity dilemma. The recognition of one actor implies the non-recognition of the other. Thus, it was impossible for Poland to recognise alleged Aryan superiority without jeopardizing its own identity. Similarly, it was impossible for the theocratic and proselytizing Iran to comply with an American power which was keen on spreading democratic values. On the other hand, egalitarian identities strengthen mutual respect, as is the case within the European Union.

I will empirically identify hubristic identities or, on the contrary, the more modest, of the great powers by examining the architecture of their new governmental buildings. I have differentiated three forms of architecture: ostentatious architecture (2 points), representative architecture (1 point) and modest architecture (0 points). Two simple criteria make this differentiation possible: the dimensions and costs of newly constructed governmental buildings and their 'regular', or, on the contrary, their 'curved' form. One can reasonably hypothesise that over-sized and rectilinear architectural dimensions transmit hubristic images of political leaders and a will to control the world, such as Adolf Hitler's *Reichskanzlei* conceived by A. Speer. Then, I shall examine if 'hubristic' architecture is associated with militarised disputes and armed conflicts between great powers, relying on the Correlates of War Project database created by researchers from the University of Pennsylvania and Michigan.[3]

My second hypothesis postulates that the heterogeneity of domestic identi-

---

3. Correlates of War 2 Project. Small and Singer (1982); Jones, Bremer and Singer (1996).

ties makes mutual recognition, and consequently peace, more difficult. Ideological heterogeneity creates another identity dilemma; seeking domestic agreement can easily spark discontent on the international stage. For example, Soviet decision-makers had to refer to Marxist-Leninist ideology in order to guarantee their reputation on the domestic front and this attempt at legitimisation sparked off fears about 'true' Soviet intentions abroad. International heterogeneity may be a source of war by the simple interest of leaders to defend their institutional position against 'domestic' revolutionary unrest. Nevertheless, beyond the strategic threat of ideological rivalry, a regime with an opposed ideology can also be an attack against self-esteem, as well as sacredly held values.

On the other hand, if a state positively identifies itself with others, a resort to force is unlikely due to the interest in not jeopardizing a positive self image. The ideological homogeneity consolidates the feeling of recognition between states by confirming their own interior values by the existence of another 'analogous' power. Thus, the feeling of common belonging – for instance within the EU – makes the recourse to force against another state immoral and as a result symbolically costly. Luxembourg should not fear annexation by its more powerful neighbours because such an action would be perceived as morally reprehensible and, as a result, costly to the image of the aggressor. It is not always easy to determine if 'ideological' heterogeneity is a source of conflict by a 'corporatist' or an 'identity' threat. The expression of spontaneous emotion or, on the contrary, strategic calculation *vis-à-vis* certain actions jeopardizing domestic 'values' may give us some clues about an actor's motivation. The degree of heterogeneity of the international system can be detected thanks to the compatibility of internal legitimacies between great powers. Are heterogeneous systems more propitious to armed conflict between great powers than homogeneous ones?

According to my third hypothesis, non-recognition of a state's universal status, such as the exclusion of great powers from major international conferences and the humiliating treatment of defeated powers, can equally encourage armed conflict. It is also necessary to characterise the method of exercising hegemonic power. Is it a unilateral or multilateral domination? Is it based on military force or on 'soft power' (as defined by one's capability of convincing another to want the same) (Nye 2002)? Even the realist E. H. Carr confirms that the stability of an international order depends in a large part on its legitimacy and the respect that it grants to dominated powers

> Any moral international order must be founded on some hegemony of power. But this hegemony, like the supremacy of a ruling class within the state, is in itself a challenge to those who do not share it; and it must, if it is to survive, contain an element of give and take, of self-sacrifice on the part of those who have, which will render it tolerable to the other members of the world community'. (Carr 2001: 51f)

Moreover, the hegemonic power's capacity to respect other states explains why a 'hegemonic power' does not trigger off counter-coalitions if it keeps the exercise of its might within reasonable limits.

First of all, I will concentrate on stable international orders, that is to say those in which war and military disputes between great powers are rare. The order of the Congress of Vienna (1815–53) and the peace between democracies after 1945 are prime examples that correspond to the principle of stable international order. I will demonstrate that stability is maintained where there is a relative match between the identities claimed by one state and the identities granted by others as well as non-stigmatisation and the inclusion of great powers within international institutions. Finally two conflicting orders shall be considered, the first being the post First World War/pre-World War II period (1919–1939) and the second being the first period of the Cold War (1945–53). The precarious feature of these orders is explained by their heterogeneity, their hubristic identities, as well as the stigmatisation and gratuitous punishment of vanquished powers.

## THE PACIFICATION BETWEEN GREAT POWERS BY RESPECT

### The Congress of Vienna (1815–1853)

The international order made by the Congress of Vienna is characterised by surprising stability to the extent that no major confrontation between the great powers emerged for ninety-nine years, with the exception of the Crimean War (1853–1856) and two bilateral confrontations on a smaller scale (the Austro-German War of 1866 and the Franco-German War of 1870). In comparison, Europe was confronted with five wars between great European powers during the revolutionary period (Carr 2001). Finally, the number of war casualties during the nineteenth century was clearly weaker than during previous centuries, as well as during the following one.[4] Paul Schroeder asserts that

> the nineteenth century has represented the most stable international order having existed since the emergence of the modern international system (Schroeder 1996)

My purpose here is to explain this durability, through temperate and shared identities and recognition between European powers.

Unlike the 'imperial' past of the European continent marked by Portuguese, Spanish and French messianism, no European power openly aspired, during the first half of the nineteenth century, for superiority over other powers. Napoleonic conquests made other European states aware of the importance of their sovereignty. The Treaty of Chaumont (1814) established the Quadruple Alliance. It proclaimed a Europe of independent states, equal in rights, status and security (Longhorne 1986; Jervis 1985; Kissinger 1973). At the time of the Congress of Vienna, the powers set up a complex diplomatic protocol in which all states agreed, regardless of their actual power, an equal rank: the 'precedence of seniority' (Bull 1995; Schroeder 1992; Nicholson 1970; Lascoumes 1991). These temperate identities convey the principle of legal equality between great pow-

---

4. Sorokin (1997) 33,645,620 casualties for a population of 238,000,000 whereas the number of casualties, during the eighteenth century, stands at 4,505,990 for a population of 135,000,000 inhabitants. The population is the one assessed in 1850, 1750. Ruloff (2003).

ers. The relatively modest image held by political leaders has been reflected in the architecture of governmental and institutional buildings constructed during that period.⁵ In Austro-Hungary, 'classical' architecture prevailed, represented by Paul Wilhelm Sprenger (1798–1854). From 1842, he led construction within the Austro-Hungarian Empire. He was recognised for functionality and for the economic characteristics of his constructions. If the place of political power is the *Schönbrunn Palace*, it became, following the Congress of Vienna, associated with the idea of 'light living'; with its festivals and 'waltzes' (Morelli 2000).

In Great Britain, Victorian architecture distinguishes itself by the renaissance of the Gothic style accompanied by other stylistic elements. The most important construction was the Palace of Westminster, conceived by A.W. Pugin and Sir Charles Barry (1836–37; 1844–52). It boasts an 'imposing' style and oversized dimensions, with its one thousand one hundred rooms, a facade two hundred and seventy-five metres long and the ninety-seven metres high St Stephen's Tower which houses Big Ben. The irregularity of its whole, its asymmetric structure (with a significant number of juxtaposed aisles), its historical eclecticism and the weak Gothic 'elevation', diminishes the impression of a gigantic structure (Gympel 2005). As regards Buckingham Palace, its splendour is strengthened by the works carried out between 1820 and 1830 by John Nash (see for instance the Mall, the one mile triumphal path leading from Trafalgar Square up to the entrance of Buckingham Palace). Nash was dismissed in 1831 and replaced by the competent and somewhat soberer Edward Blore. Aesthetic writings from that time, like those of John Ruskin, advocated moderation and architectural harmony against excessive structure, drawing inspiration from the Aristotelian ethic of the 'just middle'.⁶

In Prussia, the beginning of the century was dominated by the classicism of the royal architect Karl Friedrich Schinkel (1780–1841). Buildings, like the *Gendarmenmarkt Theater* (1818–1824), *L'Altes Museum* in Berlin (1824–1827), the Church of Saint Nicholas of Potsdam or the cathedral of Berlin, embody an austere and rigorous style though without being 'spectacular' or over-sized (Melvin 2002). Schinkel's ideal was respect of functionality and the harmonious clarity of ancient designs. The Charlottenhof Palace, built between 1826 and 1829, looks more like an Italian villa than a palace. As regards France, Louis XVIII as well as Charles X, preferred the Palais des Tuileries' more modest environment, to the Napoleonic Invalides and the Palace of Versailles. 'Classical' constructions, such as Henri Labrouste's library, Sainte Geneviève (1845–1850), preferred functionality in order to promote educational dimensions (Melvin 2002).

Lastly, among the powers of the Pentarchy, Russia has without doubt the most dramatic showcase of power. The new Great Palace of the Kremlin was built between 1837 and 1851 by A. Ton. Ton was assigned to demonstrate the splendour

---

5. For the literature: Poirrier (2006); Melvin (2002); Monnier (2001); Morelli (2000); Hipp and Seidl (1996); Mumford (1972).

6. "There is virtue in the measure, and error in the excess…" quoted by John Ruskin, *Unto His Last and Other Writings*, London, Penguin Classics, 1989, p. 107.

of the Russian aristocracy. The dimensions of the palace highlight this attempt; one hundred and twenty-five metres long, forty-seven metres high and twenty-five thousand metres squared. Even the private apartments were splendidly decorated. Although the exterior of the palace is imposing, it remains in 'simple and elegant' classicist style (Morelli 2000). In St Petersburg, for the sumptuous Tsarskoïe Selo Palace, the builder was concerned chiefly with the upkeep of the building.

To conclude this point, within these European powers, the architecture of their governmental and institutional buildings during the first half of the nineteenth century were often 'prestigious', but in comparison with previous periods, considered proportional and 'functional'.

The homogeneity of the international system was another factor of stability. The compatibility of domestic institutions was a source of collective identification and peace. Unlike the eighteenth century, monarchies had slowly developed a common belonging. This awareness of a collective identity had its origin in the French Revolution in 1789. The fear of contagious revolution was still strong. Lord Castlereagh, the British Foreign minister, remarked that once revolution has been undertaken, another can swiftly follow.[7] According to Henry Kissinger, the balance between powers had shifted from a 'physical' nature to a 'moral' one, as powers sought to regulate their relations in referring to accepted values (Kissinger 1994). The preamble of the Holy Alliance between Austria-Hungary, Russia and Prussia states that, 'Conforming with the Words and Scripture of the Holy Saints who allow all men to regard themselves as brothers, the three contracting Monarchies are now united by real and indisputable links of Brotherhood, and are hereafter Compatriots' (Berstein and Milza 1995). Metternich noted in 1824, in a letter to Wellington, 'For a long-time now, Europe has had for me the quality of a fatherland' (Kissinger 1994: 86).

This collective identity progressively became much more than the defence of the dynastic identities against the force of liberalism. For example, Prussia refrained from exploiting German nationalism against Austria-Hungary and Alexander I and Nicholas I of Russia refrained from taking advantage of the weaknesses of the Ottoman Empire. As H. Kissinger observed:

> Had Prussia sought to exploit German nationalism, it could have challenged Austrian pre-eminence in Germany a generation before Bismarck. Had Tsars Alexander I and Nicholas I only considered solely Russia's geopolitical opportunities, they would have exploited the disintegration of the Ottoman Empire far more decisively to Austria's peril... . (Kissinger 1994: 85)

The three central powers remained, for a long-time, linked to the common feeling of monarchist solidarity. In 1849, Russia intervened in Austria's favour when the latter was confronted by revolutionary unrest in Hungary. Pierre Renouvin stated that

---

7. '... *one revolution was made the means of giving birth to another.*' Quoted by Sir Harold Nicholson (1970:155).

the Russian government, nonetheless, demands nothing; it sent, without any compensation, an army of 150,000 men. It was an important step because Russia could have considered leaving Austria to collapse giving her more freedom to act in the important Balkan region (Renouvin 1994: 207)

Similarly, Germany cooperated with Russia in the suppression of the Polish uprising. Prussia and Austria-Hungary avoided in 1850 (Olmütz) a war over the German issue not only because of the Russian threat, but also from the pressure of the Prussian Old Guard conservatives (Geiss 1988: 108). A war against Austria was perceived as being 'immoral' and so incompatible with Prussian honour. In 1873, Germany, Russia and Austro-Hungary signed the Alliance of the Three Emperors.

As regards to the recognition of an equal dignity between great powers, the 'punishment' of France was moderated by the concern to set up the foundations of a stable peace. Within the Treaty of Paris (1815), France was to give up all of its conquests and retreat to its pre-revolutionary borders. From 1816, the seven hundred million francs compensation claimed from France was divided by six. Loans were guaranteed by British banks and unlike previous occurrences, the defeated power was not excluded from the Concert of Power at the Congress of Aix-la-Chapelle in 1818, but was included. The original one hundred and fifty thousand strong occupational force was evacuated. According to Castlereagh, France's overzealousness could have severely damaged Europe, but the Allies 'took the chance to secure the peace that all the powers of Europe so strongly desired' (Kissinger 1994).

For the great powers, the peaceful evolution of their identities is due greatly to their 'inclusion' in the Congress of Vienna. Alexander's Russia caused trouble with imperial ambitions within Orthodox Europe. But this was 'truncated' by the other great powers who brought up this issue at the great international conferences. As for the style of exercising power, one must acknowledge the 'multilateral', concerted and moderated characteristics of British domination. Some institutional mechanisms, such as the organisation of meetings and regular consultations were put into place following the 1814 Treaty of Chaumont, in order to collectively manage conflicts of interests and territorial disputes (Battistella 2006: 57). Thus Austria's intervention in the German states where liberal movements were growing was authorised by the Congress of Carlsbad (August 1819) and of Vienna (1820). Facing national unrest in Spain, Portugal and the Kingdom of Naples-Sicily (1820), the Congress of Troppa permitted the Holly Alliance to fight the revolution on the Iberian Peninsula as well as in Italy. As for the revolution in Greece (from 1821), the Holy Alliance was opposed to it at the Congress of Verona in the name of monarchical solidarity. All of these actions, even if some of the powers, such as Russia, may have been reluctant, were concerted efforts. Consensus, at least at the beginning, characterised the Congress.

This confirms John Ikenberry's judgement, according to which international society only turns out to be effective and durable when it can rely on a capable power that supports the creation of institutions to regulate the work of the international system, relying in a large part on self-restraint. It is not the hegemony itself which is the originator of peace, but its ability 'to engage in strategic auto-restriction, reassuring its partners and thus facilitating cooperation' (Ikenberry 1981). This description of a 'good' hegemonic power applies perfectly to nineteenth century Great Britain. In Europe, Great Britain did not exploit its vast power in order to impose its will. Far from feeling scorned, other great European powers considered Great Britain's use of its naval power as tolerable, indeed beneficial.[8] The Congress of Vienna put into place a system of collective security where all subjects were under the guarantee of all powers and not only a few individual powers.

Nonetheless, the system gradually weakened from the strains of revisionist powers. In 1848 with the accession of the French Second Republic, monarchical solidarity was no longer an uncontested reference. Under Lamartine's rule, the government of the Second Republic developed a 'revolutionary' strategy to weaken the Austro-Hungarian monarchy. When Napoleon III came to power, established powers were suspicious of him. Far from going out of their way to integrate him into the scope of the great powers, they reserved an almost discriminatory treatment for him because for other powers he was not regarded as a 'brother', but merely as a 'friend'. Feeling snubbed, Napoleon III aimed to overthrow the Vienna order in order to re-establish France's honour. He encouraged Italian unity in 1859 and pushed Prussia in confronting the faltering Austro-Hungarian Empire. Napoleon III felt that France was being unfairly isolated from the international system. Paradoxically, he strengthened German power which eventually put an end to French hegemonic ambitions in Europe. Napoleon III had nothing to gain with such provocations. His attitude is partially explained by the lack of consideration from the other great powers towards him. As regards the stigmatisation of vanquished powers, Bismarck took care not to humiliate Austria-Hungary in 1866. Contrary to his own political instinct, he annexed in 1871 Alsace-Lorraine under pressure from his Chiefs of Staff and proclaimed German unity in great pomp at the Hall of Mirrors at Versailles. As a result, a structural adversity existed between France and Germany until the First World War (Renouvin 1994; Kissinger 1994).

**Alternative explanations for the stability of the Congress of Vienna**
Classical analyses of European politics give little attention to the normative foundations of the order of Vienna. According to the hypothesis of hegemonic peace, Great Britain's hegemony guaranteed the stability in the European order. From this, the decline of British power at the end of the nineteenth century went hand in hand with an increased probability of world war.

Contrary to this interpretation, it is arguable that the peaceful or bellicose effects depend on what the declining hegemonic power 'produced'. Scornful behaviour from dominant powers, that offends state identities, such as at the time of Louis XIV or Napoleon, inevitably triggers off resistance from the dominated powers even though they have an 'interest' to submit without resistance. And yet, the 'soft' domination of Great Britain was so discreet that it was hardly perceived

---

8. Schroeder (1996: 575) 'It kept the sea lanes open, encouraged and protected commerce, and, as will be seen, was not used to monopolize overseas expansion for Britain'.

to be a hegemonic power by other European states. In the same way, Great Britain did not have a role identity that was incompatible with the affirmation of other great powers. Despite its maritime hegemony (but not on the European continent), Great Britain reacted carefully to provocations, as shown by her patient behaviour towards Russia, who was always inclined to try to destabilise the Ottoman Empire. Such restraint is not so evident. Louis XIV, the Sun King, went so far as to wage war on the Netherlands in response to satirical pamphlets published there which criticised his reign (Cornette 2005: 79).

For peacekeeping purposes, it is necessary that the hegemonic power is viewed as a benign power. In spite of an increase in potential power, Great Britain never sought to unilaterally dominate the international stage and refused to pursue territorial conquests on mainland European. The logic of hegemonic peace also suggests that it was the decline of British supremacy which revealed her challengers' ambitions and at the same time forced Great Britain to defend herself against this aggression with a preventive war. Even so, England was by far the most pacifying great power on the European continent in July 1914. For another school of thought, the stability of the 'Viennese' system was due to its ability to maintain the balance on the European continent. According to William Pitt's plan, the British Prime Minister, Central Europe should have been strong enough, via the setting up of bigger and allied states, to resist French and Russian expansion. The creation of the German Confederation with thirty or so states under the auspices of Austria and Germany matched Pitt's objective. For Henry Kissinger, the Confederation was too powerful to be attacked by France, but was too weak and decentralised to attack its neighbours (Kissinger 1994). German unity shattered these balances. In other words, Germany was not able to become the rival power of Great Britain without jeopardizing the European balance of power (Geiss 1990). The growing instability of this system was demonstrated above all by the upheaval of the balance of forces on the European continent following the revolutions or the affirmations of independence, firstly Italian (1859) and then German (1871). Germany transformed itself from a Confederation of thirty-nine states (from 1815) to a united state with immense resources. As the new centre of power with rapid growth, both demographic (from forty one million people in 1871 to sixty-four million in 1914) and economic, Germany had to engage in imperialist expansion and the construction of a powerful navy.

This interpretation does not take into account that the balance of power on the European continent was already disrupted during the first half of the nineteenth century. The weakening of Austro-Hungary did not have major consequences because, as we have seen, neither Russia nor Prussia were willing to take advantage of the growing weakness of the Danubian monarchy. The old feeling of solidarity prevailed over ambitions of power. The system of regular consultation between great powers survived even after German unity (see for instance the Congress of Berlin in 1878) for a period of roughly twenty years, which is far from being a negligible period. Bismarck's Germany declared itself 'saturated' in order to avoid the 'nightmare of coalitions' (Bismarck 1877). Against those who yearned for colonial expansion, Bismarck objected 'This is France, this is Russia and we are right in the middle. This is my map of Africa'(Kaplan 2005: 37–38). The Bismarckian system was, because of this moderation, relatively steady. In other words, despite the upheaval of the European balance, the system remained steady as long as the dominating powers remained committed to the policy of self-restraint and maintaining the 'honour' of the other powers.

### Peace between the great democratic powers (1945–1991)

If a democracy is defined as a political regime that organises fair, competitive elections and where the opposition has a real chance of obtaining power, as well as a system in which individual rights, such as freedom of expression, are guaranteed (Ted Gurr), it would be fair to say that there are no examples of war between two democratic countries between 1945 and 1991.[9] The number of democracies has constantly increased, chiefly with the third democratic wave after 1989, strengthening considerably the democratic peace theory as it further became 'statistically' significant. Additionally, democracies have concluded strong alliances within NATO or the EU. Even after the disappearance of the Soviet threat, these alliances have continued to exist. A war within western democracies is no longer within reasonable contemplation. Europe, having been ripped apart by war over the centuries has become a haven of peace. According to my thesis, this development has been supported by temperate, homogeneous and shared identities. Cooperative behaviour and 'respect' within the democratic sphere have produced positive identifications.

After 1945 and the excesses of Nazi Germany, no 'great' democracy has had the ambition to affirm superiority over other democratic states. The United States was more an 'empire by invitation' (Lundestad) in Western Europe than a genuine superpower aspiring domination. Furthermore, states from Western countries prompted the United States to remain on the European continent (Lundestad 2005). The temperate identity among great democracies is also in the expression of governmental architecture. The Federal Republic of Germany is possibly the best example of new modesty in self-representation (Reichel 1996). The choice of the small town of Bonn with its three hundred thousand inhabitants, known as a town of retired people with an important yet 'relaxed' university is in itself an indication of the political leaders' desire to adopt a low profile on the international stage. The German parliament was sober. Its architect H. Schwippert wanted to create an architectural antithesis to the Nazis' monumental and ostentatious classicism designs. He preferred glass to stone in order to emphasise the transparency of the new German democracy. The other governmental buildings have comparable inspiration. The Chancery was at first in the Palace of Schaumburg. In 1973, the new Chancery was completed. Its symmetric façades, which are made up partly of large windows are barely distinguishable from an ordinary office block (Petsch 1977). Moreover, Chancellor Schmidt lived close to Hamburg in a modest bungalow, which amazed his friend Valéry Giscard d'Estaing. On the other hand, the architecture of the second big 'new' democracy, that of Japan, can be qualified as 'prestigious'.

---

9. See also 'Polity IV' (2005), a bank of data collected by some researchers of the University of Maryland; Gurr (2000).

The Kantei, the official residence of the Japanese Prime Minister, built in 1929, is heavily influenced by Frank Lloyd Wright. Similarly, few changes were made in the composition of the Japanese Parliament; continuity prevailed. Moreover, Japanese architecture modernised and became known for the new movement called Metabolism. Tange Kenzo supervised the installations of the 1964 Olympic Games as well as the Universal Exposition of Osaka in 1970. The Tokyo City Hall, finished in 1991 by Kenzo, conveys this technical approach; architecturally both modern and ambitious. This building, with its audacious structure is 'crowned' by twin towers, each measuring some two hundred metres (Melvin 2002).

During the same period, the continuity of governmental architecture also prevailed in Great Britain. The older government buildings, such as 10 Downing Street, are reinvested by political power. In the 1950s, there were plans to demolish the Foreign and Commonwealth Office at Downing Street in order to build a more modern complex. These projects were soon abandoned. As for Italy, the old buildings were acquired by the Republic. The *Senato della Repubblica* is still in the same residence as it was during the rule of the monarchy (since 1871). It is situated in the elegant *Palazio Madama* built by the Medici family. The President of the Council's seat has, since 1961, been the Palazzo Chigi which was Pope Alexander VII's residence (1655–1667). This elegant building is located in a very residential district.

In France, the Prime Minister lives in the Hotel Matignon whereas the President lives in the Elysée Palace in Paris. The Elysée Palace is a striking example of classicism with guards behind a monumental gate completed by four ionic columns. Since 1874, there have been minimal changes. President Vincent Auriol restored the Palace of Elysée without really modifying its appearance. Presidents Auriol, Pompidou and Mitterrand each hired interior designers to add contemporary design to the Elysée. Some projects like Le Corbusier in Marseilles demonstrate a will to break with 'monumental' architecture. In the United States, the interior of the White House was slightly modified with the arrival of the Truman administration – a presidential bunker was added. Whereas the Jefferson memorial (1939–1948) and the Gatway Arch (1959–1965) are rather spectacular (Krieger 1996),[10] the modern architecture inspired by Bauhaus (and notably Mies van der Rohe) gives more transparency and lightness to American cities. So, although governmental architecture of great western powers is 'dignified', it clearly presents a rupture with the monumental architecture of the interwar period. Federal Germany exemplifies most clearly the new sobriety in the showcase of political power.

Ideological homogeneity constitutes another factor in the pacification of relations between great democratic powers. Faced with the heterogeneity of the international system and the 'revolutionary' threat of the USSR, democracies that developed after 1945 can be said to have a shared identity. The Truman Doctrine of March 1947 was the first significant manifestation. Referring to the communist threat in Turkey, Greece and against the Western world, this speech was a mani-

---

10. Krieger, P. 'Spiegelnde Curtain Wall als Projektionsflächen für politische Schlagbilder', in Hipp and Seidel (1996: 297–310).

festo for inaugurating the community of 'free nations', or free people. Created in 1949, NATO, more than simply a traditional alliance, was a system of collective security, in which security was considered as being indivisible: one for all and all for one. This collective conscience transposed itself into the concerted structures of NATO with defence planning committees and multinational bodies. If the collective identity was primarily a quasi-instrumental method of providing better protection to Western countries against the communist threat, it subsequently became an autonomous reality. Thus, even during the Cuban missile crisis of 1962, President Kennedy experienced a degree of responsibility over Berlin, asking whether the Soviets could not be brought to account over reprisals against the city.

This positive identification was rendered possible by cooperative practices between the dominant democracies. Unlike the order of Versailles, founded on the exclusion of the German nation and the USSR from the concert of Europe, the Federal Republic was rapidly accepted within the new order of democratic powers (Lundestad 2005: 63–110). It was also well integrated within NATO and the European community. Similarly the United States was willing to economically help Germany *via* 'care' packages and by the Marshall Plan announced on the 5th June 1947 at Harvard University. American occupying troops behaved in a friendly way towards the German population. The image of the nice black American soldier giving chocolates to German children is profoundly rooted within the German collective conscious. Thus, a nation which once believed that it held the 'master race' quickly transformed its collective identity thanks to the protective and empathetic behaviour of the occupational forces. America was at the head of a benign leadership within Europe, that is to say a leadership based on consultation, soft-power and self-restraint. Georges-Henri Soutou stated that unlike the common conception, Europeans begged the reluctant Americans to bind the two sides of the Atlantic by a formal military and political commitment (Soutou 2001). The United States pursued a clear recognition strategy by setting up an institutional network in the Western hemisphere – monetary (Bretton Woods and GATT) and security (NATO) systems that aimed to guarantee cooperation between Western democracies.

Unlike other hegemonies, the United States offered its allies an opportunity to partake in co-decision. In the words of Charles Maier, American hegemony was a 'consensual empire' (Maier 2007: 146f). Americans supported the construction of the European Community and accepted, for the first time, discrimination against their own exports (Melandri 1994: 40). Americans exercised their hegemony by consent (Gaddis 2005: 61). The favourable outcome of the Cold War for American power was certainly partly due to the fact that the USSR was not concerned with installing its legitimacy in Central and Eastern Europe, but rather with pillaging the region's economic resources. Even after the disappearance of the USSR, European powers had no ambition to oppose American hegemony for they were used to its 'self-restriction' (Ikenberry 1981).

Thus, according to my interpretation, democratic peace is a consequence of a self-fulfilling prophecy. This is because cooperative behaviour between democracies has promoted shared identities, creating in turn cooperative practices.

## Alternative explanations to democratic peace

To explain democratic peace, liberal theories emphasise the peaceful nature of democratic regimes, putting forward the 'civilising' role that their internal structures have, for example, that the 'institutional' complexity of democracies impedes the decision to resort to violence. Liberal theories also claim that a country's political culture would be 'exported' to an interstate level. These interpretations barely enable us to understand why democracies often demonise authoritarian regimes, for instance Reagan's 'Empire of Evil' or G. W. Bush's 'Axis of Evil'. It is far from accepted that all conflicts between democratic and authoritarian regimes are always initiated by the latter; even the origins of the Cold War are contested. Colonial wars (Algeria, Indochina) or interventions of great democratic powers against minor states (against Allende's Chile, Chad, and Panama) can hardly be down to purely defensive considerations. Instead of rushing to assert the peaceful character of democracies, it is necessary at first to elucidate the precise meaning of 'democratic peace', i.e., the absence of armed conflicts between democracies. Democratic peace does not exclude the persistence of wars between democratic and authoritarian regimes. Democracies often adopt a 'Hobbesian' policy when they are confronted by ideological adversaries (the refusal to cooperate with other states and even possibly attempting to annihilate the opposition by branding him a sworn enemy). The American refusal to give Taliban prisoners the status of 'prisoner of war' is a good example of this 'Hobbesian' practice. On the other hand, such powers display themselves as 'Kantian' amongst their peers, i.e., they renounce resorting to force against another state, partially identifying themselves with the other's interests.

The existence of conflicting relations between Western democracies before 1945 constitutes the strongest argument against the idea of democratic peace because the threat of an armed conflict during this period was far from being ruled out. 'Democratic peace' is an historical product for, before 1945, it was a fragile phenomenon. From my perspective, the two wars which pose the most serious problem are the armed confrontation between the United States and the Philippines (1899) and alignment of the democracy of Finland with the Axis Powers during the Second World War (1941–1944). The Philippines War can be interpreted as a colonial war. The Filipino regime was not yet democratically elected and American leaders considered the Filipino resistance as evidence of their lack of civilisation rather than of a demonstration of democratic will. The Filipino leaders had, nevertheless, shown their will to establish a real democracy and proclaimed on the 23rd June 1899, the First Republic of the Philippines. Their constitution contained a 'bill of rights' and foresaw executive power assisted by a representative assembly. It was therefore not a lack of democratic will in the Philippines, but rather a racially charged ethnocentrism on the part of American leaders, that prevented a peaceful resolution to the conflict.

During the pre-bipolar period, there are significant examples of 'militarised disputes' between democracies where the resort to force was far from excluded. During the 1890s (1895–1896), Great Britain and the United States disagreed over the boundary limits between Venezuela and British Guinea. With the threat of war against Great Britain, President Cleveland strengthened American military presence. His behaviour was all the more remarkable as his foreign policy was considered as being prudent and conservative. The driving force behind American intransigence was not down to the President and his administration, but – contrary to theoretical attempts to clarify his behaviour – 'public opinion'. An employee of the British embassy in Washington noted that it would be pleasant to go to a country where it would be possible to read newspapers without finding articles accusing your country of all possible imaginable crimes everywhere. Some political leaders, like Shelby Cullon, had even imagined using force against Great Britain in order to terminate its occupation of Cornito in Nicaragua (Layne 1994). The Ruhr crisis of 1923, which involved a Franco-Belgian invasion of the Ruhr, showed that the French Republic felt that the Weimar Republic was as dangerous as the preceding Wilhelminian Germany. Certain observers believe that the peaceful resolution of these crises was facilitated by the perception of being confronted by a democratic power (Layne 1994). Yet, an armed confrontation between democratic powers was at that time possible and even foreseen. Before 1945, one must acknowledge that democratic peace was an extremely fragile phenomena and nobody at that time would have put forward such a theory. The most conflictual relations between democracies before 1945 are linked to self-representations made by democratic powers, which were much more hubristic than after the Second World War. During this period, the democratic powers were also colonial powers and their leaders saw themselves as responsible for a 'civilising' mission.

As for shared identities, if democracies present the same domestic legitimacy, then at the very least they give them no value. For the pre-Second World War period, all the evidence leads us to believe that even the notion of a supranational democratic community was practically unknown. The referential identity of great powers before 1914 was incontestably the national community and certainly not a hypothetic community of democratic nations. The two big democratic powers, Great Britain and the United States, did not feel that they belonged to a supranational community. The British policy at the time was well expressed by Lord Palmerston who famously exclaimed that England knew neither friend nor foe, only interest (Geiss 1990). Decision makers had a strong awareness of their insularity and hesitated to involve themselves in continental alliances. This identity conception was reflected by Salisbury's formula according to which 'we are all fish' (Kissinger 1994).

The other great power, the United States, had an even more noticeable consciousness of its insularity and of the ocean which split her from the 'old world'. The isolation triumphed after the First World War. Indeed, the Wilsonian idea of 'a war for democracy, justice and freedom [...] and so that the Republicans of this world can live and can last' (January 1918) heralded the potential that democracies have to establish a community of values, especially when they are confronted with a major threat (Serfaty 1986: 21). However, as soon as the war was over, most of President Wilson's supporters resorted to the traditional approach and took the US's isolationist role on the international political scene. The very use of the term 'Western World' before the Second World War is rather revealing of American identity. Whereas we think of Western democracies when this term is used, it was at that time synonymous with the Western hemisphere (i.e., the Americas) where the Monroe Doctrine of 1823 aimed to free the continent from the predators of the Old World. If, in the US, there was a supranational identity, it was indisputably geographic and not political. When President Roosevelt claimed 'I hate war' in his speech on the 14th August, 1936, he coined the phrase 'peace in the Western world' referring to the US's 'good neighbourhood' relationship with Latin America, which he felt could be used as an example for Europe. Before the Second World War, America felt that European problems were the problems of 'others'. The influential Senator Gerard Nye, a Republican from North Dakota, exclaimed in 1936

> If Europe once again explodes before our eyes, America can avoid being entangled once more in the difficulties she faced before [referring to the First World War and the US intervention in 1917], if the US is intelligent enough to learn from history. (Holbo 1967: 12)

America was content for a long time to protect the Western hemisphere against external aggression (Gaddis 1987), adhering to Jefferson's ideal of establishing 'lines' between the new and old world

> From our side, no European rifle will be heard and no American rifle will be heard on the other side. (Serfaty 1991; Powarski 1991).

As regards to politics of recognition, at least during the period between 1919 and 1925, the French Republic under Clemenceau and Poincaré had no intention whatsoever of integrating the Weimar Republic within the great powers. Before 1945, there was no 'political integration' and even consultation between democratic powers comparable to NATO and the EU. The Entente Cordiale concluded between France and Britain (1904) was not a real alliance – there was no guarantee of mutual assistance in case of aggression – but formerly an agreement on the areas of influence in North Africa (British control over Egypt and French control of Morocco). For the majority of democratic leaders, the driving force of international politics was the 'national interest' and the balance of forces and not 'ideological' solidarity. In fact, democratic leaders from that time made few differences between foreign policy of an authoritarian regime and that of a democratic regime. In 1944, President Roosevelt noted about Russians

> They still have a piece of stale bread inside their country to keep them for many years to come.... (Gaddis 1987)

This prism of 'Realpolitik' led them to underestimate Nazi Germany and the USSR's ambitions. Until 1946, the American perception of the USSR was on the whole positive. Truman noted in May 1945 that he also had many difficulties in negotiating with Churchill, maybe as much as with Stalin. At the same time, the American military strategists saw their country as a mediator between Great Britain and Russia on the European continent. At the Potsdam Conference, Truman still saw Stalin as 'Uncle Joe', with whom he could still 'do business' (Gaddis 1987).

The fragility of 'democratic peace' in the pre-bipolar period apparently confirms the realist theory according to which the democratic community is a transitional creation of the Cold War. However, the persistence of the bi-polar referential – democratic friends/authoritarian enemies – incarnated in the democratic enlargement doctrine of the Clinton administration, then the 'Wilsonism in boots' (Hassner and Vaisse 2003; Ehrman 2009) led by the Bush administration in the post-Cold War period, confirms my 'recognition' interpretation. It is because of the absence of a shared identity that democracies behaved as potential enemies amongst themselves before 1945. On the contrary, as soon as the concept of the 'Western Community' became anchored into the minds of democratic leaders, the symbolic price of a 'muscled' approach, i.e., military mobilisation against another democratic state, became so costly that this course of action was no longer realistic.

## WAR TO AVOID SHAME?

### The interwar period 1919–1939

The order of the interwar period was very short. During its existence, changing political regimes, wars (for example, the invasion of Manchuria by Japan in 1931), international crises and militarised disputes followed one another. The order of Versailles represented the perfect example of instability in an international system.

It was principally during the 1930s when Germany, Japan and Italy each developed their own hubristic national identities, alleging a racial superiority over other nations. At the moment when Hitler gained power, German nationalism was consolidated in such a way that its transformation *via* a policy of appeasement became practically impossible. The identity assigned to the national-socialist German role – the alleged racial superiority of the Germans over other nations – is crucial for understanding the origins of the Second World War. Names, such as *Führer* or *conductorre* demonstrate this pretension of superiority. These dictatorships had inflated self descriptions. Hitler, who had failed the entrance examination to the Vienna Academy of Fine Arts on two occasions, never saw his best friend Kubizek again (after 1908) because he could not own up to his second failure. The writer Eric-Emmanuel Schmitt remarked that Hitler

> saw the war as an achievement, it socialised him, granting him a role […] it offered him the model of an organisation […] He became nostalgic, bellicose, politicised and determined to take his revenge to erase the defeat. (Schmitt 2003)

The National-Socialist ambition was not simply a revision of the Treaty of Versailles (Taylor 1946). The project for a Great Germany, with vital space in the East and the domination of the 'sub-human' Slavs had been a constant part of National-Socialist objectives since the release of *Mein Kampf* (1924).[11] It was im-

---

11. Hildebrand (1976: 522–30) 'For Hitler's intention and the task of National-Socialism was not to uphold a particular economic or social structure […] Rather, notwithstanding considerations of economic expediency, it was to realize racial supremacy on a global scale'. Hildebrand (1976: 524).

possible to convert Nationalist-Socialist leaders to a system of mediation. Even the refusal to grant Poland to Germany was perceived as an unbearable insult by the National-Socialist leaders. The will to impose the image of a superior Germany on other powers and to destroy all those who opposed it was a profound driving force behind the National-Socialist foreign policy.

The strategies and conquests of Hitler corresponded more to a logic of searching for 'recognition' than economic or political gain. Against all strategic logic, Hitler continued to exterminate Jews during the war whereas the resources used for this would have been put to better use on the Fronts. It is equally significant that Hitler postponed the war against Russia for one month because he believed that it was his duty to avenge the Serbian coup d'état that took place on the 26th March 1941 in Yugoslavia which replaced the Nazi puppet government of King Paul by his successor Peter. According to William L. Shirer, this coup provoked the most violent anger in Hitler's life (Stoessinger 2000). Postponing the war, because of the Russian winter with its snow storms and arctic temperatures, was one of the fatal strategic mistakes of the Second World War. The will to avenge 'offensive behaviour' clearly prevailed over strategic rationality. As regards the Western powers, they had retained enough political will so as not to be reduced to slavery by Nazi Germany. The intention of saving 'honour' became an important factor in the Anglo-French psyche of not accepting Polish incorporation into Nazi Germany.

Confirmation of unequal identities was distinctly represented by the architecture of the period. In Germany, there was a shift towards an architecture which became increasingly hubristic as the National-Socialists gained power. George L. Mosse recalled that Hitler and Mussolini grew up in baroque environments (Mosse 2003). The Baroque style, such as one finds in the Palace of Versailles, aimed to manifest the splendour and majesty of temporal and spiritual powers. Monuments were designed to submerge observers in their overwhelming grandeur. An impression of infinity comes from the main longitudinal naves or mirrors in the Hall of Mirrors at the Palace of Versailles. Drawing inspiration from the latter, the new chancellery designed for the *Führer*, constructed in 1938 by A. Speer, included a huge hall which was twice as long as the Hall of Mirrors. Hitler demanded Speer to build grand halls and antechambers to impress his visitors. Concerning his future visitors, he exclaimed 'they come to have a taste of the power and splendour of the German Empire' (Speer 1970). The Nazis constructed huge spaces for their parades. The best known staging is indisputably the meeting of two hundred and forty thousand people at the Congress of the National-Socialist Party in Nuremberg in 1936. This meeting became famous thanks to the propagandistic film that was staged, *The Triumph of Will*, directed by Leni Riefenstahl.

Neo-classicism was another reference to the Nazi style. It was characterised by elongated buildings covered with limestone plaques and the endless alignment of high pillars and windows which were designed for intimidation. There was no ephemeral characteristic about the design, as there is in modern architecture – the Nazis above all wanted to establish permanence; the 'One Thousand Year Reich'. Thus, during the construction of the Parliament in Nuremberg, A. Speer planned to leave a small part in ruins in order to highlight the atemporal character of the whole campaign. Following the Roman and Greek examples, the German Empire had to leave architectural traces even after several millennia. In order to do this, Speer stipulated the exclusive use of 'robust' materials, such as huge stones (e.g., in marble) and iron instead of steel or glass which is unable to withstand bad weather. 'Aryan games' were to replace the Olympic Games.

In this regard, National-Socialist leaders considered the construction of a huge stadium, the *Deutsche Stadium*, with a capacity of four hundred thousand. For the Berlin Olympic Games, they had to content themselves with the construction of a more modest stadium. The National-Socialist project led to the reconstruction of Berlin by Albert Speer (1905–1981) and this project was given the title Germania. A huge ceremonial avenue, ornately decorated with an Arc de Triomphe conceived by Hitler, was to link the largest station in the world to the Grand Hall, itself an edifice surpassed by a two hundred and ninety metre high monument topped with the Nazi Eagle holding a globe. This gigantic hall should have housed huge meetings, between 150,000 and 180,000 people, in which the individual would literally be drowned in the crowd. The Reichstag and the Brandenburg gate were comparatively 'pygmy' structures. In Berlin, Albert Speer planned the demolition of entire streets. The periphery of Berlin was to form a huge cross, crowned by the 'Great Hall' at the crossroads. All the urban planning was subordinate to the objective of achieving a grandiose showcase. Hitler was well aware of the link between his architectural projects and his political objectives. He admired the Coliseum and the Circus Maximus, symbols of Roman power. Hitler wrote in *Mein Kampf*

> The architecture isn't only the verb inscribed on the stone, but it's also the expression of faith and conviction that a community has or signifies the power and the splendour of a great man or leader.

Jochen Thies, examining National-Socialist architecture, principally Germania, concluded that this architecture clearly demonstrated an ambition for worldwide domination (Thies 1982).

'Titanic' ambitions also appeared in Soviet architecture between 1919 and 1939. After ostracising modernist projects made by constructivists in the 1920s in favour of socialist realism, Stalin, in the 1930s, wanted a building constructed which was to be more than four hundred metres high and crowned by a one hundred metres statue of Lenin – making it the highest building in the world. Faced with the 'technical' impossibility of it being built, he contented himself with skyscrapers, such as the complex Vysotniye Zdaniye in Moscow, constructed in the 1930s (but only completed after the Second World War). During the reconstruction of Moscow, a large number of churches and cathedrals were simply destroyed. Lenin's mausoleum (1924–1930) and the house on the quay (a complex of apartments 1928–1931) illustrate the huge project that was Stalinist architecture. The personality cult surrounding Stalin materialised from the innumerable portraits, monuments and street names dedicated to him (Melvin 2002).

On the other hand, governmental architecture in fascist Italy, constructed from 1919 to 1939, was riddled with contradictory tendencies. 1920s Italy adhered, paradoxically, to rationalist, modernist and futurist principles (Marinetti). The Casa del Fascio (the House of Fascism of 1932–1936) with its geometric and sophisticated proportions was considered a rationalist masterpiece (Schumacher 1991). At the end of the 1930s, Italian architecture began to closely resemble that of its German ally, as the constructions became clearly more monumental. The governmental architecture in interwar Japan also presented 'prestigious' features, but without attempts to surpass the architectural grandness present in other powers. The Japanese Prime Minister's two storey building (the Kantei), built in the 1920s, was sober and inspired by modern architecture, notably that of Frank Lloyd Wright. In contrast, the national Diet (1920–1936) presents a mixed style and a rather pompous take on monumental neo-classicism. This building has nine floors with a central tower (Stewart 2003, Sadler 2009).

As for Great Britain, it was far too occupied with the consequences of the war to be concerned with government architecture. During this period, official buildings were hardly modified. Certain new impulses occurred, but only in Glasgow under the influence of Charles Rennie Mackintosh (1868–1928). During the same period, the official buildings in the United States, such as the Supreme Court in Washington (1933–1935), built by Cass Gilbert, or the Ministry of Trade (1932), embodied the 'classical' approach to governmental architecture. Some constructions, such as the Pentagon, completed in 1942, were surprisingly close to those carried out by Speer. Vertical architecture was very popular during this period, as illustrated by the Empire State Building (1931) or the Chrysler building (1930) (Wieseman 2000: 23*f*). In France, governmental architecture only marginally drew its inspiration from the 'purist' style of Le Corbusier, with the exception of the socialist mayor Edouard Herriot, future President of the Council, who created a US district in Paris (Biermann and Borngässer 2006). The Palace of Versailles was sometimes used for receptions, for example, George VI and the Queen's visit on the eve of the Second World War. In sum, the style of governmental architecture of the great powers oscillates during this period between 'dignified' and 'hubristic' showcases of political power.

As regards shared identities, the post-1919 international system was burdened by a strong ideological heterogeneity with the advent of the USSR and then the emergence of fascist countries, first Italy and then Nazi Germany. The ideological opposition to the USSR led a significant number of political leaders to under-estimate Nazi Germany. In 1930, Lord Rothermere, owner of the Daily Mail, wrote

> The transfer of political power in Germany to the National-Socialists is an advantage to the rest of Europe; it raises a further obstacle against bolshevism. (Tabouis 1958)

It was precisely this heterogeneity that delayed a coordinated fight against National-Socialism. The ideological heterogeneity also prevented a stronger alliance between the USSR and Nazi Germany. Despite the German-Soviet Pact of 1939, Russia remained National-Socialism's main enemy. Hitler's pathologic hatred of the USSR may be explained by the fact that communism was his main political adversary under the Weimar Republic: they were the only two formations to challenge the voice of the victims of the economic crisis. John Stoessinger argues that the destruction of the USSR became a real obsession for Hitler that even surpassed his desire to obtain vital space (Stoessinger 2000). Hitler said in private

> The Bolsheviks have suppressed everything that resembles civilisation and I have no problem with wiping out Kiev, Moscow, and St. Petersburg. (Tabouis 1958)

The absence of shared identity between great European democracies constituted another obstacle to the coordination against the National-Socialist threat. The Weimar Republic, the 3 Republic in France and Great Britain regarded each other with suspicion. They were also incapable of coordinating consolidated action for fighting the economic crisis, as well as the increase in Nazi Germany's power. Thus, the United States set up a new ultra-protectionist customs tariff in June 1930, as well as France and Great Britain who abandoned the free-trade approach in 1931. For a short period, a European Union project was even mentioned, but the 1939 economic crisis put an end to it. As regards American power, it turned away from Europe in order to resort back to its isolationist tradition.

The order of Versailles was based on a punitive approach towards German power, which was morally recognised as being guilty by Article 231 of the Treaty.[12] The German delegation did not even participate in the treaty discussions. Germany, on top of the loss of Eastern territories, had to accept – inter alia – the occupation of the Rhine's left bank by French troops, a reduction in the size of its army by a hundred thousand men, a prohibition on having an air force, tanks, and heavy artillery, as well as paying heavy reparations, the amount of which was yet to be determined. The treaty was a diktat and felt as such

> For the first time in history, it is through discussions between victorious powers that the treaty of peace is drawn up. (Girault and Frank 1998)

Max Weber, who was at that time a member of the German delegation, noted

> A nation can always forgive having to endure material prejudices, but never an attack against her honour, especially when it's done in the way of a predicator who wants to be right at all costs. (Weber 2002)

The Rhineland was demilitarised and the Emperor had to abdicate, which, to the Germans, felt like interference in their domestic affairs. Sir Harold Nicholson described the context in which two German delegates signed the Treaty

> 'Let the Germans in', exclaimed Clemenceau in the silence. 'They are pale. They do not look like representatives of a brutal military. One is thin with reddish eyelids, a man who plays the second violin in a provincial orchestra. The other has a lunar face and looks as if he's suffering, a senior lecturer. All of this is painful.' (Nicholson 1970)

---

12. It was a violation of what Kaplan (2005: 35) designs as rule six of the balance and power system, 'Permit defeated or constrained essential national actors to re-enter the system as acceptable role partners'.

This treaty was thus seen as a humiliation for Germany (Lebow 2008). German soldiers, entering Paris, rushed to the archives of the French Minister of Foreign affairs in order to retrieve the original French copy of the Treaty (Klein 1968: 126). Hitler ordered an armistice to be signed at Rethondes, the same place where, on the 11th November 1918, Marshall Foch received the German surrender. William Shirer was an eyewitness when Hitler noticed the sign on the monument erected in souvenir of the armistice which stated

> here, on the 11th November, collapsed the pride of the German Reich defeated by the free people which it wanted to enslave

In the distance, armed with binoculars, William Shirer observed the expression of the Fuhrer

> I have seen his face many times over major moments of his life. But today, he was impassioned with scorn, anger, hate, revenge and triumph. (Saurel 1968)

The French delegation, 'invited' into the same wagon restaurant used for the 1918 armistice, had no right to speak, but received a copy of the text detailing the conditions of the armistice. When Hitler went away an orchestra 'burst into a performance of *Deutschland über alles* and then *Horst Wessel Lied*'. It could be questioned why the victors fed the illusion that it was possible to set up maintainable peace based on the humiliation of a great power. The reason for their blindness may be explained by their own desire for revenge. The proclamation of the German Empire in the Hall of Mirrors long remained in the minds of political leaders, such as Clemenceau. Right-wing nationalism strengthened considerably after the signing of the Treaty of Versailles. Whereas the anti-parliamentarian right party received less than 15 per cent at the two elections of the Constituent Assembly on the 19th January 1919, it received 29 per cent of the vote at the 1920 Reichstag election (Berstein and Milza 1988)..

Until 1928, Germany was excluded from major conferences and international institutions such as the League of Nations. This stigmatisation of Germany was highlighted by the fact that it was still under French control. The return to the Poincaré presidency led to the French occupation of the Ruhr in 1923. The incredible inflation in Germany fed by the high amount of reparations and a deliberate policy of devaluation by the German government led to considerable political consequences. René Remond noted

> a renaissance of far right terrorism and *Freikorps* activity. Some politicians are killed by terrorists. In a couple of months, some two hundred have been victims of attacks. (Remond 2002: 142–4)

In Munich, Adolf Hitler launched a putsch which failed on the 8th November 1923. On the other hand, the French-German agreement between Prime Minister Briand and Chancellor Streseman in 1924 consecrated by the 1925 Treaty of Locarno slightly curbed German and French nationalism. In France the Action Française, which was the core of the opposition to Briand's policy, was condemned by the Vatican in 1926 and lost much of its audience. In Germany, the electoral results of the Nazis collapsed and Briand wanted to put forward the idea of collective security. The strength of the revisionist feeling became weaker in Germany after Locarno, only to become active again in 1933 (Monnet 2000). Thus, the NSDAP fell from 6.6 per cent to 6 per cent during the 1928 Reichstag elections, the same year when Germany entered the League of Nations and the great powers signed the Kellogg-Briand Pact (Remond 2002). Moreover, the transformation of Stresemann himself was also dramatic. He changed from a 'pangermanist' nationalist into a liberal, and on the whole a peaceful, nationalist

> The two men [Briand and Stresemann] combine idealism and realism, good feelings and ulterior motives. They get on well together and end up assuming their individual roles and their combined role as apostles of peace.

Locarno also turned out to be a success in German domestic policy. From 1924, another international order succeeded the order of Versailles (Klein 1968)

But this order turned out to be too fragile 'to resist the economic and social turmoil of the 1930s' (Girault and Frank 1998: 111). Stresemann died in 1929 and the economic crisis led to European countries falling back on themselves

> Everybody retreats behind their economic borders, raising custom tariffs and practising a policy of strict compartmentalisation – in a so-called "autarchy". (Remond 2002)

The 1930 elections were the first turning point for the NSDAP who obtained 18.3 per cent of the vote and then 37.3 per cent in July 1932. The Treaty of Versailles was politically exploited by the far right which organised a plebiscite against the Young Plan of 1929 (Bracher 1977). This fixed German debt to 109.6 billion Deutsch Marks, of which only 22.6 billion were to be paid unconditionally. The proposition was a difficult issue to accept psychologically; it meant spreading out payments until 1988. The Young Plan aroused within the German right-wing a wave of indignation and an awakening of nationalist resentment. Crowds discovered a young agitator, Adolf Hitler. He accused the government of having let the former victors reduce the German people into slavery for several generations. Four million signatures were gathered supporting a referendum. Less than 14 per cent of the electorate declared themselves in favour of the Young Plan and the National-Socialist Party regained popularity. The high amount of reparations was skilfully exploited by the far right, notably indicating that they were responsible for the precarious economic situation that Germany found itself in 1929. Paradoxically, it was with the Nazi's arrival to power that Western powers began to set up a durable policy of appeasement. This policy was no longer able to integrate Germany into the international order and it was uniquely interpreted as proof of 'weakness' by Nazi Germany.

The second power excluded from the order of Versailles was the Soviet Union. The United States, Japan, Great Britain and France intervened actively in the civil war in favour of the 'White' monarchic forces in order to fight against the 'Bolshevik leper'. The English and French landings on the coasts of the Baltic Sea, White Sea, Black Sea and Caspian Sea, as well as Japanese and Americans on the Pacific coast of Siberia, show a real worldwide alliance against Bolshevism. The 1920 Polish attack, crossing the plains of Ukraine, highlighted without doubt the Soviet leaders' realisation that they were surrounded by enemies. Russia was absent from the negotiations for the Treaty of Versailles. It was only recognised in 1924 by Great Britain and in 1933 by the United States. In 1927, the Soviet ambassador in Warsaw was murdered, the ambassador in Paris was expelled and in China communists were hunted and slaughtered by their nationalist allies of the Guomindang. In July–August 1928, the Komintern recommended, during the sixth Congress, the policy of class against class; all the non-communist political parties were to be regarded as 'fascists' and the social-democrats were to become social-fascists. Subsequent to its exclusion, the Soviet Union reconciled with Germany through the Treaty of Rapallo (1922) and concluded a non-aggression pact in 1926. This was the first act of recognition to a major capitalist country by the Soviet regime.

The durable exclusion of the Soviet Union from the international order encouraged the rise of a closed identity, as well as the complex of encirclement (Neilson 2006). The Bolshevik authorities drew the conclusion of unavoidable hostility with Western capitalism. British and Nazi 'plutocrats' were seen as being the same thing and the Nazis were seen as 'the last rampart against a capitalist world in distress' (Grosser 1999). The inclusion of Soviet power in the international order would have possibly avoided the occurrence of the Second World War. This fallback strategy was to impede, some years after, all efficient left-wing alliances against the rise of Nazism in Germany – a situation worsened by the fact that Stalin under-estimated this new danger from the beginning. Edouard Herriot, the French Prime Minister, stated with lucidity in 1924, at the official inauguration of diplomatic relations with the Soviet Union

> Leaving Russia outside of the European forum, is to encourage her to attach herself more and more to Germany [...] I shall sign, next October, the resumption of relations between Paris and Moscow; this will be the end of the "barbed wire fence".

But France, under Poincaré, continued with the issue of reimbursement of the tsarist debts whereas the conservative government in London accused the Soviets of supporting the 1926 Miners Strikes in Britain (Girault and Frank 1998). Great Britain broke off diplomatic relations in May 1927.

**Alternative explanations**

According to the realist perspective, the fragility of the order of Versailles lay, above all, with geopolitical balances. The constitution of numerous, weak buffer states was bound to encourage Germany and Russia to once again share zones of influence. Germany was humiliated, but far from being seriously weakened. According to Jacques Bainville, the Treaty was 'too tough for its milder parts and too soft for the tougher ones' (Keynes and Bainville 2002). From the realist perspective, the weakness of the system of collective security also promoted armed aggression. Without the involvement of American power, the system of collective security, promoted by the League of Nations, could not afford to develop a deterrent force against revisionist states. According to classic realist authors, such as H. Morgenthau, Wilsonian idealism and the illusion of the rule of law were largely responsible for the Second World War. But if the policy of appeasement encouraged Hitler to multiply his demands, is it true that a dissuasive policy would have been susceptible to discourage German aggression? If Nazi racial ideology is taken into account with its grotesque under-estimation of the Soviet Union, refusing even to take winter equipment for the Russian Campaign, it was doubtful that such a policy would have been successful (Stoessinger 2000; Stahel 2009). A 'realistic' Hitler certainly would not have invaded Poland in 1939. It was thus Hitler's hubristic self-presentation, and not the cold calculation of a power struggle, which explains the resort to armed force by Nazi Germany.

In some regards, the 1938 Munich Agreements are characterised not only by a policy of appeasement, but also by a deterrent approach with the goal of containing Nazi demands. Hitler wanted a war against relatively small Czechoslovakia. On the 22nd–23rd September, 1939 at Berchtesgaden, Hitler demanded not only the Sudetes, but also gave three days for the evacuation of the territories predominantly populated by Germans, the organisation of plebiscites in mixed territories, as well as immediate occupation by German troops. However, he was confronted by Neville Chamberlain. Being certain that if he were to attack Czechoslovakia, there would be a Anglo-French intervention, Hitler backed down. It is even likely that Hitler gave up on this idea all together, having been a 'coward' at Munich, as the French ambassador André-François Poncet suggested.[13] The historian Gerhard Weinberg also argues that Hitler had been 'traumatised' by Munich. Hitler was disappointed and even 'furious to have been deprived of his war'.[14]

Hitler's decision to attack Poland on September 1939 does not necessarily result from the incapacity of Western leaders to communicate, in a credible way, their determination for military intervention against Hitler in case of aggression (Grosser 2001). Clues are somehow contradictory, but they all indicate a belief that Hitler expected, at least in the last days of August, a Western intervention. The British ambassador warned Hitler on the 23rd August

> It was claimed that, if His Majesty's government had taken a clearer position in 1914, the following great catastrophe could have been avoided. Whether or

---

13. Quoted by Rook (2000: 74), 'did not at all believe that he had, at Munich achieved a success. He felt, on the contrary, that he had renounced his original objective, that he had compromised and capitulated. As after the invasion of Austria, he regretted having been a coward. He believed himself, or wanted to believe himself, cheated, fooled by British artifice, frustrated in the proper object of his ambition, which was to seize Prague'.

14. Weinberg quoted by Rook (2000: 75), 'Hitler conducted his foreign policy in 1939 under the personal trauma of Munich. He had shrunk from war then – and attributed such cowardice to everyone else – so he would not be cheated once again of the war he had always intended. Just as his anger at having been deprived of war in 1938 made him all the more determined to have it in 1939, so his postponement of the attack on the 25th August left him all the firmer in almost hysterical fixation to attack a few days later. He would not back off again'.

not this is a valid assertion, His Majesty's government is resolved to not allow the repetition of another tragic misunderstanding in the current circumstances. (Saurel 1968)

The Secretary of State, von Weizsäcker, Hermann Göring and the German Ambassador in London, von Dirksen, expected war to break out with Great Britain.

Hitler's behaviour was not so clear, but afterwards, subsequent to the 25th August Anglo-Polish defence treaty, even the most optimistic of National-Socialists could not deny the likelihood of British intervention in favour of Poland. General Keitel, Chief of Staff, reported that on the 25th August Hitler confirmed that Great Britain was going to defend Poland.[15] There is more. The policy of appeasement was ultimately founded on a vision of a power balance and such 'realistic' interpretations of international relations

> from the perspective of the English realpolitik [...] there was no major reason to confront, a priori, Germany. (Battistella 2006)

It is not by chance that A. J. Taylor defended the policy of appeasement assuming that Hitler was pursuing traditional objectives. As Pascal Vennesson quite rightly noted

> In the tradition of realist thought, a well conducted foreign policy based on appeasement can constitute a significant aspect of the international action of great powers. The balance of power assumes that, in the case of a modification of the distribution of power, the challenger is compensated.... (Venesson 2006)

Neither a policy of appeasement, nor a policy of deterrence, is realist *per se.*

The 'realist' cure in the form of a deterrent policy was unsuitable during the Weimar Republic. The revanchist nationalism was not a product of fate, but rather a progressive development. There is a correlation between intensification of German nationalism and the Western policy of stigmatisation. During the period of the Stresemann and Briand détente, the moderated and democratic forces of the Weimar Republic grew in influence. It was true that once the national-socialists seized power, a policy of compromise was bound to fail because nothing could change its revisionist objectives. Even if Hitler was the product of German history, German nationalism was forged from the identity of exclusion, making its stigmatisation a virtue by presenting it as evidence of German superiority.

### East-West confrontations (1945–1953)

The first question one should ask is whether the Cold War, which was also a long period of peace (Gaddis 1986), truly represented an unstable period, all the more so since today numerous analysts claim that a bipolar situation is foreseeable and stable. After all, a 'real' war has been avoided. If one considers the number of peripheral wars where the two superpowers confronted each other indirectly (the

---

15. Quoted by Rook (2000: 70), 'There's absolutely no doubt that London has realised by now that Italy won't go along with us. Now Great Britain's attitude toward us will stiffen – now they will back up Poland to the hilt'.

1950 War of Korea, the Vietnam War, Arab-Israeli confrontations, etc.), the 'military crises' between the two blocs that almost became wars (the Berlin blockade of 1948, the Suez Crisis of 1956 etc.) and the 'pactomania' between the Big Two, this confirmation becomes contestable. The increasing defence budget represented 20 per cent of the USSR's GDP, invalidating the idea of a 'calm' period. The alleged stability of the bipolar period was not taken so calmly by American and Soviet leaders.[16] The high frequency of armed conflict and militarised dispute between them is unquestionable from 1945 to 1953.

The second question is what actually caused the Cold War to reach its peak between 1947 (the Truman Doctrine and the Zhdanov Doctrine) and 1953 (the constitution of the two Germanys in 1949 and the 1950 Korean War)? Without denying the 'geostrategic' and economic oppositions as regards Germany, Central and Eastern Europe, Turkey, Greece and Iran, my main thesis postulates that 'recognition' threats were the most significant at the outbreak of the 1946/1947 conflict. Firstly, one should remember that the antagonism was characterised by the existence of two incompatible messianic ideologies (Battistella 2006). The two superpowers aspired above all to spread their communist or liberal ideology. From 1917, Soviet Russia and the United States 'claimed to construct a worldwide order founded on innovative and radically opposed principles' (Jeannesson 2002). Considering their identities as the 'protector of the free world' or 'the revolutionary birthplace', both superpowers could hardly concede any kind of superiority to the other, be it in economic, military, cultural or political fields.

The existence of revolutionary messianic ideologies is also reflected in the architecture of the great powers. In the United States, Mies van der Rohe's ideas inspired the construction of the headquarters of the United Nations, built at the end of the 1940s (Krieger 1996). As I have already outlined, the neo-classical Jefferson memorial illustrates a representative and sometimes even 'spectacular' form of architecture. In the Soviet Union, the huge Vysotnye Zdaniye sky scrapers were completed in the early 1950s. Soviet towns are characterised by a significant number of statues of Lenin and Stalin, showing a cult of personality (Golomstock 1991). As regards China, Mao's arrival corresponded to the popularisation of monumental architecture and sometimes even martial architecture, as indicated by the monument of the 'Heroes of the People' (1952–58) and the enlargement of Tiananmen Square in the early 1950s. The Great Hall of the People, completed in 1959, can accommodate ten thousand Chinese parliamentary representatives.

As I have already mentioned, in the 'declining' democratic great powers, governmental architecture became slightly more modest. In Great Britain, continuity prevailed. Public work programs originally had 'modernist' ambitions, but the shortage of materials did not make their initial intentions possible. The modernisation project for Downing Street was given up. The process of replacing monumental architecture by using glass, lightness, transparency and simple and functional constructions notably occurred in France (chiefly with Le Corbusier's, Unité

---

16. See the evocative title of the book of Soutou (2001) *La Guerre de cinquante ans*.

d'habitation), but did not really influence governmental architecture. In total, at least three 'great powers' demonstrated an ambitious representation of themselves.

Messianic ideologies triggered off an identity dilemma – it was impossible for the two superpowers to assert their identity without compromising that of their rival. The United States revived some Wilsonian idealism in the Atlantic Charter of the 12th August 1941 expressing the right of the people to freely choose their government and the establishment of durable international peace *via* an international organisation. In 1945, Truman's United States saw itself as the guarantors of a fair peace embodied by the ubiquitous institutions of the United Nations. During the Conference of Yalta (4th February 1945 to the 12th December 1945), Stalin promised to organise free elections in those Eastern countries which were controlled by the Red Army. This statement to a newly liberated Europe was, for President Roosevelt, almost sacred (Jeannesson 2002). Roosevelt and Churchill obtained in Yalta the commitment that there would be free elections in Poland in exchange for their temporary support of a principally communist coalition. But the elections of January 1947 were not exactly democratic. During this period the Chief of Staff Major Leahy was President Truman's principal advisor. He presented Truman with some aide-memoires in which he 'highlighted on the offensive language of Stalin', that insulted Truman's patriotic sentiments (Yergin 1977).

Truman's opposition to Soviet 'standardisation' in Eastern Europe resulted more from the violation of liberal principles than geostrategic considerations. Truman designated the Soviet action as a 'ruthless action'. On the 23rd April 1945, President Truman heckled Molotov over Poland to such an extent that Molotov complained of never having been treated so badly in his whole life: 'Throughout my life, nobody has dared to talk to me in that tone', to which Truman dryly answered 'Well, if you carry out your agreements I won't have to speak to you like that' (Yergin 1977: 122).

It is possibly the Polish situation which best exemplifies the antagonism of identities over the American-Soviet role at that time. Harry Hopkins, Truman's special emissary in Moscow, stated in May 1945 in front of Stalin, that he had to consider the Declaration of Liberated Europe, as well as the fact that Poland had become the stumbling block to American-Soviet relations. Stalin did not understand that the existence of an American interest in a free Poland was a question of principle.[17] Concerning his doctrine pronounced on the 12th May 1947, President Truman wrote in his memoirs that 'the moment has come to place the United States at the head of the Free World' (Jeannesson 2001). Daniel Yergin noted that the self-image of American leaders and of their nation as a protector of the free world encouraged them to be uncompromising over the Polish issue.

The Americans did not only feel responsible for everything that happened in the world. They adhered to a new and vivacious messianism, with a powerful desire to reform the world – which we call Wilsonianism. They wanted a world

---

17. Yergin (1977: 112) states that the ambassador, Averell Harriman wrote to Truman: 'Stalin does and never will fully understand our interest in a free Poland as a matter of principle'.

where liberal democracy and capitalism equaled security. Otherwise, why were they fighting against tyranny and totalitarianism? So it was for the best reasons that they opposed the Soviet Union within Europe. They saw themselves as liberators and not imperialists. (Yergin 1977: 73)

The self-proclaimed role of defender of the 'free world' quickly became 'a prison' for American decision-makers, leading to the necessity of being credible 'to avoid the moral victory of the adversary' (Grosser 1999). The stakes of credibility were also intended to deter Soviet aggression in Western Europe. This safer motivation played a role in the defence of South Korea against the aggression of North Korea and later to the same extent in Vietnam. Beyond this 'realist' security aspect, there was a 'moral', and on top of this an 'electoral' issue, to not 'lose face' in front of domestic opinion (Grosser 1999). For a long time, Soviet ambitions on the international stage remained relatively speculative. If for some, the USSR concentrated more on security, for other analysts it was still inspired by revolutionary ideals. The two theses are only partially founded and are in fact compatible. Even if the Soviet Union did not give up on the objective of a worldwide revolution, it gave priority, at the latest in 1928, to strengthening Soviet socialism. The Komintern, founded in 1919, gathered all the communist parties under Soviet direction in order to reverse the Bourgeois governments in their countries. After its suspension during the war, a comparable organisation was made under the name of the Kominform. The Soviet Union had not given up its revolutionary ambitions and carried out a policy of transforming Eastern and Central European countries into satellite countries. The Soviet policy in Germany illustrates this blend between national objectives and revolutionary ambitions. If Stalin hoped to make it wholly communist, he was not willing to pay the price because he practised a policy faithful to the precept of 'the vanquished will pay'. The historians Zubok and Pleshakov, according to recently available archives, argue that Stalin was certainly concerned about the security of the USSR, but that he was also a prudent expansionist (Zubok and Pleshakov 1996).

As regards the image and identity of the role of the USSR projected abroad, Stalin did not only have an enhanced image of the USSR's role in the world, but he also had a very hubristic image of his own abilities. In a secret speech at the twentieth Congress, Khrushchev quoted an official biography of Stalin which referred to him as the 'greatest leader and the most sublime strategist of all countries and of all time.' Stalin represented all the symptoms of a paranoid, hypersensitive megalomaniac. As such he ordered the execution of Pavel Postyshev (1938), member of the Politburo, for not having shown enough deference to him. Unlike interpretations which argued that Stalin's foreign policy was only influenced by the concern of preserving socialism in the Soviet Motherland, one should also consider his strong irritability when the 'superior image' of the USSR and his own personality were questioned. Despite ideological affinity, he was offended by the independence of Tito's Yugoslavia. Stalin designated Tito as Trotskyite and stopped all contact with him. On the 28th June 1948, Yugoslavia was excluded from the Kominform on the grounds of 'ideological deviationism'. The rejection of the Marshall Plan by the Soviet Union is another illustration of this. If the Soviet rejection was partially motivated by the fear that the USSR could exercise an influence over Western countries, it was also down to the fact that the Soviet Union could not accept help from a power deemed as being 'inferior'.

The displayed role identities also fed suspicion. According to S. Jeannesson, the partisans of the so-called 'spirit of Riga', Charles Bohlen and especially George Kennan, kicked off a decisive shift in American policy (Jeannesson 2002). The Latvian capital served as a look-out post for American diplomacy during the interwar period before the United States opened its embassy in Moscow in 1933. According to these diplomats, the USSR was a state searching for worldwide revolution, negating the possibility of coexistence which would ultimately result in their messianic objective of worldwide domination. Kennan's 'Long Telegram' sent on the 22nd February 1946 stated that

> Moscow can never sincerely suggest a community of (shared) targets between the Soviet Union and those powers considered as capitalists.

According to the School of Riga's thesis and the American ambassador in Moscow, Averell Harriman, the USSR would not settle for a buffer zone.

> Once the Soviet Union gets its hands around its neighbouring countries, it will probably try to penetrate the circles of the adjacent countries. (Kaspi 1994)

These threat perceptions shed some light on why American decision makers at the time spontaneously had the impression that the strategic independence of Turkey, Greece and Iran were significantly important for the US. Conversely, Soviet leaders should have been shaken by Churchill's Fulton speech, Sinews of Peace (Missouri, 5th March 1946) where he claimed that an 'iron curtain' had descended across the Continent. Churchill also spoke of the leadership of Anglo-Saxon nations in the world. Admiral Leahy declared that

> Mr. Churchill has bravely outlined his faith in the fundamental right of the power of the English-speaking community. (Yergin 1977)

Stalin responded to Churchill's claim that 'only English-speaking nations are superior nations' by stating that it reminded him of Hitler's speech about the superiority of the German people.

The ideological heterogeneity, that is to say the opposition of political identities of superpowers, is another reason for the Cold War. Some historians, like André Fontaine, trace the origins of the Cold War back to 1917, or the following year, when Western powers intervened against the Bolsheviks. The Soviet Union was not only a threat because of its power – the US had a nuclear monopoly until 1949 – but because of its revolutionary potential. The American perception of an insurmountable ideological opposition with the USSR became acute with the process of transforming Eastern and Central European countries into satellite states. American decision makers became convinced that Russia was particularly dangerous because of its ideologically seductive power. The journalist Mark Ethridge, a US special reporter in the Balkans, noted that

If Greece turns to communism, all of Central Asia and part of North Africa will certainly fall to Soviet influence. (Yergin 1977)

President Truman's speech of 12th March, 1947 is most evocative of the fears of contagious ideology. Even the opposing power's successes in sport were becoming an identity threat as the sportive, economic and cultural efficiency of the opposing system could question the validity of the US's own model (Battistella 2006).

On the other hand, American power prevented the 'stigmatisation' and the punishment of other great powers. This moderation is demonstrated by the effort made by America to include other great powers within the United Nations. Roosevelt refused to believe in the above reasoning based on zones of influence. Dario Battistella explains that the US, in spite of its hegemonic strength, was concerned with the institutionalisation of a dialogue with the Soviet Union:

> having an excess of resources, they tried to organise a sustainable order setting up multilateral jurisdictions for resolving disputes, starting with the United Nations. (Battistella 2006)

Even during the most intense period of the East-West confrontation, American power did not completely give up international institutions in order to manage international conflict. After the aggression from North Korea towards South Korea (1950), President Truman and his Secretary of State, Dean Acheson, immediately mobilised the United Nations. The policy of containment carried out by the Truman administration included a way to recognise Soviet power because it admitted the de facto existence of Soviet zones of influence. It was no later than 1947 that American policy distanced itself from an 'inclusive' approach. Thus, Chinese communist power was excluded from the Security Council of the United Nations in favour of the partisan Guomindang, who were now on a Taiwanese Island. From this, the use of nuclear weapons against Japan could be interpreted as a will to render, according to Burns' expression, Soviet leaders 'more manageable' within Europe (Yergin 1977). The hostility between the two powers became a kind of self-fulfilling prophecy. Each perceived their own measures as defensive whereas they interpreted the others' as confirmation of an aggressive stance.

At the beginning of 1948, the suspicious behaviour of the Western powers in establishing a 'Western' zone in Germany, with the creation of the Deutschmark, heightened a conflict which could have perhaps remained more limited. Conversely, the Soviet Union, with its policy of transforming Central and Eastern European states into satellite states confirmed the worst fears for the West. Neither American power nor Soviet power made any effort to maintain cooperation between 1945 and 1953. Certain oral acts voiced by the two superpowers were gratuitous provocations and yet had deep consequences. Attacks on 'self-esteem' are shown through especially disparaging rhetoric practices. In April 1945, at the moment of his talks with the Minister of Foreign Affairs, Mr. Molotov, President Truman did not hesitate to talk about the issue of Poland in tough language, referring to Molotov as a 'mule driver' (Miscamble 2007: Ch IV). Similarly, in a speech on the

27th October 1945, he labelled Romania and Bulgaria 'police states'[18].

The taboo around nuclear weapons was another symbolic factor, paradoxically contributing to the American-Soviet confrontation. After Nagasaki and Hiroshima, it was unthinkable that American leaders would take advantage of their nuclear superiority without 'losing face' in front of public opinion. This moral inhibition also played against conventional preventive strikes. During the 1962 Cuban crisis, the simple mention of an analogy of air strikes against Cuba, with the 'horrible' Japanese attack against Pearl Harbour, led to the rejection of this option (Gaddis 2004). This inhibition was known by Soviet decision-makers and encouraged them to support preventive peripheral wars and to carry through ideological standardisation in Central and Eastern Europe. Furthermore, despite a large gap between the US and the USSR subsequent to the Second World War – the US provided half of the world's production and three quarters of worldwide expenditure – the US could not deter the USSR from transforming Central and Eastern countries into satellite states. Indeed, American decision-makers also had doubts over the strategic usefulness of nuclear weapon against the USSR in the early 1950s. The USSR had conventional superiority in Europe and the US still did not have the capability to destroy the entire USSR with nuclear weapons. Nevertheless, the idea of a preventive war was evoked at the end of the 1940s and in the early 1950s by various men such as Winston Churchill, the Naval Minister, Francis P. Matthews and leaders of the Air Force (Lebow 1984). The 'nuclear' option was also rejected because of moral inhibitions. In 1949, the Chief of Staff and future President, Dwight D. Eisenhower, openly expressed his indignation over the idea to use a weapon powerful enough to take millions of lives (Lebow 1984). Political decision makers, both Soviet and American, skilfully fought for the support of 'worldwide opinion' to avoid being stigmatised as aggressors. These examples show the existence of a politically motivated 'symbolic strategy', using 'morality' as a tool.

*Alternative explanations*
As regards the origins of the Cold War, some analysts place importance on the security dilemma, that is to say the impossibility of proving to the other that his intentions are purely defensive (to the extent that offensive and defensives means are barely distinguishable objectively) (Grosser 1999). The Soviet Union, fearing a revival of the German revanchists, set up a buffer zone in Central and Eastern Europe. Western leaders were not sure of the Soviets' defensive motivation because the 'buffer zone' was at the same time capable of being used as a springboard for an assault against Germany. For those who claim that Stalin chiefly acted for security preoccupations, it is realpolitik which inspired his foreign policy (Jeannesson 2002). Nevertheless, should it not be forgotten that threat perceptions were precisely linked to ideological considerations? Other historians see the origins of the Cold War in American or Soviet imperialism.[19] Certain analysts be-

---

18. See the Speech, available <millercenter.org/scripps/archive/speeches>, accessed 20th June 2009.

19. For an overview of the literature: Lebow and Risse-Kappen (1995).

lieve this imperialism was caused by economic motivation and others claim it was ideological motivation (intentionalist interpretation). After 1945, the US had economic superiority (50 per cent of all coal, 65 per cent of all oil and 60 per cent of all manufactured goods in the world came from the US) as well as an impressive military advantage (with a monopoly over nuclear weapons). The use of nuclear bombs on Hiroshima and Nagasaki could also be understood as intending to intimidate the Soviet Union. If the political and economic interests in maintaining free-trade and securing raw materials played an important role in the American strategy, the 'search for peace and the extension of democracy' were also decisive. Otherwise, how would it be possible to understand Americas' indignation *vis-à-vis* Poland, which presented a limited interest and was already attributed to the Soviet zone of influence (Jeannesson 2002)? What can be said about Greece and Turkey in 1947? As regards nuclear weapons, America had not deterred Stalin from setting up a buffer zone in Eastern and Central Europe, or from encouraging North Korea to fight South Korea. In other words it is difficult to understand the Cold War by abstracting recognition concepts.

## Quantitative links between the stability of international orders and the corresponding degree of recognition

My qualitative examination of international orders can usefully be completed and verified by quantitative analysis. S. Bremer's work on armed conflict provides an important basis for such an examination.

### The stability of international orders

The number of armed conflicts and militarised disputes between great powers for each examined international order is as follows:

1815–1853 The Congress of Vienna: twelve conflicts in thirty-eight years between five powers (Great Britain, Austria-Hungary, Russia, France and Prussia). On average, each power was involved in 0.063 conflicts a year.[20]

1945–1991 Great democracies: zero conflict in forty six years between six powers (United States, Great Britain, France, Germany, Italy, Japan). On average, democratic powers had 0.000 conflicts each year between them.

---

20. See S. Bremer's data 'Militarized Interstate Dispute' (MID) (1996) in Correlates of War Project: 1. France against Spain, Russia, Prussia, Austria-Hungary during the 1823 French-Spanish war; 2. Russia, Prussia against France. Independence I of Belgium 1830; 3. France against Great Britain 1831 ('Netherlands-Belgium'). France supports the Netherlands whereas Great Britain supports Belgium. 4. Prussia, Netherlands against Belgium and Great Britain. Independence II of Belgium 1833; 5. Great Britain against Russia and the Ottoman Empire. Near Eastern Crisis 1833; 6. Great Britain against Russia 1836; 7. France against Germany, Russia, Austria-Hungary, Great Britain. Second Syrian dispute 1840; 8. Prussia (with 'German' allies) against Russia and Great Britain during the first period of the War of Slesvig Holstein 1848; 9. Russia against France, Ottoman Empire, Great-Britain; 10. Crisis of Hungarian refugees 1849, Prussia against Austria-Hungary, Russia, France; 11. Olmutz Summation (1850); 12. Austria-Hungary, Great Britain (with Italy and the Ottoman Empire) against Russia during the Crimean war 1853.

1919–1939 The inter-war period: thirty-four conflicts in twenty years between seven powers (United States, Great Britain, USSR, Germany, Italy, Japan and France).[21]

On average, each power was involved in 0.242 conflicts a year during this period.

1945–1953 The Cold War: twelve armed conflicts in eight years between five great powers (United States, USSR, China, Great Britain and France).[22]

On average, each power was involved in 0.300 armed conflicts a year.

**Self-representation**

In terms of governmental architecture as an indicator of the self-image of great powers, my classification is as follows:

– Hubristic self-image or superior image of its own community: 2 points. Indicators: grandiose dimensions in governmental buildings, sturdy materials, opulent and costly decorations, numerous and giant statues of political leaders,

---

21. 1. Great Britain, Italy, Japan, France against the USSR 1917–1920; 2. Japan against USSR 9th March 1919, 1919 Nikolaevev incident; 3. Germany against Great Britain (supporting Latvia, Estonia and Poland), March–December 1919; 4. Russia against Great Britain during the 1920 Russian-Polish War; 5. Great Britain against USSR 1918–1920. 1918–1920 British intervention in Caucasia and Transcaucasia; 6. USSR against Great Britain, Germany (plus Latvia and Poland) from 3rd January till the 1st February 1920; 7. USSR against Great Britain (plus Estonia) 1918–1919; 8. Japan against USSR 1919 about the Chinese attempt to navigate on the Amour river; 9. USSR against Japan 1920–22. Occupation of Vladivostok 1920–22; 10. France, Great Britain, Belgium, Italy against Germany. Second occupation of the Ruhr 1921; 11. USSR against Germany 10.12.-13.12.1939; 12. The USSR against Japan. Occupation of the Sakhaline islands II 28.4.-23.9.1921; 13. Great Britain against USSR. British Trawler Issue 1923; 14. Italy -France 9.12. 1925 – 19.1. 1926; 15. Italy -France 1.12. 1927–15.1.1927; 16. Italy against Great Britain, France (plus Spain). 1927 Italian demands of a share of the administration of Tangier; 17. Japan against USSR, "China Eastern Railway" 1932–35; 18. Germany against USSR 12.11. 1936; 19. Germany against France, Great Britain, United States (plus Czechoslovakia) at the time of the 1938 Crisis of Munich; 20. Italy against Germany and Yugoslavia, 1934 Dolfus issue; 21. Italy against Great Britain and Ethiopia 1934–36; 22. Germany against France. Remilitarisation of the Rhineland, 1936; 23. USSR-Japan 26.2. 1936–9.4.1936 tensions about the Amour river; 24. USSR-Japan. 5.9.1937–10.9.1937; 25. France, Belgium against Germany. Third occupation of the Ruhrland 1922–23; 26. Italy against USSR in the 1937 Spanish civil war; 27. France against Italy during the Spanish civil war on 13.8.1937; 28. Great Britain against Italy during the Spanish civil war from the 31st August to the 2nd September 1937; 29. Japan against Russia 1937. Islands of Bolhoi and of Senufa 1937; 30. USSR against Japan. War of Chankufeng; 31. Japan against Great Britain, France 1938. Blockade of Tienstin 1938–40; 32. Great Britain, France against Italy. January 1938; 33. Italy-Germany from August 1938–February 1940; 34. USSR against Japan. 1939 War of Nomahan.

22. 1. United States against USSR in Turkey 1945–46; 2. Great Britain, United States against USSR and Czechoslovakia 1953; 3. USSR against FRG and United States, Berlin blockade 1948/49; 4. France against China 14th December 1949; 5. USA against China about Taiwan 1949–1950; 6. China-Great-Britain from 18.8. till 24.8.1950; 7. France against China. 1950 occupation of Sikkim; Great Britain against USSR 3.5.1950–27.9.1950; 8. Great Britain against China 12.2.1951–8.6.1951; 9. USSR against Great Britain about Iran 6.6.1951–8.9.1951; 10. Great Britain against China 25.9.-3.10.1952; 11. United States against China at the time of the Koran war.

big squares dedicated for parades and sky scrapers ordered by the political power.
- Dignified self-image or dignified image of its own community: 1 point. Indicators: the 'prestigious' feature of governmental architecture (having significant dimensions), but an absence of attempts to surpass the architectural grandness present in other powers.
- Temperate self-image or modest image of its community: 0 points. Indicators: little is spent on governmental buildings compared with other great powers; soft materials are used to create simple and functional architecture. This grade implies an intention to break with pompous architecture.

1815–1853 The Congress of Vienna: Great Britain, Austria-Hungary, Russia, France, Prussia:

Austria-Hungary: 0 points; Great Britain: 1 point; Prussia (1815–53): 1 point; France: 1 point; Russia 1815–1853: 1 point.

On average, each great power obtained the value of 0.800 points for its governmental architecture.

1945–1991 great power democracies: United States, Great Britain, France, Germany, Italy and Japan:

Germany (FRG): 0 points; Japan: 1 point; Great Britain: 1 point; Italy (1945–1990): 1 point; France: 1 point; the United States: 1 point.

On average, each great democracy obtained the value of 0.833 points for its governmental architecture.

1919–1939 the inter-war period: Germany, the USSR, Italy, Japan, Great Britain, the United States and France:

Germany: 2 points; the USSR: 2 points; Italy: 1 point; Japan: 1 point; Great Britain: 1 point; the United States: 1 point; France: 1 point.

On average, each great power obtained the value of 1.286 points for its governmental architecture.

1945–53 The Cold War: the United States, USSR, China, Great Britain and France:

The United States: 1 point; the USSR: 2 points; China: 2 points; Great Britain: 1 point; France: 1 point.

On average, each power obtained the value of 1.400 points for its governmental architecture.

**Homogeneity and Heterogeneity in the International Order**
In terms of homogeneity (similarity of the internal systems of great powers) and heterogeneity, the two homogenous orders are the following: the Congress of Vienna (1815–1853) and the order of the great democratic powers (1945–1991).

Table 3.1: Recognition, non-recognition and Great power conflicts

| Period of great power relations* | Number of conflicts in which a great power is involved in a year | Self image in governmental architecture | Homoge-neity and awarenesss of shared identity | Harsh punishment of defeated powers | Great powers excluded in a international system | All great powers democratic | Hegemony |
|---|---|---|---|---|---|---|---|
| 1815–53 | 0,063 | 0,800 | Yes | No | No | No | No (Europe) |
| 1945–91 great power democra-cies | 0,000 | 0,833 | Yes | No | No | Yes | Yes |
| 1919–39 | 0,242 | 1,286 | No | Yes | Yes | No | No |
| 1945–53 | 0,300 | 1,400 | No | ? (all great powers are victorious) | Yes (Communist China ) | No | Yes (United States) |

* 1815–1853: Great-Britain, Austria-Hungary, Russia, France, Prussia ; 2. 1945–1991: USA, Great-Britain, France, Germany, Italy, Japan; 3. 1919–1939: USA, GB, Soviet Union, Germany, Italy, France, Japan;4. 1945–1953: USA, Soviet Union, China, Great Britain and France (Doran OK, but with Germany; criteria at least 5 per cent).

On the other hand, heterogeneous orders are the order post Treaty of Versailles (1919–1939) and the beginning of the Cold War (1945–1953).

### Stigmatisation of Great Powers in the International Order

On the issue of the number of great powers excluded from the international order, none were expelled from the Congress of Vienna (1815–1853) or from the democratic order (1945–1991). As regards the order of Versailles (seven great powers), two – Germany and the USSR – were initially excluded from the League of Nations. Throughout the Cold War (1945–1953), one power of the five (continental China) was excluded from the Security Council of the United Nations (1949–1953).

### Punitive' Peace Treaties

Another important factor of non-recognition is the instauration of international orders by punitive peace treaties. The order of Versailles (1919–1939) was formed on a punitive basis whereas the Congress of Vienna and the "democratic peace order" were initially destined to integrate all the great powers.

Table 3.1 illustrates that variables of recognition vary in accordance with armed conflicts and militarised disputes. The more the governmental self-images are modest, the more identities are shared, the more powers are included and the less peace treaties are punitive and conflict become less frequent. On the contrary, I have mixed results for the realist variable "hegemony" and the "liberal" variable "democratic regime". Thus, while the "multipolar" and "authoritarian" order of the Congress of Vienna is peaceful, the multipolar and partly authoritarian system of Versailles is much more prone to conflict. Consequently, my analysis suggests further investigation about a 'statistical' link between recognition denial and armed conflict.

### Conclusion

The analysis also suggests some ideas for understanding the post-bipolar order and its armed conflict. Interstate conflict relations have indeed slightly decreased, but we are a far cry from the hopes conceived at the end of the bipolar confrontation. With four major interstate wars, the decade from 1981 to 1991 was not less pacific than the past two decades from 1991 to 2009 with about eight major inter-state wars.[23]

This mitigated outcome of armed conflict corresponds with equally contrasting tendencies towards the development of recognition within the new international order. With regards to hubristic identities, American power has openly proclaimed its leadership on the international stage since G.W. Bush took office in early 2001. Strongly influenced by the 'neo-conservatives', the American President believed that the US was invested with a moral mission (Hassner and Vaïsse 2003). This 'new arrogance' is perhaps precisely an invitation for terrorist groups to try to

---

23. SIPRI Yearbook 2009; ISS 2009; Marschall 2005. For the 1946–2006 period, sixty-seven inter-state conflicts are registered.

demonstrate the superpower's vulnerability. In turn, the 'narcissistic wounds' of 9/11 have a direct connection with the American attacks against the Taliban (2001) and Iraqi (2003) regimes.

Conversely, the 'ideological' homogenisation after the end of the Cold War was to bestow more stability upon the international system. Few states, including China, were seen to jeopardise liberal and free-trade values. Besides, the shared identity between Western democracies subsisted after the disappearance of the Soviet Union. This explains probably why there has been no return to a 'balance of power' policy in Europe.

Nevertheless, amongst great powers, there are still two who are not fully integrated in the post-Cold War international order. Firstly, Russia does not belong either to NATO or the EU. Neighbouring Western countries and Baltic states have already been integrated within NATO. Western countries have, half-heartedly, sought to associate Russia within the G7 framework and the program of the Partnership for Peace (PfP). Western policy is also hesitant towards China. It has been integrated in the world trade order, but not in the international security system. The effects of this policy have been ambivalent. Whereas a mainstream nationalist power popular among the military, refers to the imperial tradition, other social forces, chiefly economic actors, prefer Western integration to imperial temptation. It is necessary to highlight that some entrepreneurs of morality, chiefly American power, strive to split the world into two sides: 'Rogue states were stigmatised and punished like during the period of Wilson, where he declared that a guilty nation had to pay for its crimes (Colonomos 2006; 2008). The effects of this policy seem to be have been highly counter-productive because the 'punitive' American approach towards these countries seems to have only consolidated and amplified mainstream nationalist sentiments, such as in Iran where President Ahmadinejad promotes the 'clash of fundamentalism' (Fayazmanesh 2007).

# chapter four | saving face and peace; the politics of recognition in international crises

Those who have examined the process of international crises have postulated that the peaceful or bellicose outcome of a crisis depends on its 'management' by political decision makers (Lebow 1981; Yuen Foong Khong 1992; Allison and Zelikov 2004; Yetiv 2004). Although structural causes such as socio-economic disparities and security dilemmas are among the causes of war, not all tensions result in armed conflict (Baldwin 1971; Lebow 1996; Evans 2006). There have been many crises in which the outcome initially seemed uncertain: the Moroccan Crises 1905 and 1911, the July 1914 Crisis, the Munich Crisis 1938, the Cuban Missile Crisis 1962, the Israeli-Egyptian Crisis 1967, the Iraqi Crises 1990 and 2002–2003, the U.S.-Libyan Crisis 1986–2004, the Crisis of Yugoslavia and Kosovo 1991–1995, 1999, the U.S. – Iranian Crises and even the India – Pakistan Crises. Why were some of these crises resolved peacefully whereas others led to war? 'Utilitarian' models, which dominate explanations of international crises (Jervis 1976), stipulate that war breaks out because the state that defies the status quo is not dissuaded from aggression. The ambiguity of British policy throughout the Crisis of July 1914 could have encouraged German decision makers to maintain their conflictual policy to the same degree as concessions made in Munich in 1938. However, as Richard N. Lebow points out, the analogy of Munich 1938 is probably inapplicable to many historical cases. Few decision makers wage war purely because of potential material gains. If wars were provoked only by imperialist exuberance, they would be won by the provocative power. Therefore, some (Lebow 1981) consider that a policy of reassurance, which seeks to calm others' security fears, can be sufficient to avoid war.

Following this line of logic, this chapter seeks to affirm that numerous wars could have been avoided by taking into account the security aspirations of others. But it is not only security concerns that guide decision makers in an international crisis – it is also the quest for recognition. This includes both questions of 'saving face' – prestige and honour – as well as concerns for maintaining a specific identity and the need for some measure of empathy. Contrary to the utilitarian theories of war for security (*homo politicus*), or war for profit (*homo economicus*), I start with the hypothesis that state leaders also seek to cultivate a certain image of themselves and their collectivity (*homo symbolicus*). This hypothesis holds that the peaceful or bellicose outcome of crises, fostered by actors motivated by a sentiment of military and symbolic vulnerability, depends on the presence or absence of a politics of conciliatory recognition. This takes into account the security constraints of others, but also attempts to allow them to 'save face' and take into consideration their need for 'identity' recognition and 'empathy'.

88 | causes of war

In the crises I examine, most of the decision makers acted more out of vulnerability than opportunity. The wars waged were not inevitable. The crises that led to war were managed in a manner contrary to a politics of recognition. Accordingly, I will examine four serious international crises, two of which resulted in war (the Six Day War 1967, the Iraq War 2003) and two of which did not lead to war (The Cuban Missile Crisis 1962, the U.S.-Libyan Crisis, 1986 to 2004). I will seek to determine if a change in the dependent variable (war or peace[1]) corresponds to a change in the independent variable (presence or absence of a politics of recognition) (George 1979). If the hypothesis is valid, the two crises with peaceful resolutions should correlate with a politics of conciliatory recognition, whereas the two crises resulting in war should correspond to a posture of deterrence. The term 'crisis' broadly designates relations between two states where tensions could lead to war.[2] Their interstate nature, their chronological proximity, and the protagonists' power potential justify comparisons between these crises. Thus, two asymmetrical conflicts are compared with two symmetrical conflicts.

The demonstration will be conducted in four stages. Firstly, I will define the politics of 'conciliatory recognition' in the context of 'military and symbolic vulnerability'. In the second part I will focus on the two crises that led to war by determining the effect of deterrence postures. Then I will determine whether the two crises that ended peacefully correspond closely to the imperatives of conciliatory recognition. Finally, I will test alternative explanations for the outcome of these crises. The conclusion will put the results in perspective by specifying implications for both the origins of war and conflict prevention policy.

## THE POLITICS OF RECOGNITION IN INTERNATIONAL CRISES

My thesis is that the peaceful conclusion of an international crisis strongly depends on a politics of recognition when the instigating power in a crisis acts through a feeling of vulnerability (out of fear for survival or identity) rather than opportunity (for economic or political gains). I therefore do not assume that a politics of recognition would be sufficient to appease revisionist states such as Nazi Germany.

### The Dependent Variable: Peace and War Resulting from a Crisis Initiated through a Sentiment of Vulnerability

To demonstrate the limits of threats and the virtues of a politics of recognition in the context of 'vulnerability' I will make use of two theses. First, I will focus on 'perceptual' realism (Jervis), which concerns the perception of power distribution at the origin of international conflicts (Van Evera 1999). Second, I will consider the constructivist approach, which focuses on the role identity plays when resorting to force (Katzenstein 1996). These two approaches suggest that a deterrence

---

1. This chapter holds that a politics of recognition can be said to 'succeed' if peace is maintained for five years.
2. For a bibliographical orientation: Lebow (1981); George and Smoke (1974); Dobry (1986); Lynn-Jones, Miller and Van Evera (eds.) (1990); Davis (2003); Gelpi (2003) Bially Mattern (2004).

posture can be ineffective with states who consider themselves vulnerable, either because of concerns over their military security, or concerns over 'saving face' (Goffman 1974; Buzman 1994), i.e., the self-image that the decision makers wish to project.

**Military Vulnerability**
The limits of deterrence are apparent within the rational actor model. The costs of possible reprisals must be perceived as higher than the costs of the status quo. Robert Jervis holds that threats risk being ineffective when the provocative state acts from a sentiment of vulnerability, supposing that its 'survival' is compromised by the status quo (Jervis 1976). Such a situation emerges when a state perceives that other 'rising' powers are hostile towards it. There is a great incentive to use force when the balance between offence and defence is inclined towards the former, when state decision makers believe that there would be a military advantage to a first, 'defensive' strike. In extreme situations, it could lead to preemptive war. Even the misperception of military vulnerability can have real consequences (Thomas Theorem) (Levy 1983). Decision makers who believe that their state's security situation will progressively deteriorate and who perceive other states to be resolutely hostile towards them are not easily swayed by postures of pure 'deterrence'.

*Symbolic Vulnerability*
Decision makers in a state that is markedly weaker than the deterring power often refuse concessions despite their interest in avoiding material and human losses. This insensitivity to deterrence frequently corresponds to the image that the decision makers have or wish to project of themselves and their nation. Symbolic vulnerability designates the gap between the image put forth by decision makers and that which is projected (Wolf 2008) by others. It can be defined by a simple formula: desired image > image projected by others. The actor has an image of himself that is superior to that which others have of him. The larger the gap, the greater the frustration, humiliation and loss of self-esteem. Damage is thus inflicted on identity, negatively affecting self-representation. Caving in to threats can be considered so humiliating that the decision makers prefer to lose a war rather than lose face.

*Military and symbolic vulnerability in internal opinion*
Any regime – especially democratic – is concerned about public support at least of its elites. Decision makers generally want to preserve their power. A politics of recognition is particularly likely to allay internal opinion and to exert via the latter pacific pressure when elites and an opposing state's opinion are mainly invigorated by a feeling of 'vulnerability' and not by a determination of conquest or revenge (Whystock 2006). Symbolic gestures like the kneeling of Chancellor Brandt in Warsaw in December 1971 or the spectacular visit of Egyptian President Sadat in 1977 to Israel are capable of delegitimising another state's aggressive policies (Long 2003; Tabory 1978; Osgood 1962; Lefranc 2002).

State A is especially sensitive to state B's policy of recognition, if state A's decision makers justify the existence of a crisis by the existence of a threat. The more the justifications of the state A are of defensive nature, there is a better chance that state B's politics of recognition can deconstruct the legitimisation of an armed aggression. Opinion polls provide another clue about the influenceable pacific character of internal opinion: are there still notable oppositions with regard to the recourse of armed force within public opinion and their 'leaders' during crises? (Whystock 2006).

*The Independent Variable: Conciliatory Recognition*
Rationalist approaches hold that aggression results from a cost/benefit analysis, in which the interests of states are relatively constant. In order to prevent wars, it is necessary to increase the costs of aggression via sanctions, or even to increase the benefits of a peaceful approach through material compensation (Axelrod 2004). These approaches ignore the fact that certain decision makers prize symbolic interests over material ones. They do not hold that state decision makers accord variable values to the same objects. A rocky island can thereby symbolise a great interest for certain states, considering their identity. Finally, punitive and deterrent postures do not systematically discourage actors from armed violence. On the contrary, numerous examples demonstrate that such punitive practices construct and consolidate 'exclusive' identities which in turn favour aggressive behaviour.

Contrary to these materialist perspectives, a politics of recognition based on the following premises can affect the outcome of a crisis. First, building on the work of Axel Honneth, the desire for recognition rests on fundamental human needs such as self-respect, social self-esteem (the recognition of particularity) and empathy. John Burton holds that the desire for recognition is a 'human need' and refusal to accord it can bring about aggressive behaviour (Burton 1990; 1996). Secondly, in a more constructivist vein, it seems apparent that identities that seek recognition are variable (Bially Mattern 2004). Thirdly, identities are constructed and are often that which 'significant others' make of it. A politics of recognition is thereby susceptible to construct new identities whereas a politics of 'stigmatisation' is likely to reinforce feelings of otherness. The combination of an approach based on both fundamental 'psychological' needs and constructivism is therefore possible if one clearly specifies which recognition interests are stable and which are socially constructed. If needs such as self-esteem are anthropological constants, the concrete means to satisfy them depend on the historical and social context. On the other hand, the constructivist postulate according to which identities construct interests will be difficult to sustain if elementary psychological needs are not taken into account, for example, an enhanced self-image.

At a more elementary level, a politics of recognition first requires the acceptance of the existence of others. Like a policy of *reassurance* (Lebow and Stein 1994), it seeks to reduce tensions through minor symbolic and material concessions that demonstrate their 'peaceful' intentions. In times of international crisis, restraint, the mastering of military measures and declarations of mutual recognition can help avoid an escalation of violent behaviour (Osgood 1962).

In any case, a politics of *recognition* requires *more* than simply showing others that you do not want to physically harm them. It also involves *a politics of dignity*. A politics of recognition must, at the very least, abstain from questioning the principal of sovereignty between states. Sovereign dignity also requires the confirmation of others' autonomy by respecting 'their territories', both physical and psychological (Brown and Levinson 1987). Confirmation of others' autonomy generally poses few problems for actors' identity security because it deals with conservative ambition.

The politics of recognition also respects 'identities' that manifest themselves through belief systems, religions, cultures, norms, trauma and historical memory. A politics of recognition does not oblige the other to accept their values. Finally, recognition of the other as a 'particular' being supposes an *empathetic commitment, a taking into consideration*. An emphasis on shared values can show the other that there is a partial identification with them (Wendt 1992). On the other hand, indifference and stigmatisation of the other risks becoming a self-fulfilling prophecy (Blumer 1969).

A politics of recognition can be defined as *material and above all composed of symbolic concessions aimed at confirming the other's identity*. It aims, like the policy of 'reassurance' (R. N. Lebow/J. Stein), at easing tensions by making minor symbolic and material concessions as a token of one's peaceful intentions. The objective of this policy is, first and foremost, to alter the way our intentions are perceived by others. It thus seeks to reduce a state's fears, both strategic and recognition-related, rather than its power. The restraint of military action during an international crisis is capable of preventing the action-reaction escalation. This approach draws on the fact that actors are equipped with only limited rationality and engage in conflicts arising out of exaggerated security fears. Similarly, Charles Osgood's *Graduated Reciprocation Initiatives in Tension Reduction* (Osgood 1962) aims at creating an atmosphere of mutual trust among the actors through initially unilateral measures. However, unlike these psychological approaches, *recognition* policies involve much more than merely demonstrating that one does not seek to physically harm the other. This politics is more sensitive to the 'recognition-related needs' of the other actors. *Recognition* policy typically avoids 'narcissistic injuries' during an international crisis (by offering the opponent dignified ways of backing down in a crisis) and takes into account the symbolic concerns of the other side, particularly those linked to their national identity (e.g., holy sites, national symbols and historical sensibilities). A *politics of recognition* accounts for the following symbolic-related aspects:

*Self-esteem (the 'positive face')*: At the very least, a politics of recognition, conforms to the contemporary dignity standards in international relations, respects the principle of sovereign equality among states. It is not only a matter of averting anything that could possibly jeopardise the positive identity of the other, but also to deliberately confirm it (commonly called 'flattery' in social relations). Thus, the resolution of a conflict between great powers is often promoted through the recognition of a shared right to leadership in international politics (e.g., the demarcation and allocation of zones of interest in the Cold War). Even a policy of deterrence requires taking into account the other's 'face'. In the Cuban Missile Crisis 1962, for instance, it would have been difficult for Khrushchev to retreat if the U.S. had not pledged to withdraw the Jupiter Missiles from Turkey allowing Khrushchev 'to save face'. Yet, the more actor A cultivates an inflated, 'hubristic' image of himself, the more difficult and costly will it be for actor B to confirm A's self-perception. By the same token, it would have been impossible for the Jews to recognise the identity of Nazi-Germany without consenting to their own destruction. The following questions are useful for identifying the degree of respect accorded to the other's positive face in an international crisis:

1   Can a minimal concession be proposed which would allow the other to save face, or will a solution be unilaterally imposed?
2   Concerning discourse during a crisis, are there explicit devaluations of the other's hierarchical or moral status?
3   Do the actors allow discussions to be founded on equal one-on-one negotiations?

***The confirmation of the other's autonomy*** through respect for its physical and psychological 'territories' – the 'negative face' according to Brown and Levinson (Brown and Levinson 1987):

A politics of recognition must make a special effort to account for the holiness of certain sites and territories (Jerusalem, Kosovo). Respect for a state's sovereignty is the minimum requirement for a successful politics of recognition (e.g., President Kennedy's declarations concerning Cuba's territorial integrity during the Cuban Missile Crisis). Confirming the other's autonomy generally does not threaten one's own identity-related security, as the quest for autonomy is usually 'conservative' in nature. The claim for national independence varies also as a function of the respective identity framework, ranging for instance from the endorsement of globalisation (as in the case of the Scandinavian countries) to the rejection of everything foreign (e.g., of Western music in Taliban Afghanistan). The more that state leaders conceive their territory as sacred, the more aggressively they will react towards external influences or interference. The following question is useful to identify the respect of the other's 'negative face':

In a crisis, are the demands and rhetoric of states compatible with respect for others' internal sovereignty?

***The respect for 'identity-related particularities'*** which are linked to specific belief systems, cultures and norms:

A politics of recognition is sensitive to the others' religions and historical trauma. Disregard for past injuries, as displayed by Egyptian President Nasser's incendiary declarations in the run-up to the Six Day War, will be perceived as particularly 'violent'. A politics of recognition refrains from imposing one's own values upon the other (e.g., exporting democracy). The limits of recognition are reached at the point where the recognition of particularities implies the negation of one's own existence (e.g., Iraq claiming historic rights to the annexation of Kuwait). The following question concerns the recognition of the adversary's identity in international crises:

In a crisis, are states' rhetorical demands and practices compatible with their adversary's cultural and historical references? For example, denial of the Holocaust is a denial of recognition through the negation of historical suffering

**Engagement:** There is a possibility to overcome the egoistic Hobbesian identities through a policy of empathy that promotes positive identification. A. Wendt considers that the emphasis on common values and cooperation can bring about a transformation of images of the enemy (Wendt 1992). For instance, during the Cuban Missile Crisis, President Kennedy appealed to the common destiny that connected Soviets and Americans. In the same way, 'stigmatisation' of the other is liable to become a self-fulfilling prophecy, as was the case with the 'Clash of Civilizations' thesis that became reality, as many in the West began to conceive of the 'Islamic civilisation' as our enemy. Thus, the identities of the actors depend to a great extent on how they are shaped by the 'others' ('alter casting', i.e., when a certain role is ascribed to somebody).[3] The hostile behaviour of actor A towards actor B is often the result of B's display of distrust (and thereby also of a lack of respect) towards A (e.g., the chances of being attacked by a gang of youths are presumably higher if one tries to dodge them by crossing the street). The following questions are useful to identify a 'policy of empathy':

1  Which discursive practices are employed? Do decision makers focus on an impenetrable barrier between 'us' and 'them'? Or rather do they show that they are not so different from the other by making reference to a community of shared destiny? The 'nuclear' threat that weighs on humanity is an example. Does this include others in the argumentation, i.e., the principle of communication seeking entente?

2  Do states take into account the needs of others by demonstrating minimal empathy when the population is hit by an attack or natural catastrophe: for example, Sarajevo 1914 or the 11th September 2001?

I assert that in an international crisis a politics of recognition will often be able to preserve peace. The costs of such a policy vary. It will be considerably easier to placate states that maintain democratic identities (calling for an equality of status) than those states which claim 'honour' insisting on the recognition of their superiority.

A politics of recognition can preserve peace if the state that causes an international crisis is principally satisfied with the territorial status quo and motivated by *existential fears,* i.e., by a perceived strategic vulnerability or the fear of losing face. One could put forward the hypothesis that international crises are more often

---

3.  See on this topic Blumer (1969: 13) 'It follows that we see ourselves through the way in which others see or define us – or, more precisely, we see ourselves by taking one of the three types of roles of others that have been mentioned.'

caused by states that act out of a feeling of vulnerability than by state leaders with boundless ambitions, such as Hitler.

According to R. Jervis (Jervis 1976) and James W. Davis (Davis 2000), a policy of deterrence is required when the state to be deterred provokes an international

*Table 4.1: The different aspects of a policy of recognition*

| Aspects of a policy of recognition: to be sensitive to | 1) the positive face: self-esteem | 2) the negative face: autonomy | 3) cultural particularities | 4) the degree of positive identification |
|---|---|---|---|---|
| Politics of recognition is easily feasible if | actors seek only 'equal' recognition, e.g., ex-FRG | actors are willing to open up to foreign countries, e.g., the EU member states | actors do not strive to preserve religious and cultural particularities, e.g., the Scandinavian countries | protagonists share the same values, e.g., the Western democracies |
| Politics of recognition is costly if | actors cultivate hubristic self-images, e.g., Serbia's Milosevic | actors try to ward off foreign influences, e.g., Taliban Afghanistan | actors have a high consciousness of national particularities and historical traumas' e.g., Israel | Actors exhibit different values and identities, e.g., the Cold War |

crisis solely in order to seize profit opportunities, as in the case of Nazi-Germany. Nevertheless, a policy of deterrence or coercion should always be accompanied by a form of recognition if it aims to preserve peace. Coercion based on the humiliation of the other is unlikely to succeed, even if the balance of forces clearly favours the coercive party. Even in the case of one party acting for reasons of opportunity alone (as China did against Taiwan in the Spratly Islands dispute), a policy of deterrence must be sensitive to the positive and negative face of the other (self-esteem and autonomy) if it is to be effective. The only case in which a politics of recognition does not encourage peace is when a state is preparing for a war of conquest, thus violating the principle of sovereignty of other states. Hitler's Germany is an example of such a case. However, a policy of pure deterrence would not have prevented the war. A dictator like Hitler, who based his claim to power on the alleged superiority of the 'Aryan race', would hardly have been disposed to yield to the threats of the Allied powers. When faced with such a dictator, the alternative to a politics of recognition is not a policy of 'pure' deterrence, but a mixed approach or, in the worst case, war. For the most part, the politics of recognition is better suited to preserve peace than a policy of pure deterrence. Few proponents of deterrence theory have recognised that deterrence is only effective if the other's face is saved. In short, a policy of recognition is indispensable for the peaceful management of international crises, particularly if an actor acts out of a feeling of vulnerability. The following chart shows that a politics of recognition is more likely to preserve peace than a purely deterrence-based approach.

*Table 4.2: The effects of a policy of recognition, a mixed policy and a purely deterrent policy on the preservation of peace as a function of the motivation of the instigator*

| identity-related motivation of the instigator (actor A) policy implemented by actor B | desire to be considered as superior | actor acts out of existential fears (the most common case) |
|---|---|---|
| policy of recognition | **peace but** war is maybe only postponed and will probably be more costly, e.g., Munich 1938; Western policy towards Milosevic from 1991 to 1995 | **peace** e.g., Gaddafi's management of the American-Libyan conflict after 2003 |
| mixed policy of recognition and deterrence | **peace is possible** e.g., the crises between China and Taiwan handled by the U.S. with commitment and respect for Chinese sensibilities (but this policy would not work towards extremely hubristic Nazi Germany) | **peace** e.g., Kennedy's determined, but sensitive handling of the Cuban Missile Crisis 1962, allowing Khrushchev to save face |
| policy of pure deterrence | **War breaks out immediately**, but might be less costly, e.g., the Allies guaranteeing support to Poland in 1939; the coalition against Saddam Hussein in 1990 | **War is probable** e.g., the July Crisis of 1914, the Six Day War, the Iraq War (2003) |

*Case studies*

I have chosen four international crises in which the initiators of the crisis acted mainly out of a feeling of strategic or symbolic-related vulnerability. These cases differ with regard to their dependent variable: peace or war. War broke out in two of the cases – in the Six Day War 1967 and the American war against Iraq in 2003

– whereas war could be prevented in the other two cases, i.e., the Cuban Missile Crisis in 1962 and the US-Libyan conflict (1986–2004). If my hypothesis is valid, the two latter cases must be linked with a politics of recognition while there must have prevailed a more deterrent approach in the two former cases. These four cases are all relatively recent interstate conflicts between great or middle powers. The likeness of the cases and the variation in the dependent variable – war or peace – justify the comparison.

First, I will examine the two conflicts which resulted in war, focusing especially on the effect of the deterrent postures. I will then verify whether the two conflicts with peaceful outcomes correspond more with the principles used in recognition policy.

For either conflict type, I will first assess the subjective motivations of the policy-makers. Did they perceive opportunities to make economic, strategic or symbolic gains or were they rather concerned with possible material or symbolic losses? The key test will then be whether we can detect a 'chronological correlation' between symbolic provocation and military threat from the opponent and an evolution towards an attitude more favourable to the use of force.

*Testing the hypotheses*
An analysis of only four case studies cannot be said to be representative. However, such analyses are exploratory studies that will serve as a framework that can be applied to further cases. For example, what role was played by non-recognition in the July Crisis in 1914, the build-up to the China-Taiwan Crises and that of Russia and Georgia? Case studies present important empirical material for analysis. A detailed study increases the internal validity of propositions for hypotheses analysed in a case study. Correlative studies on international crises that have been triggered by various factors are more easily susceptible of being founded on contestable facts and doubtful comparisons.

First of all, I will pay special attention to the chronological sequences of all four cases to identify the causal process and eventually the multiple factors that intervene at each phase of the crisis (George and Benett 2005). Such a distinction will allow us to see if the crises have evolutionary characters. An evolution in a crisis would constitute the first sign that actors' behaviour actually counts in its resolution. In other words, are there chronologic concordances between, on the one hand threats and recognition policy, and on the other hand, between the aggravation and appeasement of international crises (Skocpol 1979)? We have already identified the hallmarks of both recognition policies and deterrence policies. All that remains to be seen is a verification of whether or not such 'recognising' or 'intimidating' policies go hand in hand with an aggravation in the crisis. For example, what was the impact of Iraqi and Libyan reactions to the 11th September on US policy? What was the impact of the exaggerated declarations made by the Egyptian President Nasser on Israeli policy during the 1967 Crises or, on the contrary, of the US recognition of Khrushchev as an equal interlocutor in 1962? Furthermore, I will also consider the justifications and subjective motivation expressed by decision makers in internal debates.[4] In these debates, are other states (the US, Egypt, Iraq and Libya) considered as representing a threat to national identity and security, or can we deduce that these ideas are enlivened by a desire to assure a 'regional' hegemony or to assure energy interests? On top of this, does credibility in front of public opinion play an important role for decision makers?

Our test applies the congruence method (George and Benett 2005), which verifies if the cases studied correspond to the predictions made by different theories. All four cases present different results (peace or war) while the liberal variable of economic interest (oil) and the realist variable of security interests are relatively constant. On the other hand, I suggest that the presence or absence of a recognition policy goes hand in hand with a variation of the studied variable (peace of war). I will also analyse 'dissuasion' as a concurrent theory to recognition (Huth and Russett 1993). According to this theory, US aggression towards Libya and Iraq depends on the weakness of the latter two countries. 'Soviet aggression' in 1962 and Israeli aggression in 1967 would in the same way depend on 'opportunity'. In principle, the more that challenged states are able to seem credible in their capacity and desire to strike back, the more the 'instigators' should be dissuaded from engaging in a military attack. Threatening behaviour from a state should therefore bring a second state to prudence, for example, through the fear of a 'terrorist' attack against their overseas citizens or even the use of WMD. However, according to recognition theory, threats from states should, on the contrary, incite a second state to take military action. In effect, threats often constitute attacks on self-images and also fuel fears about the future behaviour of such a state. For this reason, I will use these case studies to test if threats are linked with an appeasement of international crises (as predicted by dissuasion theory) or with an aggravation (as predicted by recognition theory). I will then summarise the results of this comparison between recognition policy and 'threatening' postures. The empirical demonstration will be applied to all four cases in two steps. First, I will study the state's vulnerability that provoked the conflict (in terms of both military and symbolic threats). In the second step, I will examine the links between the effects of a politics of recognition and a deterrence policy on the progression of the four crises by establishing chronologic concordances as well as subjective influences affecting the decision makers, and by verifying if alternative explanations are as apt as the 'symbolic' explanation at explaining the outcome of these crises.

## CRISES WITH A BELLICOSE OUTCOME (LOSING FACE)

Why do states start international crises and why are they ready to engage in war? The answer is evidently variable from one case to the other, but empirical studies tend to suggest that states engage more often in a conflict because they feel vulnerable rather than because they sense an opportunity in terms of power or economy (Van Evera 1999). Thus, Wilhelmian Germany did not take advantage of Russia's strategic vulnerability at the first Moroccan crisis (1905) to start a war against the Entente, but ended up going to war in 1914 in a markedly less favourable situa-

---

4. For a similar study Tannenwald (2003).

tion. In the same way, US decision makers did not use their nuclear monopoly to dissuade the Soviet Union in Eastern Europe at the end of the 1940s, but took risks in the Cuban missile crisis against a nuclear-armed USSR. Before now, studies have mainly focused on problems relating to strategic vulnerability and have neglected the symbolic aspect. Yet this symbolic dimension is as old as international relations history and has an important place in Thucydides' account of the Peloponnesian War (Lebow 1996).

Both the crises that are presented here – those preceding the Six-Day War and the Iraq war 2003 – confirm the importance of military and symbolic vulnerability in the buildup to these conflicts.

**Military and Symbolic Vulnerability**

*The Six-Day War of 1967*
Egyptian decision makers initiated the crisis preceding the Six-Day War, but Israeli leaders launched the actual war. I will try to understand the motivations of the latter. Concerning military vulnerability, S. Van Evera affirms that during a crisis, each protagonist can believe that they possess an advantage by striking first and would garner extreme risk by expecting the other to take the initiative (Lebow 1996). This is particularly true for Israeli leaders who are confined to an exiguous territory. On the 14th May, Egyptian troops crossed the Suez Canal and headed towards the Sinai. Israeli leaders feared that an attack from neighbouring Arab countries was imminent (Stein 2000), and determined that a first strike by the Arabs would be disastrous (Van Evera 1999: 66). On the 25th May, Israeli intelligence services learned that the Fourth Egyptian Armoured Division was taking up positions in the Sinai. The same day, the Prime Minister L. Eshkol wrote to his Foreign Affairs Minister en route to Washington

> The problem of straits should this be "the Straits"? is not the greatest of our fears, but rather the danger that high concentrations of troops would pose to the security of Israel. A surprise attack on Israel is not out of the question. (Enderlein 1997: 235)

After the withdrawal of U.N. troops from the Sinai, Israel was confronted with Syrian and Egyptian troops on its borders. Israeli leaders could have believed that the pre-emptive option was their best chance of survival. The incentive to launch an offensive attack was also based on the perceived strategic benefits of a first strike. In early June 1967, Israeli air force commanders advocated war based on their conviction that a surprise attack could destroy a large part of the Egyptian air forces (Van Evera 1997: 40). In fact, their 'pre-emptive strike' destroyed 66 per cent of the Egyptian Air Force.

The premise that Israel acted purely through a sentiment of vulnerability has been questioned by certain analysts. In fact, it is not certain that Israeli leaders feared for the survival of their state, because Israel possessed two nuclear weapons (Razoux 2003). Imperial ambition seems to have been more important than security. Certain individuals, most notably members of religious parties, like interior minister M. H. Shapira or defence minister M. Dayan very probably hoped to capture 'holy' land. In any case, this argument seems to be invalid as applied to the entire government. The premise of a pre-planned purely imperialist war is not compatible with the change in the Israeli government's attitude throughout the crisis. The cabinet was opposed to engaging in war untilthe 27th May, with seventeen ministers against and one in favour (Bar-Zohar 1968). Otherwise, could the possession of a nuclear weapon really have saved Israel under any circumstances, considering the Soviet nuclear umbrella to which Syria and Egypt could avail themselves?

Israeli decision makers were also vulnerable to symbolic challenges. R. N. Lebow recalls the Holocaust syndrome in the construction of Israeli identity, which is often accompanied by 'exaggerated fears for the survival of the nation' (Lebow 1981). In the Israeli imagination, the memory of Auschwitz teaches the lesson to fiercely resist against aggression from the outset. However, the government was considered to be too soft and conciliatory towards Arab states by parts of the population and the military. Rabin concluded on the 28th May that,

> It is becoming more and more obvious that in this country the only force on which we can count on is the army. (Bar-Zohar 1968)

Egypt's strategic vulnerability can also partly explain why President Nasser decided to set off a crisis by demanding the withdrawal of the UN forces, closing the Straits of Tiran to Israeli shipping and repeating his inflammatory declarations towards Israel. According to Pierre Razoux (2003), the Egyptian leaders were informed about Israel's nuclear program. The nuclear research centre of Dimona, located in the northern Negev desert, had been chosen for the development of a nuclear bomb, and carrier rockets which had been ordered from Marcel Dassault were to be delivered before the end of 1967. While the actual danger of a nuclear strike against Egypt was not imminent, the existence of such a nuclear program was decisive for the Egyptian perception of Israel's intentions. There was no doubt in the minds of the Egyptian decision makers that the Israelis could aggressively use their nuclear capacities

> What mattered was the perception that Nasser and his entourage had of the nuclear threat. The Egyptians themselves never doubted that they represented the primary target of a possible Israeli nuclear strike. (Razoux 2003: 40)

Egypt was then further alarmed on the 12th May by rumours that Israel was preparing a surprise attack against Syria. This false intelligence report had been propagated by the Soviets, who had sent an according telegram to a number of Arab capitals. Moscow was thus hoping to strengthen the Syrian regime by fuelling Arab-Israeli-hostilities. Yet it is not sure whether the Egyptian leaders actually believed that an Israeli attack was imminent. General Fawzi, the Egyptian Chief of Staff, who was sent to Damascus to determine the veracity of the threat, remarked that 'the Russians must have been having hallucinations' (Hazan 1989: 16). Nasser was also considering conquering the port of Eilat so as to connect Egypt with Jordan. However, Nasser reckoned that such an intervention 'was only feasible as long as Israel did not possess nuclear weapons', that is to say, before the end of 1967 (Razoux 2003: 14).

On either side, symbolic-related vulnerabilities played a key role and were maybe even more important than strategic vulnerabilities. The beginning of the crisis is described by Anwar Sadat in the following manner

> Nasser seemed to be in favour of such a measure [close the Port of Aqaba] to stamp down Arab opposition to his policy and to maintain his popularity in the Arab world. (Enderlein 1997: 231)

King Hussein of Jordan criticized the Egyptian's lack of solidarity, not only regarding the Palestinians, but also regarding the Syrians, tied to Egypt by a pact of mutual assistance. The Egyptian army was considered a paper tiger. In his autobiography, Anwar al Sadat explains Nasser's active part in triggering the war by considerations of prestige (Enderlein). Indeed, we can only understand Nasser's provocations if we take into account the role identity that Nasser conferred to Egypt: Nasser's image of Egypt was that of the strong and virile nation that leads and unites the Arab world. He was a kind of modern pharaoh. His self-image, however, was challenged by the other Arab leaders, for instance King Hussein of Jordan. The latter never missed an occasion to denounce Egypt's inaction not only regarding the Palestinians, but also regarding Syria, which was tied to Egypt by a mutual defense pact. Also, the Egyptian army was considered a paper tiger. According to Pierre Milza: 'Nasser's about-face can be explained by the Rais' concern to spruce up his image, somewhat tarnished by his military failures in Yemen and his moderation towards Israel' (Milza 1996). The loss of prestige is also emphasized by the historian Pierre Hazan

> Nasser is in trouble. The once-rising star of Pan-Arabism is now on the decline. Syria and Jordan scoff at Egypt's inaction towards Israel. Gamal Abdel Nasser, anxious to clean up his image, dramatically raises the stakes. (Hazan 1989: 15)

Moreover, Nasser could not ignore the strong identity bonds between the socialist Arab states without losing face. He could not possibly have shown himself indifferent to Syria's call for solidarity. In his speech on Egypt's Independence Day, on the 23rd July, Nasser tried to retroactively assign an Arab and revolutionary meaning to the war against Israel

> We all know that this war began with the Israeli wish to invade Syria. It was clear for us that in this policy, Israel was not alone, but was supported by the forces losing patience with the Arab revolutionary movement. (Hazan 1989)

As a matter of fact, the other Arab leaders overtly played with pan-Arab and revolutionary references in order to draw Nasser into the conflict. And Syria did not fail to remind Nasser to comply with his duty of intervention, as laid out in their mutual defense pact. The other Arab heads of states showered Nasser with sarcasm, sneering that 'the Egyptian army was capable only of bombing fellow Arabs in Yemen and of quelling Palestinians living in Egypt'. Thus, upon receiving the false telegram from Moscow, Nasser ordered the large-scale mobilisation of the armed forces, appealing to the 'socialist solidarity' that unites Damascus and Cairo (Razoux 2003).

## American Decision Makers Confronting Iraq in 2001–2003

Among the four crises examined, the Iraq war embodies most what R. Lebow (1981) calls 'hostility justification crises': a pretext to wage a war that has already been decided on. The hypothesis of an imperialist war, characterised by strategic, economic, and offensive ideological objectives, is justified by the existence of a coalition between 'ideological' neo-conservatives grouped around P. Wolfowitz and R. Perle in addition to representatives of the armament and oil industry – D. Rumsfeld and D. Cheney. This group of decision makers has long sought to overthrow the Saddam Hussein regime (Ruloff 2003).

Nevertheless, American decision makers were not unanimous. More classic conservatives such as C. Powell, his assistant secretary R. Armitage, those in charge of the military, C. Rice and G. Tenet were more reluctant to go to war (Yetiv 2004: Daalder and Lindsay 2005). The head of Central Command and the Joint Chiefs of Staff also expressed their concerns. They were supported by former members of the 'Bush 41' administration such as the former Secretary of State J. Baker and former National Security Advisor B. Scowcroft, Rice's former boss. On the 5th August 2002, Secretary of State C. Powell expressed his reluctance to the President during a dinner (Woodward 2003: 355). The President was apparently somewhat swayed by his arguments. On the 7th September 2002 during a meeting between T. Blair and G. Bush at Camp David, British diplomats found Vice-President Cheney rather silent. This could have indicated the ineffectiveness of his bellicose rhetoric at that precise moment.[5]

One cannot dismiss the security and recognition components of the American Iraqi policy, even if they were based on erroneous assumptions. If one refers to the documents published by intelligence services as well as to testimonies of IAEA and UNSCOM inspectors, journalists and American politicians, it is difficult to deny the sincerity of political leaders' security fears. The assumption that Iraq possessed weapons of mass destruction was not absurd on the basis of then available information and psychologically understandable in the post-traumatic climate of the 11th September. The fact that decision makers deliberately exaggerated the Iraqi threat does not prove that they believed that Saddam Hussein was not a threat. Above all, false information from the intelligence services explains the belief in the existence of WMD. The National Intelligence Estimate of October 2002 concluded

> Iraq is pursuing its WMD program, and is making missiles which surpass the range of 150 km established by the United Nations resolution.[6]

The CIA arrived at similar conclusions, viewing the acquisition of high-resistance aluminium tubes and the purported purchase of uranium from Niger as evidence

---

5. Peel, Graham, Harding, and Dempsey 2003.
6. National Intelligence Estimate, Oct. 2002.

that Iraq was trying to enrich uranium for military purposes. On the 21st December 2002, CIA director G. Tenet asserted to President Bush, who had begun to have doubts about the solidity of the case that it possessed 'concrete' certainty of nuclear activities in Iraq ('It's a slam dunk case'). The President retrospectively asserted to Woodward that the comments of Tenet 'were determinant'. Even French intelligence services held that Iraq possessed weapons of mass destruction (Blix 2005: 210). One cannot ignore the Iraqi regime's past history in the matter. During the war against Iran, the Iraqi regime used chemical weapons on a large scale against Iranians. The Kurdish insurrection in Halabja in 1988 was repressed using mustard gas and neurotoxin agents. In 1991, the IAEA inspectors led by David Kay discovered that Iraq had secretly enriched uranium without being detected (Blix 2005: 48). In 1995, the defection of a son-in-law of Saddam Hussein, General H. Kamel, led the IAEA inspectors to discover that Iraq had well placed stocks of chemical and ballistic weapons. In addition, the inspectors had discovered the admission of thousands of tons of chemical products and other raw materials to Iraq. In 1996, they had updated two hundred containers of production equipment for glass partitions for a VX factory.

The vulnerability of American leaders included a second aspect related to recognition. Many American politicians considered their status as a major democratic power to be challenged by Iraq. Since the Cold War, this image of being a major power assuring respect of global liberty has been so deeply anchored in the American collective memory that it remains even after the bipolar confrontation. The 11th September 2001 did not only mean the loss of three thousand human lives, but also inflicted a tremendous narcissistic wound on US power. The fact that Iraq was practically the only state in the world not to condemn the attacks comforted the vision of American leaders. In his address on the 11th September 2001, G. Bush proclaimed: 'America was targeted because it is the brightest beacon of liberty and progress in the world' (Ritter 2002). Saddam Hussein not only maintained his belligerent status after the first Iraq war, but also challenged American power on multiple occasions. This includes an assassination attempt against Bush's father and the refusal to allow IAEA inspectors to access possible WMD sites despite US warnings. The war against Iraq was a means for American power to eliminate a leader that had consistently challenged its authority. H. Kissinger remarked that the Iraqis had symbolically showed that one could challenge the United Nations by the violation of 17 UN resolutions.[7] The comments of the American president reflect a concern to preserve the power of American credibility against Iraq. G. Bush remarked with C. Rice at his presidential ranch in Crawford Texas on the lst January 2003: 'The United States cannot allow themselves to remain in this position while Saddam enjoys himself leading the inspectors by the nose!'. In the next few days after the New Year, Bush probably made the final decision to go to war. With C. Rice, he made his intentions clear

> Far from losing confidence [referring to Saddam Hussein] he is more and surer of himself. [...] We will surely have to go there. (Woodward 2004: 378 *f*)

---

7. Kissinger quoted on the web page of Sheer (2006).

The American president was particularly offended because of the manly image that he attempted to project. One must remember that the President's father had been called a 'wimp' by his opponents. Retrospectively, G. Bush admitted his refusal to back down once he had proclaimed his objective 'to disarm' Saddam.

As for the 'vulnerability' of American public opinion, it had prepared the Americans for war for security and 'dignity' and not for regime change. American decision makers who justified in favour of an armed intervention were all focused on the existence of weapons of massive destruction, the supposed links between Saddam Hussein and Al Qaeda and the possible implication of Iraq in the 11th September attacks. Key speeches from President Bush on the 29th January 2002 and on the 1st June 2002 and from Colin Powell on the 5th February 2002 as well as the 17th September 2002 document (National Security Document), are the illustration (Janieson 2007; Cashman 2007; Kaufman 2004).

Admittedly, the support from American public opinion for a war against Iraq all through the period between September 2001 and March 2003[8] was often significant. However, everything leads to a belief that public opinion support remained very intently conditioned by the belief that Iraq constituted a security threat and an 'offence' for the United States. Investigations show that American public opinion approval for the recourse to armed force against another state depends on the accuracy and the stakes of the operation (Jentleson 1992), on the number of human losses[9], the probability of success (Gelpi, Feaver and Reifler 2005), the consensus of the political elite (Larson 1996) and multilateral support (Kull 2003).

Particularly for the Iraqi case, a large majority of Americans were victims of at least one major distorted perception of the conflict. Or they assumed that Saddam Hussein had weapons of massive destruction and that it was implied in the 11th September attacks or they considered that the United States benefited from the support of international opinion. On the other hand, those questioned which did not share any one of these three distorted perceptions were mainly opposed to the war (Kull 2003). The support from American opinion also depended on 'patriotic' emotion. The attacks of the 11th September produced a strong feeling of humiliation among Americans (Saurette 2006). Thus, according to Gallup Polls, in November 2001 74 per cent of those questioned were favourable to a resort to armed force against Iraq whereas they were 'only' 50 per cent in August 2002.[10] Finally in June 2004, at the time when The National Commission on Terrorist Attacks Upon the United States (the 9/11 Commission) revealed that Iraq did not have any link with Al Qaeda that a majority of people polled began to consider the war in Iraq as an error.[11] This data suggests that an Iraqi politics of recogni-

---

8. Gallup Poll, 8th–10th February and 19th–21st August 2002; 13th–16th September and 10th–11th December 2002. < www.gallup.com/poll/1622/iraq.aspx>

9. Mueller (1973). However, see the discussion between Gelpi, Feaver and Reifler (2005) and Klavenas, Gelpi, Reifler (2006).

10. See in connection Diedhiou (2004: 87).

11. Gallup poll.

tion could considerably have weakened the support of American and international public opinion for the war.

**The quest for recognition against threats**
What effect was produced from states assuming deterrent postures when others felt vulnerable? In neither case did we find proof that credible dissuasion could have avoided war. On the contrary, the firmness showed by both the Egyptian and Israeli leaders in 1967, and by Saddam Hussein in 2002/2003, led to an uncontrollable and ultimately military escalation.

*The Six-Day War*
Nasser, displaying his new determination, opted not only for the simple withdrawal of UN troops from the Sinai (that it obtained on the 18th May), but days later decreed (22nd May) the closure of the Tiran Straits to Israeli navigation (Milza 96: 201f). Egyptian troops advanced to the Israeli border. Nasser had sent close to 100,000 men and 600 tanks to the Sinai desert. This was added in addition to a treaty between King Hussein of Jordan, Egypt, and the commando units of El-Fatah in northern Israel, signed on the 30th May. The flights over the Israeli nuclear power plant of Dimona carried out by two Mig-21 fighters on the 17th May 'unleashed a firestorm within the Israeli general staff' (Razoux 2006: 23). The fear of an attack against this plant was perhaps one of the principal causes for the Israeli decision to wage a 'preventive' war (Oren 2002: 76). On the 21st May, L. Eshkol established 'a moderate code of conduct aiming to defuse the crisis' (Razoux 2006: 23) during a meeting of the committee of defence. The threatening posture of Nasser collided with the Holocaust and Masada syndrome.[12] Instead of intimidating Israeli leaders, the threats of annihilation hurled by Arab leaders and Radio Cairo announcers revived the trauma created by the memory of genocide. Arab radio then intensified their insults towards the Zionists (Guerdon 1970).

Nasser's decision to close the straits of Tiran on the 22nd May played a critical role in the crisis. This decision involved the blockade of all maritime traffic bound for the Israeli harbour of Eilat (Guerdon 1970). Although Nasser certainly knew that this decision could induce war, he hoped that it could be avoided. Trapped by a wave of nationalism, the Egyptian president did nothing to indicate the narrow limits of its objectives. The Israeli general staff estimated 'that a red line had been crossed' (Razoux 2006). At that moment, the decision to go to war had not yet been taken, because the Israeli cabinet maintained hope of British or even American support to contain Egypt. The 26th May was another turning point. On that day, Nasser asserted that the Gulf of Aqaba was only a small part of a broader problem: Israeli aggression. Stoessinger (2000: 132) reported, 'the response in Israel was electric'.

Paradoxically, the clumsiness of Eshkol himself is at the origin of the radicalisation of Israeli policy. On the 27th and 28th May, the Israeli government was still reluctant to go to war (Hazan 1967: 28). President Johnson promised inter-

---

12. Reference to the destruction of the last Jewish household by Roman legions in the year 73AD.

national action and intended to open the Gulf of Aqaba to vessels of all countries (Bar-Zohar 1968: 168). On the evening of the 28th May, L. Eshkol spoke live on state radio. Exhausted and poorly prepared, the Prime Minister mumbled and gave the impression of being indecisive, incapable of withstanding the pressure from Arab States. Leaders of the general staff met with Eshkol that evening, showing themselves to be inflexible and determined to go to war. General Sharon said to the Prime Minister: 'Your procrastination will cost us thousands of deaths' (Hazan 1967). Egypt's rhetorical and military provocations explain to a good extent why Israeli officials eventually came to favour the military option. One can also ask if Israel's postures and those of its Arab neighbours did not also lead Egyptian leaders to adopt their risky strategy. Since 1957, Nasser had pursued a rather cautious policy towards Israel, entrenching himself behind the 3,400 UN Blue Helmets, but he abruptly abandoned this policy in May 1967. In order to understand this shift, we must take into account the conflict between Palestinians and Israelis, which also affected Syria and Jordan. On the 13th November 1966, following a series of raids conducted by the Palestinian Fatah from Lebanese, Syrian and Jordanian territories, Israel launched an attack against the Fatah stronghold of as-Samu in Jordan. King Hussein then explicitly accused Nasser of cowardice and of instigating the Jordanian fedayeen against Israel, all the while holding back the fedayeen in his own country and hiding 'timidly behind the UN forces' (Hazan 1967).

On the 7th April 1967, the Israeli air force attacked the Golan Heights at the Syrian border following Syrian artillery strikes against the Kibbutzim in the valley below. Syria sent up its MIGs, six of which were shot down by Israeli fighters. It was at this point mainly the Syrian leaders who were eager to push the Egyptians to further escalate the conflict with Israel: 'Revolutionary Syria is sneering at Nasser's timidity. Even the moderate Hashemite kingdom is taunting the great Nasser who is calling for an Arab rebellion outside of Egypt while locking up Palestinians in his own country' (Hazan 1967). The relationship between the young King Hussein and Nasser was contentious,

> especially as Jordan was supporting Egypt's opponent Saudi Arabia in the endless Yemen conflict. (Razoux 2003:18)

Nasser's loss of prestige in the Arab world was by now undeniable. He needed to find a way of restoring his compromised image. Nasser chose to adopt a more provocative attitude toward Israel, but failed to control the effects of his nationalist rhetoric. As Radio Cairo fittingly remarked: 'Nasser is a man: When provoked, he never backs down (Guerdon 1970).

It seems that Nasser eventually got caught in his own 'nationalist' trap. Once he himself had fuelled anti-Israel resentment among the Arab world, it was difficult to withdraw from the conflict

> Nasser, who always displayed a certain realist prudence, is overwhelmed by the enthusiasm of his people and yields to the pressure of the Palestinians who have waited nine years to return to their land ceded to the Zionists with impunity.

Thus, on the 14th May, in spite of Egyptian forces being sent in the direction of the Sinai, the other Arab leaders, especially the regime in Amman, continued on 'taunting the Rais for yet another showy, but empty gesture' (Razoux 2003). The Syrian leaders accused Egypt of 'hiding behind the Blue Helmets of the United Nations Emergency Force' (Howard, Hunter 1967). As a result, Nasser was tempted to raise his bet in order to present himself as a 'virile' leader. After the closure of the Tiran Straits on the 22nd May, the point of no return seemed to have passed. Algeria, Morocco, Kuwait, Saudi Arabia and Iraq, though far from being on good terms with Egypt, offered to send soldiers. In the face of this pan-Arab enthusiasm, Nasser, whose popularity was now at its height, could not call for peace. On the contrary, Nasser, who was now caught in the cycle of escalation, allowed the fedayeen to carry on with their raids from Gaza. As Pierre Hazan points out

> Having reached the zenith of his popularity, the Rais cannot retreat without being labelled an infamous traitor. (Hazan 1967: 22)

Nasser's task is made difficult by the rhetoric of Israeli officials who obfuscated their intentions regarding Egypt by alternating denials of military intentions with threats of retaliation. On the 14th May, General Rabin announced that Damascus will have to pay for its bellicose attitude. Likewise, the Israeli Prime Minister threatened Egypt by claiming that any restriction of the freedom of navigation in the Red Sea will be sanctioned and warned Syria that a continuation of terrorist activities was bound to provoke a military reaction. Instead of calming down the situation, these announcements caused indignation among the Arab states and were interpreted as a token of Israel's 'will to get rid of the Syrian regime'. The Arab suspicion persisted as Israel's rhetoric towards Syria remained 'tense'. On the 16th May, the Egyptian general staff was on the highest level of alert.

All the evidence suggests that Israel's deterrence strategy was doomed to fail as Nasser overestimated the military capacities of the Arab states and thus had a flawed perception of the balance of forces. Nasser was deceived by the numerical superiority of the Arab forces that indeed had twice as many tanks and assault rifles at their disposal as well as three times as many supersonic bombers and interceptors (Lebow 1981: 212). At the end of May, the Egyptian General Mourthagi declared

> Five days will be enough for us to destroy the small state of Israel. Even if it does not come to war, Israel will collapse as it cannot shoulder the burden of mobilisation. (Hazan 1967: 30)

More important, however, was probably the 'recognition-related' resistance against Israel's deterrence policy, which was a humiliation in the eyes of the Egyptians. In his speech on the 22nd May, Nasser announced the closure of the Gulf of Aqaba and declared: 'The Jews are threatening us with war. We reply to them: "Go ahead. We are ready!"' (Bar-Zohar 1968: 90).

Moreover, the UN authorities, and the Secretary-General Birman U Thant in particular, did not take into consideration dignity-related aspects in their mediation. A more sensitive negotiation on the part of the UN Secretary-General could have prevented the clash of Arab and Israeli troops. In fact, Nasser had not challenged the UNEF's presence at the most critical places, including Gaza and Sharm

El Sheikh. But, instead of temporising, U Thant issued an ultimatum to Nasser requiring the Rais to opt either for the continued presence of the troops at these positions or for their wholesale withdrawal, thus ruling out the possibility of a redeployment. U Thant even made the ultimatum public, putting Nasser into an even more complicated situation. Now being faced with the choice between a complete withdrawal and the humiliating status quo, President Nasser opted for the latter. The retreat of the Blue Helmets from Sharm El Sheikh had particular fatal consequences. Without the UNEF, the Egyptian forces were now directly facing Israeli ships passing through the Straits of Tiran. Pierre Hazan (1967: 20) states

> Nasser makes a fool of himself in the eyes of the Arab world if he accepts this situation. He, the hero of Arabism who has always called for the destruction of the Zionist state, stands idle while enemy ships pass by just a few cable lengths from his forces? So the straits must be closed to Israeli shipping.

Likewise, Pierre Razoux asks

> Could Nasser possibly have acted differently without losing face, now that ships flying the Israeli flag were cruising within the range of his troops at Sharm El Sheikh? (Razoux 2003: 24)

The diplomatic efforts by the other actors, such as France or the United States, were not conducive to calming Israeli and Arab fears, either. For example, when General de Gaulle met on 24th May with Abba Eban, the Israeli foreign minister, the French President showed himself insensitive to the closure of the Straits of Tiran: 'Do not go to war. To my mind, whoever shoots first opens the hostilities' (Hazan 1967). Moreover, de Gaulle decided to stop the delivery of weapons to Israel. Rather than to dissuade Israelis from entering into a conflict with Egypt, de Gaulle's indifference in the face of the injuries suffered by Israel caused major outrage among Israeli officials. They were more and more convinced that they could not count on anyone but themselves. Even the United States and Great Britain eventually indicated that they would confine themselves to diplomatic protest. Pierre Hazan opinionated

> The leaders of the great powers are making big mistakes which have fatal consequences. By ignoring both the psychological motives of the protagonists and the strategic situation, they make war possible in the first place, and then more probable. (Hazan 1967: 133)

Indeed, the definite decision to go to war was presumably taken on the 3rd June, on the day Israel's Foreign Minister Eban returned from Washington. On the 2nd June, President Johnson sent Eban a message clearly pointing out the limits of what the Americans were willing to do

> Our leadership is unanimous that the United States should not move in isolation. (Razoux 2003: 203)

At the end of a long meeting, in the course of which the Minister of Foreign Affairs adopted the viewpoint of the General Staff, the decision in favour of war was taken by twelve votes to two.

## The War Against Iraq

Before the 11th September, Iraq was a secondary priority for US foreign policy. Only the neo-conservatives warned against Saddam Hussein (Daalder and Lindsay 2003). Ex-Secretary of the Treasury, Paul O'Neill, removed by George Bush, indicated that the American 'hardliners' already had, at the time of the first meeting of the *National Security Council* in January 2001, projects for an intervention in Iraq (Suskind 2003). The President had particular resentment with regard to Saddam Hussein who he also accused of an assassination attempt against his father in 1993. During the electoral campaign in 2000, the President had considered in an interview with the journalist Jim Lerner that his father should have eliminated the Iraqi regime in 1991. Already at that time he determined that Saddam Hussein was a challenge to American authority: 'He just needs to know that he'll be dealt with in a firm way' (Draper 2007). It is also true that the American administration financed subversive actions for regime change in Iraq just as the previous administration (Lemann 2004). However, for the majority of American decision makers, including the President, Iraq could be contained by other means. The Secretary of State, Powell, affirmed in February 2001 that the United States had succeeded in maintaining Saddam in his 'box': 'We have kept him constrained, kept him in his box' (Powell 2001). Iraq's reaction after the events of the 11th September was therefore crucial. While Iraqi television evoked the 'lesson inflicted on arrogant America', Saddam Hussein declared on the 12th September that the United States had reaped the 'thorns sown by their leaders throughout the entire world' (Wihaib 2004: 224).[13] He was the only Arab leader not to denounce the attacks. On the 13th September 2001, Saddam Hussein sent an open letter to Americans and Westerners.[14] He emphasised the reactive character of the events of the 11th September while distancing himself from designating it as an act of aggression.[15] He compared the cowardice of American leaders with the courage of the perpetrators of the 11th September attacks

> As for those who acted on the 11th September, 2001, they did it from a close range, and with, I imagine, giving their lives willingly, with an irrevocable determination.[16]

---

13. 'Solidarité sans faille des capitales étrangères', *Libération*, Thursday the 13th September 2001 'La BCE se veut rassurante elle', *L'Humanité*, 14th September 2001.

14. 'Open letter from Saddam Hussein to the American peoples and the Western peoples and their governments' <www.infoimagination.org/ps/iraq/spch091301.html> – accessed October 2008.

15. 'Many countries of the world have suffered from America's technological might, and many peoples do recognize that America had killed thousands or even millions of human beings in their countries' (Open letter...).

16. 'There is, however, one difference, namely that those who direct their missiles and bombers to the targets, whether Americans or from another Western country, are mostly targeting by remote controls, that is why they do so as if they were playing an amusing game. As for those who acted on the 11th September 2001, they did it from a close range, and with, I imagine, giving their lives willingly, with an irrevocable determination' (Open letter...).

These provocative declarations fed American suspicion. The emotions aroused by the attacks did not favour nuance (Burbach, Tarbell 2004; 126). On the 14th September, a day after the open letter of Saddam Hussein to the Americans had been published, G. Bush met with his principal advisers at Camp David, the weekend retreat of American Presidents. P. Wolfowitz opined that 'several countries in the world' support terrorism and especially Iraq (Laurent 2004: 123). Some days later, the president declared with C. Rice: 'Iraq is on my agenda. I think that they are in involved' (Woodward 2003: 53). On the 21st November, in the middle of the war against the Taliban, the President was briefed by Secretary of Defence D. Rumsfeld on a possible plan of attack against Iraq. They asked T. Franks, head of CENTCOM, 'to study the means that would be necessary to protect America while overthrowing Saddam Hussein' (Woodward 2003: 17). The declarations of Saddam Hussein were likely to inflict narcissistic wounds on American leaders. The very 'passionate' comments of the American president towards the Iraqi leader emphasise the 'identity' character of the opposition to Iraq. In March 2002, the president stated to Rice: 'Fuck Saddam. We're taking him out' (Daalder and Lindsay 2005). In his speech of the 7th October 2002 in Cincinnati, the president revealed: 'We know that after the 11th September Saddam Hussein's' regime gleefully celebrated the terrorist attacks on America'.[17] Early on, the American administration had envisioned armed force against Iraq and the provocative declarations of Saddam Hussein were consequential. If in February 2002, 'no one seemed in a hurry to pull the trigger' (Woodward 2003), Saddam Hussein was in the crosshairs of the American administration, both as a security threat and as a challenge to its authority and national honour.

Even after the approval of UN Security Council Resolution 1441 on the 8th November, and the admission of IAEA and UNMOVIC inspectors to Iraq on the 18th November 2002, Saddam Hussein continued his obstructions, further feeding suspicion. While the threat of war intensified, Iraq refused flyovers of their territorial airspace by U2 spy air planes. Under the pretence of daily attacks by the United States and Great Britain in no-fly zones, it could not guarantee the safety of the British and American air planes. Iraq also aroused media hype about the inspectors who had visited a Baghdad mosque and were accused of asking questions on the possible presence of underground shelters (Blix 2005: 196).

A third phase begins in June 2002 when the option of a possible war becomes probable, but still can be avoided. A majority of the administration prefers from this date – and the President included – a war against Saddam Hussein. However, under pressure from the British ally and Colin Powell, the president initially decides to engage in a multilateral process inviting Iraq to open to UN inspections. It is unlikely that the President could have started the war with the possibility of Iraq's full and unconditional cooperation with the UN. The third phase begins with the speech from President Bush at *West Point Academy* on the 1st June. This speech announces without ambiguity that the option of a war is taking shape. The

---

17. 'We know that after the 11th September Saddam Hussein's regime gleefully celebrated the terrorist attacks on America' <www.whitehouse.gov>.

President exposes his concept of 'pre-emptive' war against 'proliferating' states and everyone understands that Iraq is targeted (Bush 2002). According to Hubert Védrine, it is during the summer of 2002 that the Bush administration decides

> that following the attacks of the 11th September, it should be ready to launch a preventive attack against any identified enemy likely to present a threat to the United States

This appreciation is reinforced by Richard N. Haas. When Haas expressed to Rice in June 2002 about the reservations of the cogency of an intervention against Iraq, she curtly rejected: 'Save your breath'. The President would already have made his decision. From then on, the famous Downing Street Memo recalls a July 2002 meeting between the head of intelligence service MI6 and its counterpart Tenet of the CIA as well as the other members of the administration. According to this report, officials were ready to engage in this war to prevent Iraq from providing weapons of mass destruction to terrorists (Danner 2006: 71).

However, the American administration was divided on the fact on whether or not it was necessary to involve the U.N. in the Iraqi process. For the *hardliners*, resorting to the U.N. was, as best, useless. On the 27th August 2002, the *New York Times* reports remarks of Vice President Cheney according to whom, 'the Iraqi nuclear threat justifies an attack'. On the 8th September 2001 even Condoleezza Rice seemed to position herself on the side of falcons by evoking, on CBS, the risk of an American nuclear mushroom cloud (Milbank, Allen 2003). It is, however, Colin Powell who establishes himself, thanks to the British ally, with a multilateral approach. He exposes to the President on the 5th August all the problems associated with the 'bellicose' option (Woodward 2004). He convinces him to take the Iraqi affair before the U.N. Security Council with the intention to vote on a resolution obligating Iraq to accept the return of inspectors. The President decided, against Cheney and Rumsfeld, to vote for a U.N. resolution that allowed for the return of IAEA inspectors in Iraq. The Security Council Resolution 1441 of the 8th November, demanded from Iraq a complete and accurate declaration of its entire arsenal of weapons of mass destruction as well as the return of the UNMOVIC inspectors. It is clear that the President did not expect Iraqi cooperation and sought at the outset, international support. However, as Powell had announced, in the possibility of the full and total cooperation of Iraq, the President should accept it rather than regime change.

The toughening of the American position during this third phase can be partially designated to the Iraqi 'non-cooperation' between the months of November 2001 and May 2002. For Iraq, there was never seriously a question, in its negotiations with the U.N., of resuming inspections in accordance with Resolution 1284. In January 2002, Saddam Hussein, in front of the General Secretary of the Arab League, Amir Foamed, spoke about the inspections as an affront. On March 2, 2002, the meeting between Kofi Annan and Iraqi authorities was marked by Iraqi complaints with regard to discriminatory practices (Blix 2005: 60*f*). New meetings between the 1st – 3rd May and on the 5th July were also without result. On the contrary, Hans Blix was accused of acting under American influence. All in all, the Iraqi policy was during this period a 'policy of firmness', refusing the security transparency and challenging America's power status. This policy of firmness, exploited by the neoconservatives, corresponds to a hardening of the American position.

The final possibility for Iraq to avoid war lay in the December declaration. On the 7th December, Iraqi authorities asserted their conformity with resolution 1441: an 11,807-page report asserting that the Iraq did not possess any weapons of mass destruction. This report was not very credible and even clumsy, according to many experts. Iraq had previously declared possession of 8,500 litres of anthrax in addition to several tons of VX gas to UN inspectors (Yetiv 2004). The Iraqi declaration essentially presented older documents and was a reconfiguration of a declaration presented to UNSCOM in September 1997. Certain passages and documents were repeated in the report to increase volume. For H. Blix, this nearly 12,000-page declaration revealed an aggressive attitude of Iraqi authorities, which seemed to say: 'You are demanding too much information. Hold, take that and you unravel' (Blix 2005: 175).

This Iraqi policy of 'challenge' contributed to the toughening of the American position and the ultimate alignment of President Bush with the 'hard-liners'. In addition, one can particularly observe in greater detail a chronological logic between the 7th December declaration and the American decision to enter into war. After this date, even Colin Powell seems to resign himself to war as well as the British ally. Baghdad's lack of clarity convinced the Bush administration that Saddam by no means intended to carry out disarmament (Daalder and Lindsay 2005). After the 7th December declaration, Cheney determined that Iraq had not respected its engagements and that recourse to armed force was thus justified (Cashman 2007). The more moderate members of the US government from then on were convinced that Iraq played cat and mouse with U.N. inspectors and that the only means of completely disarming the country was through armed intervention. On the 18th December, President Bush held a private talk with J. M. Aznar. Regarding the Iraqi declaration, G. Bush noted that: 'The joke has lasted enough and we will end it. He is a liar and has no intention to disarm'. During this last phase, American decision makers' motivations were also explained by many different type of motivations. For Cheney and the neoconservatives, Saddam Hussein's behavior constituted a chance to advance their advocacy for war. For the President and moderate decision makers, the perceived Iraqi threat was not only a bureaucratic justification to eliminate Saddam Husssein. The National Intelligence Estimate of the 1st October 2002 reached the conclusion that Saddam Hussein possessed chemical and biological weapons as well as ballistic missiles surpassing the authorized 150km and was continuing to develop the nuclear program (Cashman 2007: 317).

However, declarations from American decision makers also suggested that during this 'terminal' phase, the desire to 'save face' played more and more a crucial role. Thus, at the end of autumn, the American power had deployed 60,000 men and at the end of December 200,000. It became almost impossible to withdraw them without appearing to have 'lost' the crisis. G. Bush pointed out to C. Rice at his presidential ranch in Crawford at the beginning of the new year in 2003 that

> The United States cannot allow to remain in this losing position while Saddam is having fun leading inspectors by the end of their noses! (Cashman 2007: 318)

At the end of December, when Condoleezza Rice was questioned by the American President as to whether or not it was necessary to engage in war, she especially referred to the credibility of American power (Woodward 2003). She insisted on the fact that the United States was engaged in coercive diplomacy and that the President should carry out his threat to remain credible. This was also the opinion of ex-Secretary of State Henry Kissinger, initially sceptical, but now in a position which he assessed from then on: 'You can't cock the gun as you have and not pull the trigger' (Cashman 2004: 375f). For the sake of credibility, the behaviour and the remarks of the US president and its entourage betray a strong 'emotional' component. The feeling prevailed that Saddam Hussein would try to ridicule American power by his manoeuvres of avoidance. The US president was undoubtedly particularly sensitive to offences because of the virile image which he tried to project. Bob Woodward thus added his somewhat aggressive reaction *vis-à-vis* the Saudi Ambassador Prince Bandar who had questioned the American determination to start a war against Iraq

> Bush was fulminating... Bush could not tolerate that someone suspected him of being hesitant. "I repeat to you, you will not have to wait long".... .

All in all, the progressive evolution of the crisis towards the war cannot be understood without the American-Iraqi interactions after the 11th September. The policy of Iraqi 'non-recognition' contributed to the outbreak of war by reinforcing American neoconservative sales pitch, by nourishing security fears and especially by doubting the image that the American decision makers wished to project of their nation. But American declarations during this period also suggest that throughout this 'final' phase, the motivations of face played a more and more determinant role. Thus, at the end of the autumn, the American power had deployed by the end of December almost 200,000 soldiers. It had become almost impossible to withdraw them without appearing as the 'loser' of the crisis.

## CRISES WITH A PACIFIC OUTCOME (SAVING FACE)

If deterrent postures are often ineffective when they concern states that feel vulnerable, there is nevertheless an alternate policy that aims to diminish others' security fears while confirming their identity through symbolic recognition. The two cases that I will now present show that it is often possible to appease the state in question without making compromising material concessions.

### Vulnerable yet pacific states

*Khrushchev and the 'Missile Gap'*
The Cuban missile crisis began on the 14th October 1962 by the discovery of Soviet ballistic equipment on the island by an American U2 spy plane. In addition to SS4 and SS5 missiles with a range surpassing 2,000km, the Americans

detected the presence of 42,000 Soviet troops on the island (Dufour 1996: 148). How can one understand the decision of Soviet leaders to install missiles in Cuba? The Soviet initiative could have been an attempt to rectify what they considered as a global imbalance. At the heart of Soviet preoccupation was the viability of the German Democratic Republic, renewed American nuclear testing and the nuclear imbalance with the United States (Lebow and Stein 1994). The Soviets noticed that the famous 'missile gap' was increasingly in their disfavour. While the United States possessed 300 missiles and 1,600 long-range bombers, the USSR possessed only 100 missiles and 300 bombers. This power struggle had been going on since the summer of 1961 when US Corona satellites revealed that they possessed four times more ICBM intercontinental missiles than the Soviet Union (Pious 2001). Objectively, American power had a first-strike capability against the Soviet arsenal (Khrushchev 1971).

Next, the Soviets feared that their ally Cuba was not assured an appropriate level of security –Krushchev 1971). New documents 'lend credence to Khrushchev's claim that a primary Soviet motivation was the defence of Cuba against a US invasion'.[18] The American attempt to overthrow the Castro regime in 1961 was a recent memory. The American President had not renounced this objective and on the 30th November 1961 had authorised operation Mongoose advocating acts of sabotage and infiltration against the Castro regime. At last, according to the Soviet general secretary, the Americans had

> surrounded our country with military bases [...] we are only giving back to them – on a smaller scale – their courtesy'.[19]

For N. Khrushchev, American missiles deployed in Turkey were particularly threatening. He had asked in vain for their removal during his encounter with Kennedy in Vienna.[20]

Prestige also affected Soviet behaviour. A close advisor of Khrushchev, O. Troyanowki, confirmed

> Khrushchev was always anxious about our prestige, he was afraid that Americans would force us to back down somewhere'.[21]

For Y. Haine, 'Moscow was seeking an equal status, a credibility equivalent to that of Washington' (Haine 2002: 4). Khrushchev's obsession with prestige was even greater since he considered that the United States had refused to grant the USSR

---

18. Chang and Kornbluh (1992): 'The documents lend credence to Khrushchev's claim that a primary Soviet motivation was the defence of Cuba against a US invasion. For years, US analysts have dismissed this as a face-saving, after-the-fact rationale'.

19. Accessed 8 Jan. 2006, <http://cgi.cvm.qc.ca/APHCQ/scripts/aphcq.pl?get&Bulletin/Dossiers/La%20crise%20des%20missiles%2àde%de%20Cuba%20en%é0octobre%201962.htm>.

20. Quoted by Johnson and Tierney (2004: 364), 'You are worried over Cuba. You say that it worries you because it lies at a distance of ninety miles across the sea from the shore of the United States. However, Turkey lies next to us'.< www.conflits.revues.org/index310.html>

21. Haine ( 2002 n. 35): 'Khrushchev was always anxious about our prestige, he was afraid that Americans would force us to back down somewhere'.

'great power' status at the Vienna summit in 1961. In September of the same year, Khrushchev noted to a member Kennedy's cabinet

> it's been a long time since you could spank us like a little boy – now we can swat your ass. (May and Zelikov 2000: 39)

The flyovers in Soviet airspace by U2 planes irritated Khrushchev's virile self-image: 'They were making these flights to show up our impotence'.[22] According to him, 'The USA simply wanted the USSR to sit like a schoolboy with his hands on his desk'[23]. Khrushchev could not tolerate the 'arrogant violations' of Russian sovereignty by the United States that showed their refusal to treat the Soviet Union on an equal basis' (Haine 2003: 3 *f*).

In October 1961, the US Secretary of Defence revealed that the missile gap was in favour of the United States. Khrushchev considered it 'as a gratuitous humiliation' (Khrushchev 1971: 4). American decision makers were aware of this identity dimension related to the nuclear arsenal (Garthoff 1987). Cuba's protection constituted an 'identity' issue for the Soviet Union. The self-image of a great Communist power, homeland of the socialist revolution, was at stake (Ganser 2002). In addition, Cuba risked turning towards China (Haine 2004).

Khrushchev 'attempted to compensate for this strategic inferiority by a nuclear challenge' (Haine 2004). During the Cold War, Khrushchev believed nuclear weapons to be synonymous with prestige and 'modernity'. Khrushchev considered the presence of Jupiter missiles in Turkey to be another insult. The American historian J. Gaddis (1998) reported that when Khrushchev received visitors while on vacation in Bulgaria, he looked at the horizon towards Turkey and told his guest that there were missiles pointed at his dacha. It was apparently during a visit to Bulgaria in April 1962 that Khrushchev developed the idea of doing the same to the Americans (Pious 2001).

In 1962, Khrushchev's prestige was weakened in the eyes of the military and the broader public, to the extent that some even spoke of a Kremlin legitimacy crisis (Johnson, Tierney 2004). In 1960, there was an important debate over the drastic reduction of military expenditure and an increase in the price of food staples. Its allies, China and Cuba, were expecting more 'firm' behaviour from the Soviet Union (Grosser 2001: 156).

### The Case of American-Libyan Relations (1986–2004)

For many years, the American government considered Colonel Gaddafi's regime as a threat. In 1973, it withdrew its ambassador. From 1981 onwards, the US government designated Libya a terrorist state. In 1986, the U.S. military even bombed Tripoli, killing Gaddafi's daughter in the process (Perrin 2004). In July 2001, the

---

22. Khrushchev (1971: 504), 'We were more infuriated and disgusted every time a violation occurred. We were sick and tired of being subjected to these indignities. They were making these flights to show up our impotence'.
23. Krushchev (1971: 504), 'The USA simply wanted the USSR to sit like a schoolboy with his hands on his desk'.

United States reimposed five years of unilateral economic sanctions on Iran and Libya. Resorting to armed force against Libya was not out of the question. In May 2006, Assistant Secretary of Defence D. Welsch announced the return of full diplomatic relations with Libya (Blanchard 2006).

How can we understand this antagonism, followed by this spectacular resolution? First, in US eyes, the Libyan regime was the embodiment of a 'rogue' state. In the early 1970s, Libya had sought uranium, nuclear power plants and ballistic technologies through the intermediary of China at first, then Egypt and Pakistan. In 1981, Libyan leaders refused an offer of uranium enriched to 20 per cent proposed by a CIA agent under false identity. Libyan leaders considered that this offer was not 'good' enough (they wanted 80 per cent enrichment) illustrating their serious desire to equip themselves with nuclear weapons.[24] Nevertheless, the embargo imposed in 1992 by the international community after the Libyan involvement in the Pan Am attack over Lockerbie Scotland, limited the possibilities for Libya to acquire nuclear weapons. Its nuclear capabilities remained limited to a ten megawatt research reactor in Tajura, equipped with the assistance of the Soviet Union at the beginning of the 1980s. In March 2002, Gaddafi proclaimed that Arab nations should have the right to make nuclear weapons because of Israeli nuclear development.[25]

Libya was involved in numerous terrorist attacks against the United States. On the 5th April 1986, a bombing attack in Berlin perpetrated against the 'La Belle' disco frequented by American soldiers was ordered by Colonel Gaddafi (Dufour 1996). In April 1986, the Reagan administration authorised aerial strikes on targets in Tripoli and Benghazi. On the 21st December 1988, an attack on Pan Am flight 103 Boeing 747 over the Scottish town of Lockerbie claimed 270 victims. In 1991, the involvement of Libya in this attack was proved. On the 27th November, an Anglo-American joint declaration demanded the extradition of suspected Libyan agents. On the 19th September 1989, a DC-10 belonging to the French company UTA crashed over the Ténéré desert in Niger, claiming 171 victims. Once again Libyan authorities were allegedly involved (Lewis 2001).

In addition, Libya represented a 'symbolic' threat to American power. It embodied contempt for human rights and military authoritarianism of the most brutal kind. Gaddafi asserted himself as a champion of anti-American diatribes while presenting himself as a victim of 'American terrorism'. Shortly after taking power in 1969, Gaddafi asked the United States to close their military bases on Libyan territory. American diplomatic personnel were withdrawn from Libya in 1979 after a crowd (probably 'inspired' by governmental leaders) had attacked and burned the American embassy in Tripoli. Presenting himself as a hero of the anti-imperialist struggle, Gaddafi proclaimed that the Gulf of Great Syrtis was Libyan and therefore it forbade access to American vessels. In June 1981, President Reagan took the decision, on the advice of then Secretary of Defence C. Weinberger, to

---

24. *SIPRI Yearbook 2004.*
25. *SIPRI Yearbook 2004*, chapter 15.

challenge Libya by organising a Naval Air Force manoeuvre in the Gulf of Great Syrtis. He feared that the authority of American power would be questioned in the region. During skirmishes with Libyan forces, a Libyan aeroplane was shot down. It didn't matter if Gaddafi's Libya asserted itself as the champion of Arabic unity, Islam, non-aligned countries, or the anti-imperialist struggle. American leadership was brought into question (Lahwej 1998).

### The Politics of Conciliatory Recognition

How was war avoided in these two international crises? As opposed to a policy of 'pure' dissuasion, leaders were able to calm the fears of the other actors through a policy of consideration, which in each case presented certain similarities. The Cuban crisis remains the case where the deterrent factor played the most important role. With the blockade, President Kennedy chose a policy of moderate firmness. At the beginning of the crisis, he thought that military mobilisation would force the Soviets to withdraw their missiles (Rosen 2005: 58). Nevertheless, this deterrent posture was accompanied with multiple concessions that allowed Khrushchev to withdraw without 'losing face' (Lebow and Stein 1998).

### The Détente of American-Soviet Relations

American government policies regarding the Soviet Union were characterised by an effort to avoid escalating conflicts. President Kennedy understood that the use of the military as an instrument of intimidation could be a double-edged sword, while creating an incentive for preemptive or preventive strikes. Kennedy ordered the American navy to tighten the naval blockade around the island in order to avoid a precocious interception of Soviet vessels (Allison and Zelikov 1999). Through these precautions, he had more time to negotiate a diplomatic solution with Soviet leaders. In any case, on the 27th October President Kennedy intervened to prevent American military officers from retaliating for the destruction of their spy plane by Cuban anti-aerial defence (Pious 2001: 96).

As for the mutual recognition of potential belligerents, the respect given by President Kennedy to the territorial integrity of Cuba greatly facilitated the resolution of the missile crisis. In addition, the President was skilful in calling upon the UN and its general secretary to negotiate an embargo on military supplies to Cuba in violation of a naval blockade. The process of negotiation within the UN meant that the recognition was not a diktat, but a compromise between equal partners.

As for politics of recognition in the strict sense of the term, the American government paid great attention to 'face management'. T Sorenson considered that it was essential 'to give' Soviet leaders 'an exit door' (Sorensen 1966: 734). One fact should be noted about respect for 'equal dignity': despite its immense strategic superiority, the American government abstained from giving an ultimatum to the Soviet Union. President Kennedy considered that

> There is one thing I have learned in this business and that is not to issue ultimatums. You just can't put the other fellow in a position where he has no

alternative except humiliation. This country cannot afford to be humiliated neither can the Soviet Union.[26]

The choice of a blockade rather than aerial strikes and, *a fortiori*, a massive invasion, was dictated by Soviet decision makers to withdraw their missiles from Cuba 'with dignity' (Sorensen 1966: 721 *f*). American decision makers also wanted to present a good image of American power. They feared the analogy of the 'odious attack' of the Japanese on Pearl Harbor[27]. As for the tightening of the blockade around Cuba, it was the British ambassador to the United States Ormsby-Gore who had the idea. Initially, the blockade had to span 700 to 800 miles, while Ormsby-Gore proposed the reduction of 'the blockade' to 500 miles. T. Sorenson described the American motivation in this way

> Khrushchev had serious decisions to make and every additional hour would help to find a way to conduct an honourable withdrawal...? (Sorensen 1966: 731)

The flexibility in the application of the blockade around Cuba was intended to save face for Soviet decision makers. Thus, on the 24th October, the President gave the order to allow the passage of the vessel Bucharest heading for Cuba. Against the advice of military officers, the President decided to give more time to Khrushchev in order to avoid pushing him 'into a corner from which he cannot escape' (Kennedy 1999: 76). Even on the 25th October, the former commander allowed the passage of the East German civilian vessel *Völker-Freundschaft* (White 2001: 216), despite the quarantine. On the other hand, on the 26th October, the vessel *Marcula* was intercepted by the American navy. The choice of this vessel was carefully thought through. Robert Kennedy explained the choice

> He was demonstrating to Khrushchev that we were going to enforce the quarantine and yet, because it was not a Soviet-owned vessel, it did not represent a direct affront to the Soviets, requiring a response...[28]

Perhaps the most crucial moment of the crisis was the detention of Americans after the destruction of their spy plane on the 27th October 1962 by Cuban anti-aerial defense. A muscular response would probably have driven Soviet leaders to

---

26. Quoted in Kratochwil (1987: 50), 'There is one thing I have learned in this business and that is not to issue ultimatums. You just can't put the other fellow in a position where he has no alternative except humiliation. This country cannot afford to be humiliated neither can the Soviet Union. Like us, the Soviet Union has many countries which look to her for leadership and Khrushev would be likely to do something desperate before he let himself be disgraced in their eyes'.

27. Kennedy (1999: 49), 'The strongest argument against the all-out military attack, and no one could answer to his satisfaction, was that a surprise attack would erode if not destroy the moral position of the United States throughout the world'.

28. Kennedy (1999) 'The Marcula had been carefully and personally selected by President Kennedy to be the first ship stopped and boarded. He was demonstrating to Khrushchev that we were going to enforce the quarantine and yet, because it was not a Soviet-owned vessel, it did not represent a direct affront to the Soviets, requiring a response [...] our decision to board a non-Russian vessel [...] does not carry a public humiliation'.

launch hostilities in order to save face. T. Sorensen (1966: 740) recalled

> He [the president], again insisted that the Russians be given the time to reflect on what they would do.

Secretary of Defence, Robert McNamara opined

> If the president had gone ahead with the air strike and invasion of Cuba, the invasion forces almost surely would have been met by nuclear fire, requiring a nuclear response from the United States.[29]

We know today that nuclear warheads had already been transported to Cuba.

The United States had also proposed substantial concessions to Khrushchev. In addition to the guarantee of Cuban sovereignty, they proposed the withdrawal of their Jupiter missiles several months after the crisis. The negotiated agreement between R. Kennedy and the Soviet ambassador Dobrynin, on the 27th October, remained tacit. The President had quickly recognised the necessity of offering the Soviets substantial compensation to allow them to honourably extricate themselves from the crisis. The Jupiter missiles deployed in Turkey were 'exchange objects' because of their proximity to Soviet borders (May and Zelikov 2000).

On the 27th October, American leaders took another decision, clever enough to allow the Soviets to save face. They responded favourably to Khrushchev's first letter, while ignoring the second one, which demanded an American commitment to withdraw Jupiter missiles from Turkey. In this manner, American decision makers did not need to rush their Soviet counterparts while opening the way for a negotiated solution. In his response on the 27th October, the American President proposed that the Soviet Union immediately withdraw its missiles under the aegis of the UN while the United States and their allies committed themselves not to invade Cuba. Nevertheless, for fear of weakening his position in American public opinion, President Kennedy did not publicly negotiate the agreement within the framework of the UN (Johnson and Tierney 2004).

This American politics of recognition also took into account respect for the special status of Soviet power. Khrushchev and Kennedy had come to an agreement during the crisis to not question each other's 'ideology'.[30] In his letter dated the 26th October, Khrushchev sought to de-emphasise 'ideological and economic problems' in order to highlight what was shared by the two powers: their need for survival.

In terms of empathy, American decision makers put themselves in the Soviet leaders' shoes, above all to understand what their intentions were.[31] Secretary of

---

29. McNamara, *The Fog of War* (2005 documentary): 'If the president had gone ahead with the air strike and invasion of Cuba, the invasion forces almost surely would have been met by nuclear fire, requiring a nuclear response from the United States'.

30. 'I am concerned that we both show prudence and do nothing to allow events to make the situation more difficult to control than this.' Cited by Mark White (2001).

31. Kennedy (1999: 124) 'During the crisis, President Kennedy spent more time trying to determine the effect of a particular course of action on Khrushchev or the Russians than on any other thing of what he was doing.'

Defence McNamara learned a special lesson from the crisis.

> We must try to put ourselves inside their (our enemies) skin and look at us through their eyes, just to understand the thoughts that lie behind their decision and their actions.[32]

At the time of the decisive 27th October debate within the Ex-Comm, this empathetic logic enabled the understanding the security needs of Soviet power that strongly weighed in favour of maintaining peace. The argument given by the former American ambassador to Moscow 'Tommy' Thompson, had convinced the President, that Khrushchev wanted to avoid the conflict, but that he needed a concession in order to say to his compatriots 'I saved Cuba. I stopped an invasion'.[33]

The strongest example of empathy was probably provided by Soviet leaders themselves after the destruction of the American U2 spy plane on the 27th October by anti-aircraft defences, without Moscow's authorisation. Khrushchev had understood that the absence of a strong reaction towards the death of an American pilot was likely to make the Americans more belligerent

> The Cuban and Soviet personnel on the island were celebrating the shooting of the spy plane, but Khrushchev and his colleagues in Moscow were shocked because they realised that Washington would hold Khrushchev responsible for the action, although it was really Colonel Voronkov, a replacement for the commander of the anti-aircraft SAM, who took this fatal decision under Cuban pressure.[34]

The thesis that the Cuban Missile Crisis was solved through a politics of recognition is not totally incompatible with the more 'realist' thesis that a peaceful resolution was reached because both actors feared their mutual destruction. Indeed, the evidence is that Kennedy's and Khrushchev's moderation can partly be explained by their determination to avoid an armed conflict that might have resulted in a nuclear apocalypse. When Khrushchev approved the American proposition on the 28th October, he was certainly motivated by the fear that the Americans were preparing major retaliatory strikes after the loss of a plane and its pilot (Lebow and Stein 1987). Moreover, deterrence is also compatible with the saving the other's face as long as the deterrence policy is not carried out in an overtly coercive manner.

However, the resolution of the conflict is best explained by a politics of recognition rather than by the effects of force and coercion. According to the traditional explanation, the United States could impose a solution in their favour because of their immense conventional superiority (Bundy 1988). Seen from this angle,

---

32. McNamara, *The Fog of War*: 'We must try to put ourselves inside their (our enemy's) skin and look at us through their eyes, just to understand the thoughts that lie behind their decision and their actions.'

33. See McNamara, (2005) *The Fog of War* 'He (Thompson, T. L.) said to Kennedy: 'The important thing for Khrushchev, it seems to me, is to be able to say: "I saved Cuba. I stopped an invasion"'.'

34. McNamara 'The Miracle of October: Lessons from the Cuba Missile Crisis.'

Khrushchev ordered the installation of the missiles because he did not believe that the US would offer resistance. Similarly, he withdrew in fear of American military potential. First of all, as we have seen, American policy was compatible with saving the positive face of the Soviet leaders: the US made material concessions (namely not to invade Cuba and to dismantle the Jupiter Missiles in Turkey) so as to allow Khrushchev to exit the crisis with dignity. No ultimatum was issued and the more defensive blockade option was preferred to the invasion option. The dialogue was continued in an empathetic manner while ideological considerations were left aside. All this helped dispel the security worries of the Soviet Union. Moreover, the American decision makers were unquestionably driven by their concern not to debase the other side. The maxim 'Don't humiliate your opponent' was lesson number six that Kennedy drew from the Cuban Missile Crisis (Kennedy 1999). In his diary, Robert Kennedy writes about the President: 'What guided all his deliberations was an effort not to disgrace Khrushchev, not to humiliate the Soviet Union, not to have them feel they would have to escalate their response. Likewise, in his speech at the American University in 1963, President Kennedy himself stated as the lesson from the crisis that one

> Must avert those confrontations which bring an adversary to a choice of either a humiliating retreat or a nuclear war. (Kennedy 1999: 124–26)

It is quite remarkable that the President realised that the Soviet Union might engage in a nuclear war if its honour was compromised. Robert Kennedy argued along the same line

> Neither side wanted war over Cuba [...], but it was possible that either side could take a step that – for reasons of 'security' or 'pride' or 'face' – would require a response by the other side, which, in turn, for the same reasons of security, pride, or face, would bring about a counter response and eventually an escalation into armed conflict. (Kennedy 1999: 62)

Khrushchev and Kennedy had little confidence in the merits of deterrence and balance of power policy (Lebow and Stein 1987: 170). History proved them right. Indeed, Ernesto 'Che' Guevara as well as Fidel Castro at that time declared that they would prefer the nuclear apocalypse to dishonour (Blight and Lang 2005).

And finally, there is a 'chronological correlation' between the resolution of the crisis and the most substantial American concessions. There is no doubt that the meeting on 27th October between Robert Kennedy and Anatoly Dobrynin marked the decisive turning point of the conflict. Although Kennedy insisted that the dismantlement of the Jupiter Missiles must be kept secret, everything points to the conclusion that this concession was crucial in the eyes of the Soviets. Robert Kennedy added that his request for a reply on the following day was 'just that – a request, and not an ultimatum'. On the 28th October at 10 o'clock, Secretary of State Dean Rusk informed R. Kennedy that the Soviets had accepted the American proposition. In short: the thesis according to which Khrushchev backed off while Kennedy remained firm is untenable (Pious 1989).

## The Appeasement of Relations Between America and Libya

A major turning point in Libyan American relations came in 1999 when the United States accepted the trial of suspects in the Libyan attacks over Lockerbie by a Scottish tribunal in the Netherlands (chosen as territory which was 'neutral despite the embargo'). Libya in turn accepted the extradition of the Libyan suspects to The Hague. The trial opened in 2000. In April 1999, this concession led to the suspension of the UN Security Council sanctions against Libya. Enacted in 1992, they had imposed an embargo on aerial transportation and the weapons trade (Perrin 2004).

Starting in 2000, Libya presented itself as a champion of the anti-terrorist struggle while playing the role of intermediary in two liberations: one of western hostages held on the Philippine island of Jolo in 2001, and one of European tourists held by Islamic groups in Algeria in 2003. Libya signed several international conventions against international terrorism, for example, that of The Hague against hijacking (1970), or of Cairo (1998) for the elimination of terrorism. At the time of the 11th September attacks, Gaddafi seized the opportunity, in contrast to Saddam Hussein, to express his compassion towards the American people. He offered humanitarian assistance to the victims of the catastrophe.[35] Libya also approved the American war against the Taliban.[36] Colonel Gaddafi expelled Abou Nidal from his territory.

This policy of 'reassurance' was a crowning success. Libya was thus not included as a member of 'the axis of evil' in the American President's State of the Union Speech of the 29th January 2002. Perhaps the recognition by Libya of its responsibility for the Lockerbie attacks was the most important one in the normalisation of American-Libyan relations. On the 15th August 2003 Gaddafi sent an official letter to the UN

> Libya as a sovereign State has facilitated the extradition of the two suspects accused of having sabotaged Pan Am 103 and accepts responsibility for the action of its official.[37]

On the 13th August 2003, an official agreement between Tripoli, London, and Washington was signed in which Libya recognised its responsibility. It committed itself to paying $2.7 billion to the families of the victims. In exchange, members of the Security Council – and later the United States (that had previously abstained) – approved the lifting of sanctions with Resolution 1506 on the 12th September. The United States struck Libya from the list of terrorist states (Hadaad 2004: 176).

---

35. See: Statement by the Leader of the Revolution on the 11th September. 'Irrespectively of conflict with America it is a human duty to show sympathy to the American people and be with them at these horrifying awesome events...'. Also see developments of his son Saif Aleslam al Qadhafi (2003).

36. See the interview given by Colonel Gaddafi in Newsweek of the 20th January, 2003. <www.time.com/time/world/article/0,8599,1195852,00.html>

37. (2003) 'Libyan Payment to Families of Pan Am Flight 103 Victims', *American Journal of International Law*, 97 (4): 989.

Gaddafi tried to show American leaders that he was also opposed to radical 'Islamists'. In an article destined for the American public in summer 2003, his son S. Aleslam wrote

> It should be noted that Libya has never been sympathetic to Islamic radicalism. Though deeply Islamic, its religious practices do not resemble those of so-called fundamentalist societies [...] Libya issued an arrest warrant for Osama Bin Laden.[38]

This divided loyalty in the fight against Islamic fundamentalism was essential for lending credibility to Libyan attempts to normalise relations with Washington. Saddam Hussein had missed an opportunity. He could have emphasised, for example, the secular character of his state in a much clearer manner than the Libyan leader. Libyan leaders were even resolved to recognising the special role of the United States as a democratic superpower. During his speech on the 31st August 2003, Colonel Gaddafi declared

> I told Arab leaders that America wanted to declare the war on the dictatorial systems. The United States announced: "We are against the dictatorships!" [...] But this is all very well! This is also exactly what we believe. (Hadaad 2004: 175)

From then on, the only obstacle to complete normalisation of Libyan-American relations was American suspicion of a possible attempt by Libya to develop nuclear weapons as well as chemical and biological weapons. Through a public declaration by Colonel Gaddafi in December 2003, Libya announced its intention to definitively renounce weapons of mass destruction, to dismantle its program of biological, chemical and nuclear weapons, as well as to eliminate all ballistic missiles with a range greater than 300km, all under international inspection[39]. On the 27th December 2003, the director of the IAEA, Mohammed El Baradei, arrived in Tripoli with his team of experts. According to his declarations, Libya appeared very far from being able to produce nuclear weapons and enrich uranium.[40] In March 2004, Libya signed the additional protocol of the Nuclear Non-Proliferation Treaty. These concessions led to a progressive normalisation of Libyan-American relations. On the 20th September 2004, President G.W. Bush lifted many economic sanctions against Libya and also authorised the resumption of the air traffic between the two countries.[41]

Besides security concessions (terrorism, proliferation of WMD), the satisfaction of symbolic demands (Lockerbie) was the most decisive factor in the softening of the US position regarding Tripoli. In contrast to liberal explanations

---

38. It should be noted that Libya has never been sympathetic to Islamic radicalism. Though deeply Islamic, its religious practices do not resemble those of so-called fundamentalist societies.
39. SIPRI Yearbook 2004, chapter 15, *op. cit.*
40. 'U.N. Nuclear Chief Welcomed in Libya', *The New York Times*, 28 December 2003, p. 12.
41. (2005) 'United States Lifts some sanctions on Libya', *The American Journal of International Law*, 99 (1): 253–54.

favouring economic and especially energy interests in the United States, business interests, which campaigned in 2001 for the lifting of sanctions, did not succeed in facing down other interest groups, such as the 'American Israeli Public Affairs Committee' or the family of the 270 victims of Flight 103. Libya had always been associated with Anti-Israeli and terrorist positions. At that time, the moral and domestic costs of normalisation were too great for American leaders (Hadaad 2004). In 2001, the Bush Administration claimed without ambiguity that Libya, previous to any normalisation, had to assume its responsibility for the attack and to compensate the families of the victims.

In Libya's case, it was probably not only the Iraq War which led Libya to abandon its nuclear program, given that American-Libyan negotiations had been under way since 1999.[42] The Iraq War, however, certainly made Libya intensify its security efforts. It was in March 2003 that Libya declared its intention to abandon its WMD programmes.[43] The trilateral negotiations and discussions as well as the dispatch of British and American experts to Libya had long been kept secret. On their visit to Libya, these experts had been informed about the state of its nuclear, biological, chemical and ballistic programmes. One could even speak of 'clandestine' inspections, deliberately concealed from the public[44]. As all of this was taking place out of the public eye, it was easier for the Libyan leaders to save face. Moreover, Colonel Gaddafi could point to the fact that he himself had, during the Cold War, called for the denuclearisation of the Middle East and Africa.[45] Thus, the US's deterrent posture could exert indirect pressure on Libya without jeopardising Libya's 'face'. It is conspicuous that the Bush Administration was indulgent with Libya while displaying great determination and ruthlessness in its efforts to thwart the nuclear ambitions of Iraq and North Korea. Gaddafi's policy of rapprochement is therefore not solely the result of his fearing an American attack (Djaziri 1999).

The improvement of the non-proliferation regimes, too, seems to have borne fruit. In January 2001, parts of a SCUD missile destined for Libya were stumbled upon at London Gatwick Airport (Lewis 2001, Martinez 2006). The acquisition of weapons of mass destruction had undoubtedly become increasingly difficult. A major reason for Libya to reverse its policy was to avoid stigmatisation by the international community. Such 'stigmatisation' occurred only in 1992 when the UN

---

42. 'Selon son fils, le colonel Kadhafi n'a pas renoncé au nucléaire à cause de la guerre contre Saddam', *Le Monde*, 11 February 2004.

43. (2001) 'U.S./U.K. Negotiations with Libya regarding Nonproliferation', *The American Journal of International Law*, 98 (1): 195–97.

44. See Gaddafi's speech on the 19th December, 2003: 'During talks held between Libya, United States and United Kingdom [...] the Libyan experts briefed their counterparts on materials, equipment and programmes, such as centrifuges and containers transporting, that might be used to produce internationally banned weapons'. <www.time.com/time/world/article/0,8599,1195852,00.html>

45. Gaddafi's speech on the 19th December p. 196: 'In view of the international climate that prevailed during the Cold War and the tension that has gripped the Middle East region, [Libya] called on the countries of the Middle East and Africa to make those regions a zone free of weapons of mass destruction'.

issued Resolution 748 imposing multilateral sanctions on Libya. As a 'symbolic punishment', the sanctions imposed by the UN and the suspension of air traffic between Tripoli and other western capitals were effective.

In the end, the symbolic costs of Libya's exclusion from the international community were deemed to be high by the Libyan leaders. In 1995, for instance, Libya was not invited to the Euro-Mediterranean Conference in Barcelona, which brought together the littoral Mediterranean states. However, as pointed out by Jamie Calabrese, these sanctions would not have yielded success if the western powers had not at the same time signalled that diplomatic rehabilitation was possible if Syria collaborated. It was then after 13 years of sanctions that the Americans and British took the initiative to offer Libya reintegration into the international community. The first step towards Libya's opening was taken at the end of 1998: U.S. Secretary of State Madeleine Albright gave her consent to Libya's proposition to open the trial against the two Lockerbie suspects on neutral ground in the Netherlands. British diplomacy played a key role: it was during the visit of the British Foreign Secretary to Sirteee on the 2nd August that Libya agreed to negotiate compensation payments to the Lockerbie victims and formally promised to renounce terrorism (Perrin 2004). 'To rejoin the community of nations' was the main objective of Libya's diplomatic efforts (Hadaad 2003) and the Americans had evidently understood this desire for recognition. On the 19th December, President Bush announced Libya's symbolic reward in the following terms

> As the Libyan government takes these essential steps and demonstrates its seriousness, its good faith will be returned. Libya can regain a secure and respected place among the nations, and over time, achieve far better relations with the United States.[46]

By contrast, the UN sanctions against Libya between 1992 and 1999 seem to have had only minor effects, given that Libya's export volume, estimated at $7.5 billion in 1993, actually witnessed some growth during this period, reaching, for instance, $10.1 billion in 1996 (Chevallier-Bellet 1999).

*Alternative Explanations*
The idea that coercive procedures favour war appears as the one of the most important lessons learned from analysing these four crises. Of course, Kennedy's and Khrushchev's moderation was also dictated by a concern to avoid a nuclear apocalypse at all costs (Lebow and Stein 1987). Dissuasion is compatible with saving face if it is not accompanied by explicit threats. On the other hand, these case studies refute the idea that getting out of a crisis depends only on the firmness of the protagonist. In the crisis preceding the Six-Day War, we can see the obvious failure of an intimidating posture. The turning point came precisely at the moment that Prime Minister L. Eshkol seemed incapable of withstanding the pressure from Arab States. As for the crisis between the United States and Iraq (2001–2003), it was not the apparent weakness of Iraq that caused the United States to invade. In

---

46. *American Journal of International Law*, 98 (1) : 197.

any case, the policy of firmness did not in itself resolve the Cuban crisis and even less the U.S.-Libyan conflict. According to a traditional explanation, Khrushchev withdrew because he respected American military capacity (Bundy 1988) and the firmness of the American President (Scott, Smith 1994). This interpretation does not withstand scrutiny because there is a chronological correlation between the resolution of the crisis and American concessions. The 27th October encounter between R. Kennedy and A. Dobrynin marked the decisive turn of the crisis. Even if the dismantling of Jupiter missiles had to remain secret, everything indicates that this represented a substantial concession for the Soviet leaders (Pious 2001). R. Kennedy stated that his wish to get a response the next day was 'a request and not an ultimatum'. As for the crisis between Libya and the United States, any rapprochement between these two countries would have been in vain without Libya assuming responsibility for the Lockerbie attacks.

Explanations for war in terms of profit must also be nuanced. In both belligerent crises, considerations about material conquest – the recovery of 'holy land' for Israel or energy supplies for the United States – were of course not absent. Nevertheless, the decision to go to war was made during the crisis and cannot therefore be reduced to lasting motives. In both cases, a minority of decision makers were always in favour of war at any cost. In Israel, the cabinet was long opposed to going to war. It was only towards the 28th May that a belligerent majority showed itself. As for the Iraqi crisis, at least before the 11th September, entering a conflict was not an option. Even until the declaration made in December 2002 there was a chance to preserve peace. On the other hand, the resolution of the crises is linked to material concessions in addition to security and economic issues. The material gains obtained also had an effect on identity. Kennedy's concessions were largely intended to guarantee Khrushchev an honourable way out of the crisis (Ting-Tooney 1990; Kennedy 1999). Similarly, Libyan financial compensation to the victims' families represented recognition of their moral responsibility.

Finally, utilitarian approaches do not take into account the real effect on the damage to identity inflicted by events that do not have great meaning if they are reduced to their material effects. Thus, the declarations of Saddam Hussein on the 11th September were not materially expensive to the United States, but they constituted a questioning of their image. The politics of recognition criteria of the cases examined vary greatly. These variations correspond to the belligerent or peaceful way out of the crisis. The differences can be categorised in this way

1. *Recognition of Existence*: All policies based on understanding presuppose mutual recognition between both potential belligerents. President Kennedy's commitment to respect Cuba's territorial integrity facilitated a resolution of the crisis. At the same time, Colonel Gaddafi recognised the United States while condemning international terrorism and assumed Libyan responsibility for the Lockerbie attacks. On the other hand, Nasser's negation of the Israeli state in 1967 and by Saddam Hussein after the 11th September attacks, contributed to the escalation of these crises. Assuring others their right to exist also supposes mastering military operations during the crisis. President Kennedy intervened

directly in military operations while ordering the American navy to tighten the naval blockade around the island of Cuba (Stein 1991). As for Colonel Gaddafi, he removed all incentive for a pre-emptive war by the United States by renouncing nuclear weapons. On the other hand, in the 1967 crisis, the gathering of UN forces and the deployment of the Syrian and Egyptian forces on Israeli borders created a security dilemma for the Hebrew state. Similarly, Saddam Hussein playing cat and mouse with the AIEA inspectors maintained suspicions of his intentions regarding American power

2. *Recognition of Sovereign Dignity*: Sovereign dignity implies abstaining from issuing ultimatums, explicit threats, and activities that devalue the others' hierarchical or moral status during a crisis. The ease of saving face also depends on the commitments made by states faced with public opinion. American policy at the time of the Cuban crisis is clearly illustrative: refraining from ultimatums as well as injurious declarations and acceptance of the Soviet Union as an equal[47]. This diplomatic tact was even more crucial since Khrushchev was excited by his ally. Che Guevara as well as F. Castro declared themselves willing to accept a nuclear apocalypse rather than disgrace (Blight, Lang 2005). From 1999 onwards, Colonel Gaddafi led a policy that was attentive to the prestige of American power. On the other hand, at the time of the 1967 crisis, President Nasser increased his boastful declarations to the point that it was difficult to back down. Saddam Hussein put himself in a comparable position regarding his own domestic opinion. Saving face requires leaving the opponent with an honourable way out by proposing minimal concessions. President Kennedy offered Khrushchev a success which enhanced his prestige by proposing the withdrawal of Jupiter missiles from Turkey. As for Colonel Gaddafi, his security and economic concessions to the United States were so important that it was impossible not to present them as a success for American policy. On the other hand, at no moment in the crisis did Nasser or Saddam Hussein offer their opponent a concession

3. *Recognition of a Particular Identity*: The ignorance or 'contempt' displayed by religions, memories, or political regimes can unleash and perpetuate armed conflicts (Braud 2004). The recognition of special identities shows an awareness of historic and cultural knowledge. During the Cuban crisis, President Kennedy as well as General Secretary Khrushchev minimised their ideological differences while emphasising peaceful coexistence. Colonel Gadaffi even saluted the American policy of world 'democratisation'. On the other hand, the denial of recognition was particularly flagrant in the case of Egyptian leaders in 1967. The effect of the Egyptian declarations of 'death' and 'the annihilation of Israel' was amplified by Israeli memory of the Massada and genocide during the Second World War

---

47. Stein (1991: 62) 'for the same reasons of security, pride, or face, would bring about a counter response and eventually an escalation into armed conflict'.

4. *Recognition through Empathy*: The lack of empathy with respect to certain states, as well as indifference to their destiny, constitutes a denial of recognition which can lead to war. The reactions of Iraq and Libya to the 11th September attacks played an important role in the crisis. The absence of intersubjective argumentation and the lack of sincerity promoted a feeling of contempt while suggesting that the other considers them as objects of manipulation (Risse 2000). The feeling of decision makers that the other is making fun of them can induce aggressiveness. This was the case for American decision makers such as Colin Powell who thought that Iraq was not being honest by playing cat and mouse with the IAEA inspectors. Empathy is favoured by an emphasis on shared identity (Wendt 1999). Kennedy and Gaddafi both put forward a common destiny with their opponent: the former by emphasising the threat of nuclear apocalypse, the latter by stressing shared opposition to radical forms of Islam

*Conclusion*
The central premise of this chapter is that states seek not only security (*homo politicus*) and prosperity (*homo economicus*), but also the confirmation of a certain identity (*homo symbolicus*).

Even a decision maker who is emotionally indifferent to the offences of his state would have difficulty being unaware of them. Political leaders risk losing the support of both public opinion and their entourage if they are unaware of the emotions expressed about an offense to their community. The more public and organised character of differentiated entities' foreign policy renders political decision makers more vulnerable to losing face and also more susceptible to emotional influence coming from 'below'. During the 1967 crisis, Egyptian as well as Israeli decision makers had to constantly 'outbid' each other's rhetoric and military capacity because of their volatile public opinion. A second difficulty associated with policies cautious toward provocation lies in the fact that a humiliated and weak state risks losing a part of its authority on the international scene.[48] Reputation and credibility are at the heart of realistic reasoning over the capacity of a state to deter aggression from another (Schelling 1960). If a reputation for weakness depends on multiple variables (Mercer 1996), many political leaders consider that a policy of conciliation could undermine their authority. Thus, the intransigent attitude of the United States regarding Iraq is largely explained by the American administration's fear of losing face (and thus leadership) in the international community. There is certainly a 'cold' symbolic interest for state decision makers to defend a positive self-image of their political entity.

Another objection consists of the assertion that a recognition policy would be ineffective if decision makers of the adversarial state have an appetite for material gains. Nevertheless, a policy of recognition increases the moral costs of armed aggression for the aggressor. Thus, Colonel Gaddafi's recognition policy towards

---

48. On this subject see Mercer (1996).

American power removed any pretext for going to war from American decision makers. The possibility of 'hard-liners' in the American administration going to war would have been significantly reduced if Saddam Hussein had accepted the IAEA inspections without restriction and publicly announced his condemnation of the 11th September.

The analyses of war through the recognition *problématique* provides not only alternative explanations to traditional approaches, but also suggests new ways of preventing war. The principal working hypotheses has attempted to explain the practical implications of the prevention and resolution of international conflict. Globally, a recognition-related approach takes into consideration how decisions impact on the self-image and self-esteem of a state leader and his population. Contrary to the liberal and realist approaches, which postulate that war can be avoided when the strategic and economic benefits of war are inferior to those of peace, the recognition-approach invites us to consider the symbolic aspects of violence. What are the conditions under which war is a means to enhance a state actor's self-image? War, according to the main thesis, will become an option when the perceived net recognition benefits of war are superior to the perceived net recognition benefits of peace.[49] There is a recognition net benefit when an actor improves his self-image as conveyed by significant others. Without claiming that it is possible to exactly quantify the recognition benefits of war and peace, the assumption that decision makers only consider economic and strategic costs of war is unrealistic. Leaders calculate, subconsciously at least, the symbolic costs and gains in war. As it has be noted, symbolic calculations have their own particular logic and therefore cannot be approached in the same way as material benefits. One may argue that for decision makers, losing a war always signifies humiliation and thus a loss of face. If this were true, we could indeed confine our calculations to determine the power benefits of war and peace because the more powerful would always be the most 'honourable'. However, we know that state leaders may obtain reputation and national support even in military defeat – especially when confronted by an overwhelming power (Jervis 1988). National leaders and populations may even prefer physical annihilation to dishonour, the oldest example of which is when the Melians resisted the Athenians in 416 BC in the name of justice and pride.

In conflict prevention, the recognition-perspective puts emphasis on the significance of avoiding humiliation for the adversary. Humiliation is an inextricably subjective notion. This assumes that one puts oneself in another's shoes by taking their values and their 'identity reference' into account[50]. Coercive or dissuasive postures are rarely successful when they do not allow an honourable way out. This study confirms the thesis that war is probable when the symbolic costs of

---

49. For more on 'materialist' rational choice perspectives, see Fearon (1995), Cashman and Robinson (2007) and Sobek (2009). For a discussion of 'symbolic rationality', O'Neil (2001).

50. This notion is similar to that used by cognitive analyses of public policies. See Muller (2000: 44).

peace[51] are higher than the symbolic costs of war. Conversely, it is more probable that peace is maintained when the symbolic costs of war are higher than those of peace[52]. Thus, politics of recognition should consist of diminishing the symbolic costs of peace while elevating those of war. If the risk of being humiliated in the international scene is minimised (diminishing the symbolic costs of peace) and when war becomes morally unacceptable by removing the 'value' assigned to violent behaviour (increasing the symbolic costs of war), peace will be more likely than war. This process of 'civilianisation' is comparable to the internal national pacification that results from both a de-legitimisation of violence and promotion of a shared identity[53].

Unlike the classical realist and liberal perspectives, this approach suggests that the progressive pacification of interstate conflicts within a prosperous and 'institutionalised' world of the OECD is largely due to the development of peaceful norms and shared identities that transform war into a morally costly exercise. Further, saving face via multilateral and institutional behaviour, as well as the decline in coercive, dissuasive and 'arrogant' policies within the 'first world', reduce the symbolic costs of peacemaking. Thus, in spite of the United States' military hegemony, Western countries showed little opposition (for decades, 1945–2001) to an American leadership then perceived as benign.

My four hypotheses on the origins of war implicitly put forward a way to prevent war through managing symbolic interests. According to the first, that of war for prestige, leaders with hubristic identities who are attached to a superior image and/or preoccupied with affirming virile norms are more sensitive to feelings of non-recognition. Hubristic leaders are also more inclined to take risks than those who have been socialised in pacific values in order to reinforce their charismatic image. For this reason, it is difficult to satisfy their claim for recognition. However, two paths are still available for conflict prevention. In the long term, a peace process must aim to promote civil and egalitarian values in the international system. This process must weaken actors who are attached to virile and non-egalitarian values[54].

Contrary to the realist paradigm, a recognition approach does not assume that all state actors can be deterred. In fact, it is unclear as to whether hubristic lead-

---

51. I define symbolic costs as 'attacks on self-images'. This is a parallel with Alexandro Pizzorno's 'moral cost', defined as 'losing recognition'. This is the starting point for his idea that 'moral costs are much higher when a person is situated in a strong circle of recognition. When one is isolated [...] when one 'floats' through other places, there is a stronger possibility that the moral costs are low'. See Pizzorno (2000: 142).

52. On the non-use of nuclear weapons after Hiroshima and Nagasaki, a similar argument is proposed by Tannenwald (1999) and Price (1997).

53. On 'internal' pacification: Deloye and Ihl (1993), demonstrating that this notion is founded less on brute force (the monopolisation of violence in a Weberian sense) than on 'the business of civic acculturation', which delegitimises outbursts of violence by increasing the symbolic cost for the actors.

54. On 'internal' identity-related violence: Crettiez (1999).

ers and actors who attempt to affirm their glory or superior values on humanity, such as Louis XIV, Napoleon, Hitler, Milosevic, Saddam Hussein, Kim Jong-Il, Ahmadinejad, as well as the Al Qaida suicide 'terrorists', will renounce when their lives are in danger.

In order to create sustainable peace, actors who are detached from a humane legitimacy must not be allowed to hold weapons of mass destruction (Tannenwald 1999: 42). However, the fundamental question is about knowing how such hubristic actors, who support aggressive values, can be weakened. The answer must be variable and will depend on a careful analysis of domestic support and their international disruptive capacity. The least problematic strategy is the peaceful promotion of democracy, as democratisation reinforces civil values. Democratic ideals such as 'one man, one vote' and the consensual and procedural principles in conflict resolution support a culture of peace.[55] This long term conflict prevention strategy is comparable to the liberal approach in international relations. However, taking into account the recognition dimension leads us to criticise militarised liberalism; that is to say the forced exportation of democracy. Such action can be humiliating for the submitted nation and as a result, can prove to be counter-productive. In other terms, one must make use of multiple 'soft-power' techniques in order to promote democracy and to take into account symbolic dimensions. The more pacific values are diffused in an international system, the more war becomes morally costly and therefore unacceptable. Thus, Nina Tannenwald comes to the conclusion that the development of the 'nuclear taboo' has considerably slowed US willingness to use nuclear weapons since 1945 (Tannenwald 1999). Indeed, from a purely strategic point of view, deploying strategic nuclear weapons to take out political leaders' bunkers is far from absurd. Contrary to popular belief, disarmament and non-proliferation treaties are not actually ineffective. The more a norm is institutionalised and durable, the lower the probability that this norm will be violated because of the moral costs attached. In the same way, the more egalitarian concepts replace the quest for superiority in terms of recognition, the more symbolically acceptable it is to maintain peace. The sensitivity towards attacks on honour is drastically reduced when hubristic identities are weakened. Non-state actors such as epistemic communities, peace movements or NGO humanitarians also contribute to the promotion of peaceful values and the stigmatisation of virile values, as well as the use of force. When state leaders are confronted with actors preoccupied with their strength and pride they should be aware that 'resoluteness' could be interpreted as a declaration of war. If the short term aim is to avoid armed conflict with such states or groups (either for strategic reasons or in hope of a benign domestic turnaround in the enemy state), then behaviour that can jeopardise the state's grandiose image, as well as openly coercive and dissuasive actions that bring their reputation into play, should all be renounced[56]. When faced with a lead-

---

55. See to this end Russett (1993).

56. Coercive processes are even more compromising for the other's face than dissuasive postures in that they do not only aim to prevent the other from performing an action, but also to modify their behaviour. See Vennesson (2000).

er as proud as Saddam Hussein, if the objective of the Western power was to avoid war, they should have anticipated his narcissistic difficulty in accepting IAEA inspections, notably at presidential sites. 'Rambo-style' inspections only provoke resistance. The breakdown between the Western community and Iran, which has worsened since 2003, seems to stem from Iranian refusal to allow foreign powers to dictate their national 'destiny'[57]. Once again, the threats made after the 9/11 attacks by President Bush to North Korea and Iran that branded them as the 'axis of evil' have only exacerbated these states' nuclear ambitions[58]. It is evident that leaders who claim a quasi-divine status find it hard to back down in front of their domestic public opinion. A short term peace strategy must therefore address symbolic appeasement, by diminishing the 'costs' necessary to maintain peace from hubristic leaders and thus remove their pretext to resort to armed hostility.

The second hypothesis states that conflicts are more frequent between states that lack a shared identity, perceiving themselves to be radically different to each other[59]. This opposition can be based on their internal legitimacy and their values, as well as on the lack of a shared identity. Hence, this hypothesis reminds us that violence is never purely instrumental. It contains 'a principle of non-legitimacy' (Wieviorka 2005: 211) and as a result, it frequently assumes a disqualification of other states as 'rogue' or 'terrorist' actors[60]. The promotion of shared identities encourages peace because violence against a similar actor is symbolically costly. In the same way, the symbolic cost of peace is lower when other actors share our values. Cooperative interaction, empathy, cultural and economic exchange, interdependence, common ecological threats, political homogeneity as well as a moderated exercise of hegemonic power are all factors that favour the long-term creation of such common identities (Wendt 1999). A strategy that promotes shared identities, for example, via cooperative practices (Wendt 1999: 163), challenges realist and liberal arguments by affirming that only a community of strategic or economic interests would be capable of promoting peace. However, the existence of democratic peace, as well as the durability of certain alliances and international interstate organisations like NATO and the EU, invalidates this proposition.

Our third and fourth hypotheses relate to a politics of recognition that implicitly contains recommendations for conflict prevention. They stress the idea that non-recognition can result from violations of international norms or of a state's universal dignity; such as attacks on an actor's status (Doran 1991), honour, and autonomy (denying an actor's political and historical uniqueness). The effect of such non-recognition on the origins of war can be both immediate and distant. For the latter, the formation of exclusive identities by stigmatisation transforms progressively into a 'distinctive and idealised hubristic identity', such as the powerful and resentful identity formed because of the Treaty of Versailles in national-

---

57. On security and identity: Neumann (1999) and Hopf (2002).
58. See Bigo, Bonelli and Deltombe (2008).
59. For the literature: Adler and Barnett (eds.) (1998); Pouliot (2010).
60. On the problematic use of the term 'terrorist', see Sommier (2000: 85).

socialist Germany. A politics of recognition appeases both identity and security related fears. The long term prevention of inter-state war has been promoted by humility after 'successful' wars, through the integration of all the great powers in the international concert, through the multilateral exercise of power and through the respect of sovereignty.[61]

In the short term, within a context of international crisis, a politics of recognition rests dually on the classic 'reassurance' approach (restrained military measures) and on the less examined politics known as 'facework', which means working to save or to restore the other's 'face'. A politics of recognition is prudent with dissuasive and coercive postures. It abstains from moral and status-related denigration that can be seen as attacks on an actor's 'face' (for example, threats and ultimatums such as those addressed to Serbia in July 1914 (Lindemann 2001) or to Saddam Hussein in March 2003). More positively, a politics of recognition attempts to affirm the right to existence as well as the principles of equal dignity and sovereignty. Thus, the guarantee of American sovereignty accorded to the Cuban state was decisive in the resolution of the 1962 crisis. Such a politics of recognition must also take into account other actors' historical and cultural particularities or otherwise the results may be dramatic (for example, the volatile consequences of Nasser's denial of Israel's genocide trauma in 1967).[62] In this way, President Kennedy understood how difficult it was for the Soviet Union to drop a 'socialist' ally. Conflict resolution must therefore be culturally and ideologically acceptable for the adversary. On an 'affective' level, conflict resolution must try not to come across as indifferent to the other actor's lot as, for example, the 'cold' reaction from the Entente powers after the 1914 Sarajevo attacks and the jubilant reactions from Saddam Hussein after 9/11. Such an approach implies caution and compassion when other actors are exposed to grave events such as attacks and natural catastrophes (such as was the case for Colonel Gaddafi after 9/11). Lastly, affective empathy is also favoured by highlighting shared norms and identities (for example, belonging to the same human race threatened by ecological and nuclear apocalypse).

Lastly, state leaders who manipulate national sentiment and who mobilise their military in order to coerce and intimidate[63] can rapidly find themselves in a situation in which it becomes difficult to step back without losing face. This suggests that diplomatic leeway is radically reduced when a crisis has reached a certain stage. In an era where domestic opinion must be taken into account, it is necessary to envisage 'cooling off' mechanisms in order to overcome symbolic escalation. The July 1914 crisis, as well as the crisis preceding the Six Day War in 1967 demonstrate that nationalist provocations are considerably amplified by the existence of 'spectators', such as the media and public opinion. To confine a crisis, it

---

61. See also Doran (2010).
62. See (1998) Dieckhoff's plea in favour of a politics of 'consideration' between Israelis and Palestinians resting on political equity and the recognition of the other's historic and cultural specificity.
63. See Bigo (2010).

*Table 4.3: Approaches to War and Peace*

|  | Realist Approach | Liberal Approach | Recognition approach | Synergy between the approaches |
|---|---|---|---|---|
| Origins of war | Imbalance; hegemony decline. | Greed of atavistic elites; authoritarian values; absence of institutional regulation; weak level of interdependence. | Hubristic identities; negative identification; non-recognition of dignity; non-recognition of identity. | Authoritarian values are as much a source of war for the liberal approach as for the recognition-approach; according to realists and "recognition" – analysis, brutal, hegemonic domination can lead to war because of 'power balance' discrepancies for the former and 'dignity' discrepancies for the latter. |
| Conflict prevention | Peace by deterrence. | Peace by democratisation; peace by trade; peace by international institutions. | Peace by delegitimising virile and unequal values; peace by shared identity; peace by recognition of a state's universal dignity; peace by a state's particular dignity; peace by empathy. | The liberal and recognition approaches believe that international institutions favour peace via optimising information (liberal) and the capacity to lower the symbolic costs of domination and increase the symbolic costs of violating rules (recognition). |

is necessary to avoid provocation and rhetorical engagement which is capable of putting actors in a situation where their face is engaged in front of international and domestic opinion. 'Secret' negotiations are thus useful in defusing crises, well away from the pressures of national and international communities.

The precedent developments in terms of symbolic interests could suggest their compatibility with the rational choice model. However, symbolic interests are not simply measured in terms of losing prestige in front of the electorate and political allies, but they are also defined by psychological, affective costs, when the self-image that an actor claims to hold no longer corresponds with the image reflected back by others.[64] The feeling of humiliation is in itself a powerful catalyst leading to aggressiveness. Thus, in a head-to-head meeting between two heads of state, one will be able to offend the other without this offence being relayed by the media and without the electoral consequences. Nevertheless, there is an elevated probability that such a humiliated leader will seek out vengeance by force to re-establish his honour. For national-socialist, Wilhelmian, and Israeli-Arab political actors, as well as for Saddam Hussein and George Bush, a resort to armed force was also a way of putting an end to psychological discomfort created when the roles claimed for these actors were not confirmed by others on the international scene.

A comparison of the recognition approach to the origins of war and conflict prevention with other paradigms is summarised in the Table 4.3.

Thus, this study provides evidence for the general thesis that non-recognition matters in international politics. All of our cases are related to international conflict and are therefore 'hard' cases for recognition because scholars expect that in such issues physical survival should easily come before vanity. The perspective of recognition suggests an alternate means to the carrot and stick approach in the pacification of contentious powers such as China, Russia, North Korea, or Iran. One should examine in greater detail the recognition needs and aspirations of these states. In addition, it is above all the inclusion of these powers in international institutions and their acceptance as 'worthy' international actors that could calm their revisionist aspirations, instead of qualifying them as a 'hateful pygmy'. Such politics of recognition is also aimed at internal audiences of the aggressive state in order to delegitimise the war option for the decision makers of theses states. The politics of recognition is not expensive, but its benefits can be huge.

---

64. On the 'psychological dimension of recognition', see Braud (1996), Saurette (2006), Wolf (2008).

# Bibliography

## NEWS ARTICLES:

'Colonel Gaddafi', *Newsweek*. Accessed 20th January 2003 http://cgi.cvm.qc.ca/APHCQ/scripts/aphcq.pl?get&Bulletin/Dossiers/La%20crise%20des%20missiles%2àde%de%20Cuba%20en%é0octobre%201962.htm

'La BCE se veut rassurante elle', *L'Humanité*, 14th September 2001.

'Last Words of a Terrorist' *The Observer*, 30th September 2001.

'Libyan Payment to Families of Pan Am Flight 103 Victims', *American Journal of International Law*, 97 (4) 2003: 989.

'Open letter from Saddam Hussein to the American peoples and the Western peoples and their governments'. Accessed Oct. 2008 www.infoimagination.org/ps/iraq/spch091301.html

'Selon son fils, le colonel Kadhafi n'a pas renoncé au nucléaire à cause de la guerre contre Saddam', *Le Monde*, 11 février 2004.

'Solidarité sans faille des capitales étrangères', *Libération*, Thursday 13th September 2001

'Statement by the Leader of the Revolution on 11th September.' Accessed October 2002 www.mathaba.net/news/news1/usa/mq1.shtml

'U.N. Nuclear Chief Welcomed in Libya', *The New York Times*, 28th December 2003.

'United States Lifts some Sanctions on Libya', *The American Journal of International Law*, 99 (1) 2005: 253–54.

'U.S./U.K. Negotiations with Libya regarding Non-proliferation', *The American Journal of International Law*, 98 (1) 2004:195–97.

'We know that after September the 11th Saddam Hussein's regime gleefully celebrated the terrorist attacks on America'. Accessed November 2002 www.whitehouse.gov

## BOOKS AND JOURNALS:

Abdelal, R. Yoshiko, M., Alastair, I. and McDermott. R. *Measuring Identity: A Guide for Social Scientists*, Cambridge: Cambridge University Press.

Abrams, D., Wetherell M., Cochrane S., Hogg, M.A. and Turner J.C. (1990) 'Knowing What to Think by Knowing Who You Are: Self-Categorization and the Nature of Norm Formation, Conformity and Group Polarization', *British Journal of Social Psychology*, 29: 97–119.

Adler, E. and Barnett, M. (eds) (1996) *Governing Anarchy: A Research Agenda for the Study of Security Communities*, Cambridge University Press; (1998) *Security Communities*, Cambridge: Cambridge University Press

– (1998) 'A Framework for the Study of Security Community', *Security Communities*, 62.

Albertini, L. (1952) *Origins of the War of 1914*, Oxford: Oxford University Press.

Albin, C. (2001) *Justice and Fairness in International Organization*, Cambridge: Cambridge University Press, p. 26.

Alexander, J. C. (2004) 'Cultural Pragmatics: Social Performance between Ritual and Strategy', *Sociological Theory*, 4 (22): 527–573.

Allan, P. and Dupont, C. (1999) 'International Relations Theory and Game Theory: Baroque Modeling Choices and Empirical Robustness', *International Political Science Review*, 20:1.

Allan, P. and Keller, A. (eds.) (2006) *What is Just Peace*, Oxford: Oxford University Press.

Allen, W. (1984) *Nazi Seizure of Power: The Experience of a Single German Town 1922–1945*, New York: Franklin Watts.

Allison, G. (1971) *Essence of Decision*, Boston: Little Brown.

Allison, G. and Zelikov, P., (2004) *Essence of Decision: Explaining the Cuban Missile Crisis*, New York: Longman.

Anderson, B. (1991) *Imagined Communities*, London: Verso.

Anderson, E. (1930) *The First Moroccan Crisis, 1904–1906*, Chicago: University of Chicago Press.

Anghie, A. (2007) *Imperialism, Sovereignty and the Making of International Law*, Cambridge: Cambridge University Press.

Ansart, P. (2002) *Le Ressentiment*, Brussels: Bruylant.

Aoun, E. (2003) 'The European Foreign Policy and the Arab-Israeli Conflict', *European Foreign Affairs Review*, 8 (3): 289–331.
Aron, R. (1976) *Penser la guerre*, Paris: Gallimard, vol. 1 and 2
– (1984) *Paix et guerre entre les nations*, 8th ed., Paris: Calman-Levy.
Ashley, R. (1986) 'The Poverty of Neorealism' in Keohane, R.O. (ed.) *Neorealism and Its Critics*, New York: Columbia University Press.
Ashley, R. K. (1988) 'Untying the Sovereign State: A Double Reading of the Anarchy Problematique', *Millennium*, 17 (2): 227–262.
Assmann, A. (2006) *Der lange Schatten der Vergangenheit: Erinnerungskultur und Geschichtspolitik*, Munich: Beck.
Aurelius, M. (1964) *Meditations*, Harmondsworth: Penguin.
Austin, J. L. (1962) *How to do Things with Words*, Oxford: Clarendon Press.
Axelrod, R. (2004) *The Evolution of Cooperation*, New York: Basic Books.
Aycoberry, P. (1981) *Nazi Question: An Essay on the Interpretations of National Socialism, 1922–75*, New York: Pantheon.
Badie, B. (1999) *Un monde sans souveraineté*, Paris: Fayard.
Badie, B. and Smouts, M-C., (2002) *Le retournement du monde,* Paris: Presses de Sciences Po.
Bajorek, J. (2009) 'The Offices of Homeland Security, or, Hölderlin's Terrorism', *Critical Inquiry*, 31 (2): 874–902.
Baker, K. M. (1990) *Inventing the French Revolution: Essays on French Political Culture in the Eighteenth Century*, Cambridge: Cambridge University Press.
Baldwin, D. (1971) 'Thinking about Threats', *Journal of Conflict Resolution* 15 (1).
Barker, R. (2007) *Making Enemies*, Basingstoke: Palgrave Macmillan.
Barlow, I. C. (1971) *The Agadir Crisis*, Hamden: Archon Books.
Barnes, B. (2001) 'Practice as Collective Action' in *The Practice Turn in Contemporary Theory*, New York: Routledge.
Bartelson, J. (1995) *A Genealogy of Sovereignty,* Cambridge: Cambridge University Press.
Bar-Zohar, M. (1968) *Histoire Secrète de la Guerre d'Israël*, Paris: Fayard.
Battistella, D. (2003) *Théories des relations internationales*, Paris: Presses de Sciences, Po.
(2006) *Retour de l'état de guerre*, Paris: Armand Colin.
Baudrillard, J. (2001) 'L'Esprit du terrorisme.' *Harper's Magazine*. Accessed January 2009, http://harpers.org/archive/2002/02/0079058.
Baumeister, R. F. (2006)'Gewalttätig aus Grössenwahn', *Spektrum der Wissenschaft*, 4: 70–75.
Baumeister, R. F., and Leary M. R. (1997) 'The Need to Belong: Desire for Interpersonal Attachments as a Fundamental Human Motivation', *Psychological Bulletin*, 117: 497–529.
Beck, A.T. (2000) *Prisoners of hate; The cognitive basis of anger, hostility, and violence*, New York: Harper Paperbooks.
Becker, J.-J. (2004) *L'année 14*, Paris: Armand Colin.
Behnke, A. (2004) 'Terrorising the Political: 9/11 Within the Context of the Globalisation of Violence', *Millennium*, 33 (22): 279–312.
Bell, C. (2008) *On the Law of Peace: Peace Agreements and the Lex Pacificatoria*, Oxford: Oxford University Press.
Berenskoetter, F. (2007) 'Friends, There Are No Friends? An Intimate Reframing of the International', *Millennium – Journal of International Studies*, 35 (3): 647–676.
Berlin, I. (1991) *The Crooked Timber of Humanity: Chapters in the History of Ideas*, London: Fontana Press.
Berstein, S. and Milza, P. (1988) *L'Allemagne 1870–1987*, Paris: Masson.
– (1995) *Histoire du XIX siècle*, Paris: Hattier.
Betts, R. K. (1987) *Nuclear Blackmail and Nuclear Balance*, New York: Brookings Institution Press.
Bially Mattern, J. (2001) 'The Power Politics of Identity', *European Journal of International Relations*, 7 (3): 349–397
– (2004) *Ordering International Politics: Identity, Crisis and Representational Force*, New York and London: Routledge.
– (2007) 'Representational Force Meets 'Realist' Force. Thoughts on the relationship between linguistic and material forms of coercion', 9e Congrès de l'AFSP, Toulouse, 5th–7th September, 2007.
Biermann, V. and Borngässer, B. (2006) *Théorie de l'architecture*, Taschen: Paris.

Biersteker, T. and Weber, C. (eds.) (1992) *State Sovereignty as a Social Construct*, Cambridge: Cambridge University Press.
Bigo, D. (1997) *Polices en réseaux*, Paris: Presses de Sciences Po.
- (2010) *Policing Insecurity Today: Defense and Internal Security*, London: Palgrave Macmillan.
Bigo, D., Bonelli, L., and Deltombe T. (2008) *Au nom du 11 Septembre*, Paris: La Découverte.
Blainey, G. (1973) *The Causes of War*, New York: Free Press.
Blanchard, C. (2006) 'Libya: background and US relations', CSR Report for Congress. Accessed August 2009, http://fpc.state.gov/documents/organization/109510.pdf
Blättler, S. (2004) 'Die Rechte von Frauen im Streit zwischen Menschenrechtsuniversalismus und Kulturrelativismus'. Accessed 13th November 2004 www.ai-aktionsnetz-heilberufe. de/docs/texte/texte/weitere_texte1...blättler-2004%20Menschenrechte-frauenrechte-Streit.pdf
Blättler, S. and Marti, I. M. (2000) 'Rosa Luxemburg and Hannah Arendt: Against the Destruction of Political Spheres of Freedom', *Hypotia*, 20 (2): 88–101.
Blight, J. M. and Lang, J. (2005) *The Fog of War*, New York: Rowman and Littlefield Publishers.
Blix, H. (1989) 'Hobbesian Fear', *Political Theory*, 17 (3): 417–431.
- (2005) *Disarming Iraq*, New York: Pantheon Books.
- (2008) *Why Nuclear Disarmament Matters*, Cambridge: MIT Press.
Bloom, W. (1990) *Personal Identity, National Identity and International Relations*, Cambridge: Cambridge University Press.
Blumer, H. (1969) *Symbolic Interactionism*, California: University of California Press.
Bock, G. and James, S. (eds.) (1992) *Beyond Equality and Difference*, London: Routledge.
Boltanski, L. and Thévenot, L. (1991) *De la justification; Les économies de grandeur*, Paris: Gallimard.
Borradori, G. and Derrida, J. (2003) 'Autoimmunity: Real and Symbolic Suicides: A Dialogue with Jacques Derrida', in *Philosophy in a Time of Terror: Dialogues with Jurgen Habermas and Jacques Derrida*, Chicago: University of Chicago Press.
Boudon, R. (1976) *La logique du social*, Paris: Hachette.
Boulding, K. (1965) *The Image: Knowledge in Life and Society*, Michigan: University of Michigan Press.
Bourdieu, P. (1979) *La distinction*, Paris: Le Minuit.
- (2003) *Raisons pratiques*, Paris: Seuil.
Bracher, K.D. (1970) The German Dictatorship, New York: Praeger.
- (1977) *Die Auflösung der Weimarer Republik*, Dusseldorf: Droste.
Braud, P. (1996) *L'émotion en politique*, Paris: Presses de Sciences Po.
- (2004) *Violences politiques*, Paris: Seuil.
- (2007) 'Les violences symboliques dans les relations internationales', Congrès de l'Association Française de Science Politique (AFSP), Toulouse, Table ronde *Les violences symboliques dans les relations internationales*.
Bremer, S. (1996) 'Militarized Interstate Dispute' (MID) in *Correlates of War Project*.
Broszat, M. (1987) *Hitler and the Collapse of Weimar Germany*, New York: Berg Publishers.
Brown, P. and Levinson, S. (1987) *Politeness: Some Universals in Language Use*, Cambridge: Cambridge University Press.
Brubaker, R. and Cooper, F. (2000) 'Beyond 'Identity'', *Theory and Society*, 29 (1).
Bülow, B. (1931) *Memoirs of Prince Von Bülow*, 2, Boston: Little, Brown.
Bukovansky, M. (1997) 'American Identity and Neutral Rights from Independence to the War of 1812', *International Organization*, 51: 209–243.
- (1999) 'The Altered State and the State of Nature: The French Revolution and International Politics', *Review of International Studies*, 25 (2): 197–216.
Bull, H. (1995) *The Anarchical Society*, 2nd ed. Houndmills: Macmillan.
Bullock, A. (1962) *Hitler: A Study in Tyranny*, New York: Harper & Row.
Bundy, G.M. (1988) *Danger and Survival*, New York: Random House.
Burbach, R. and Tarbell, J. (2004) *Imperial Overstretch: George Bush and the Hubris of Empire*, London and New York: Zed Book.
Burg, S. L. and Shoup, P. (1999) *The War in Bosnia-Herzegovina: Ethnic Conflict and International Intervention*, Armonk: M.E. Sharpe.
Burton, J. (1985) 'Miscalculation in the North Atlantic. The Origins of the Falkland's War', in Jervis, R., Lebow, N. and Stein, J. (1985) *Psychology and Deterrence*, Baltimore: John Hopkins University Press.

- (1990) *Conflict: Human Needs Theory*, New York: St. Martin's Press.
- (1990) *Conflict: Resolution and Prevention*, New York: St. Martin's Press.
- (1996) *Conflict Resolution. It's language and processes*, London: Scarecrow Press.
- (1998) 'Conflict Resolution: The Human Dimension', *The International Journal of Peace Studies*, 3 (1)

Bush, G W. (2002) 'President Bush Delivers Graduation Speech at West Point'. The White House. Accessed Sep. 2008, http://georgewbush-whitehouse.archives.gov/news/releases/2002/06/print/20020601-3.html

Bush, R. (2004) *At Cross Purposes: U.S.-Taiwan Relations Since 1942*, Armonk: M.E. Sharpe.

Bushman, B.J and Baumeister, R. F. (1998) 'Threatened Egotism, Narcissism, Self-Esteem and Direct and Displaced Aggression: Does Self-Love or Self-Hate Lead to Violence?', *Journal of Personality and Social Psychology*, 75 (1): 219.

Buzan, B. (1991) *People, States and Fear*, 2nd ed., New York: Harvester Wheatsheaf.

Cabin, P. and Dortier, J.- F. (2005) *La Sociologie*, Paris: Editions Sciences Humaines.

Cadier, D. (2006) *Identité et Sécurité dans l'Estonie post-soviétique*, mémoire I. E. P. Toulouse Master II, (under my direction).

Cai Zhengwen, and Rongxi Wu (1989) 'Evaluations and Suggestions on Foreign Relations of the ROC', in *ROC White Papers on Defense and Foreign Policy*, Taipei: Yeqiang Publishing House, pp. 63–90.

Caillé, A. (1989) *Critique de la raison utilitaire*, Paris: La découverte.

- (2004) *Présentation*, in 'De la reconnaissance: Don, identité et estime de soi', *Revue du Mauss*, 1: 5–30.

Campbell, D. (1989) *Writing Security: United States Foreign Policy and the Politics of Identity*, Minneapolis: University of Minnesota Press.

Caplow T. and Venesson, P. (2000) *Sociologie militaire*, Paris: Armand Colin.

Carr, E. H. (2001) *The Twenty Years' Crisis 1919–1939*, London: Palgrave Macmillan.

Cashman, G. (1993) *What Causes War? An introduction to theories of international conflict*, San Francisco: Lexington books.

Cashman G. and Robinson L. C. (2007) *An Introduction to the Causes of War*, Lanham, Boulder, New York: Rowman and Littlefield Publishers.

Cederman, L.E and Daase, C. (2006) 'Endogenizing corporate identities', in Guzzini, S. and Leander, A. (2006) *Alexander Wendt and its critics*, London: Paperback.

Chang Jaw-ling. (1995) 'How Clinton Bashed Taiwan-and Why', *Orbis*, 39 (4).

Chang, L.and Kornbluh, P. (1992) *The Cuban Missile Crisis 1962*, New York: The New Press.

Chao Linda and Myers, M. (1994) 'The First Chinese Democracy: Political Development of the Republic of China on Taiwan, 1986–1994.' *Asia Survey*, 34 (3): 213–230.

Chao Linda, Myers, M. and Jialin Zhuang (2002) 'A China Divided Since the Turnover of Political Power in Taiwan', *Cambridge Review of International Affairs*, 15 (2): 115–122.

Charillon, F. (1999) *La politique étrangère à l'épreuve du transnational; Une étude des diplomaties française et britannique dans la guerre du Golfe*, Paris: L'Harmattan.

Chen Shui-bian (2007) *President Chen Shui-bian's Letter to UN Secretary-General Ban Ki-moon*, Taipei: ROC Office of the President.

Chevallier-Bellet, B. (1999) 'L'économie extérieure libyenne depuis 1969, entre isolement et ouverture', in Pliez, O. *La nouvelle Libye*, Paris: Karthala.

Chien You-Hsin (2002) *The ROC's 2002 Report on Foreign Policy*, Taipei: Ministry of Foreign Affairs.

Childers, T. (1983) *The Nazi Voter: The Social Foundations of Fascism in Germany, 1919–1933*, Chapel Hill: The University of North Carolina Press.

Chirot, D. (1994) *Modern Tyrants*, New York: Free Press.

Christensen, T. J. (2007) 'A Strong and Moderate Taiwan U.S.-Taiwan Business Council', Annapolis: American Institute in Taiwan.

Clausewitz, C. von (1955) *De la guerre*, Paris: Minuit.

- (1998) *Théorie du combat*, Paris: Economica.

Cohen, R. (1991) *Negotiating Across Cultures: Communication Obstacles in International Diplomacy*, Washington: United States Institute for Peace.

Cohen, S. (1986) *La monarchie nucléaire*, Paris: Hachette.

- (1994) *La défaite des généraux*, Paris: Fayard.

Cohrs, P. (2008) *The Unfinished Peace after World War I: America, Britain and the Stabilisation of Europe, 1919–1932*, Cambridge: Cambridge University Press.

Coleman, J.S. (1973) *The Mathematics of Collective Action*, London: Heinemann.
Colonomos, A. (2006) 'La morale dans les relations internationales', *Sciences Humaines*, Grands Dossiers (2);
- (2008) *Moralizing International Relations*, London: Palgrave Macmillan.
Connolly, W. (1995) *Ethos of Pluralization*, Minneapolis: University of Minnesota Press.
Copeland, D. (1999) 'Economic Interdependence and War', *International Security*, 20 (4).
- (2000) *The Origins of Major War*, Ithaca and London: Cornell University Press.
Copeland, D. C. (2000) *The Origins of Major War*, Ithaca: Cornell University Press.
Cornette, J. (2005) *Absolutisme et Lumières 1652–1783*, Paris: Hachette.
Cornil, F. (2000) 'Listening to the Subaltern: Postcolonial Studies and the Poetics of Neocolonial States', in *Postcolonial Theory and Criticism*, Chrisman, L. and Parry, B. (eds.) Cambridge: D.S. Brewer, pp. 37–55.
Correlates of War 2 Project, http://cow2.la.psu.edu
Craig, G. A. 'Germany, 1866–1945.' in *Oxford History of Modern Europe*, New York: Oxford University Press, 1978.
Crawford N. C. (2000), 'The Passions of World Politics; Propositions on Emotion and Emotional Relationships', *International Security*, 4.
Crettiez, X. (ed.) (1999) *L'Europe à l'épreuve des séparatismes violents*, Paris: La Découverte.
Crowe, E. (1928) 'Memorandum on the Present State of British Relations with France and Germany, 1st January 1907, in *British Documents on the Origins of the War, 1898–1914*, London: His Majesty's Stationary Office.
Daalder, I. H; Lindsay, J.-M. (2005) *America Unbound*, New York: John Wiley and Sons.
Dahrendorf, R. (1967) *Society and Democracy in Germany*, New York: Doubleday.
Danner, M. (2006) *The Secret Way to War*, New York: New York Review Books.
Davis, J.W. (2000) *Threats and Promises; The Pursuit of International Influence*, Baltimore: John Hopkins University Press.
De Cremer, D. (2002) 'Respect and Cooperation in Social Dilemmas: The Importance of Feeling Included' *Personality and Social Psychology Bulletin*, 28 (10):1335
De Mesquita, B. (1981), *The War Trap*, New Haven: Yale University Press.
Dehio, L. (1959) *Equilibre ou hégémonie de l'Europe d'hier au monde de demain*, Paris: Seuil, trans. German 'Gleichgewicht oder Hegemonie'.
- (1962) *The Precarious Balance Four Centuries of the European Power Struggle* [1948], New York: Vintage Books.
Deloye, Y. and Ihl, O. (1993) *La civilité électorale: vote de forclusion de la violence en France*, in Braud, P. (ed.) *La violence politique dans les démocraties occidentales*, Paris: L'Harmattan.
Derrida, J. (2001) *On Cosmopolitanism and Forgiveness*, London: Routledge.
Deutsch, K., Eberwein, W.-D. (1995) 'The future of International Warfare', *International Political Science Review*, 16 (4).
Devin, G. (ed.) (2005), *Faire la paix*, Paris: Pepper.
Devin, G. and Gautier, C. (2003) 'Mondialisation et droit international public', in Laroche, J. (ed.) (2003) *Mondialisation et gouvernance mondiale*, Paris: IRIS-PUF.
Dieckhoff, A. (1998) *Israéliens et Palestiniens: L'épreuve de la paix*, Paris: Aubier-Montaigne.
Diedhiou, M. 'Dilemme de la sécurité et guerre préventive: Le cas de l'opération 'Liberté en Irak', Mémoire DEA, I.e.,P. de Toulouse 2004–2005.
Diephouse, D. J., and Held, J.(1983) (eds) *The Cult of Power: Dictators in the Twentieth Century*, New York: Columbia University Press.
Djaziri, M. (1999) 'La Libye: les élites politiques, la stratégie de 'sortie' de crise et la réinsertion dans le système international', *Annuaire de l'Afrique du Nord*, 38.
Dobry, M., (1986) *Sociologie des crises politiques*, Paris: Presses de la Fondation nationale des sciences politiques.
Doosje, B., Ellemers, N., and Spears, R. (eds.) (1999) 'Commitment and Intergroup Behaviour.' in *Social Identity, Context, Commitment, Content: An Introduction*, London: Wiley Blackwell.
Doran, C. (1991) *Systems in Crisis*, Cambridge: Cambridge University Press
- (2010) 'World War I from the Perspective of Power Cycle Theory: Recognition, "adjustment Delusions", and the "trauma of Expectations Foregone"', in Lindemann, T. and Ringmar. E. (eds.) *The International Politics of Recognition*, Boulder: Paradigm.

Dorpalen, A. (1964) *Hindenburg and the Weimar Republic,* Princeton: Princeton University Press.
Draper, R. (2007) *Dead Again. The Presidency of George W. Bush,* London: Free Press.
Drazen, A. (2001) *Political Economy in Macroeconomics,* New Jersey: Princeton University Press.
Druckman, D. (1994) 'Nationalism, Patriotism, and Group Loyalty: A Social Psychological Perspective', *Mershon International Studies Review,* 43–68.
Dufour, J.-L. (1996) *Les Crises internationales de Pékin-1990 à Sarajevo – 1995,* Paris: Editions Complexe, p. 148.
Dumbaugh, K. and Sullivan, M. P. (2005) *China's Growing Interest in Latin America,* CRS Report for Congress.
Eakin, P. J. (1999) *How Our Lives Become Stories: Making Selves,* Ithaca: Cornell University Press.
Eberwein, W. D., Hubner-Dick, G., Jagodzinski, W., Rattinger, H. and Weede, E.,'External and Internal Conflict Behaviour Among Nations, 1966–1967, *Journal of Conflict Resolution,* 23: 715–742.
Edelman, M. (1985) *The Symbolic Uses of Politics,* University of Illinois Press.
Edwards, E.W. (1963) 'The Franco-German Agreement on Morocco, 1909', *English Historical Review,* 78 (308).
Ehrman, J. (2009) *The Rise of Neo-Conservatism: Intellectuals and Foreign Affairs, 1945–1994,* Yale University Press.
Einsel, W. 'Carl von Clausewitz'. Accessed 16th November 2006, www.clausewitz-gesellschaft. de/uploads/media/Vortragstext_Einsel.pdf
Eley, G. (1984) 'The British Model and the German Road: Rethinking the Course of German History Before 1914.' in *The Peculiarities of German History: Bourgeois Society and Politics in Nineteenth-Century Germany,* Blackbourn, D. and Eley, G. (eds.), Oxford: Oxford University Press.
Elias, N. (1997) *Les Logiques de d'exlusion,* Paris: Fayard.
Elman, C. and Fendius, M. (eds.) (2001), *Bridges and Boundaries. Historians, Political Scientists, and the Study of International Relations,* Cambridge, Massachusetts: MIT Press.
Enderlein, C. (1997) *Paix ou guerres; Les secrets des négociations Israélo-Arabes 1917–1997,* Paris: Stock.
Epictetus (1961) *Epictetus: Selections from His Discourses as Reported by Arrian and from the Fragments* in Heinemann, H. (ed.) Cambridge: Harvard Univeristy Press.
Evans, G. (2006) 'Prévenir les conflits: un guide pratique', *Politique Etrangère,* 1: 93–104.
Evans, R. J. (1987) *Rethinking German History: Nineteenth Century Germany and the Origins of the Third Reich,* New York: HarperCollins.
Eyck, E. (1967) *A History of the Weimar Republic, Two Volumes.* Cambridge: Harvard University Press.
Farrel, T. (2002) 'Constructivist Security Studies: Portrait of a Research Program.' *International Studies Review,* 4 (1): 49–72.
Favre, P. (2006) *Comprendre le monde pour mieux le changer,* Paris: Presses de Sciences Po.
Fayazmanesh, S. (2007) *The United States and Iran; Sanctions, Wars and the Policy of Dual Containment,* London: Routledge.
Fearon J. D. (1995) 'Rationalist Explanations of War', *International Organization,* 49: 379–414.
Feaver, D. (1992) 'Command and Control in Emerging Nuclear Nations', *International Security,* 17 (3): 160–187; (1996) 'Managing Nuclear Proliferation: Condemn, Strike, or Assist?', *International Studies Quarterly,* 40 (2): 209–233.
Feldman, D. (ed.) (1967) *German Imperialism, 1914–18: The Development of a Historical Debate,* New York: John Wiley & Sons.
Ferguson,A. (1773) *An Essay on the History of Civil Society.* Edinburgh: Cadell,T.; Kincaid, Creech and Bell. Accessed Feb 2009 www.archive.org/details/anessayonhistor01ferggoog
Feron, J. D. (1995) 'Rationalist Explanations for War', *International Organization,* 49 (3).
Fest, J. (1974) *Hitler,* New York: Harcourt Brace Jovanovich.
Finley, M. I. (1978) *The World of Odysseus,* New York: Viking.
Finnemore, M. and Sikkink, K. (1998) 'International Norm Dynamics and Political Change', *International Organization,* 52 (4).
Finnemore, M. (1996) *National Interests in International Society,* Ithaca: Cornell University Press.

- (2003) *The Purpose of Intervention*, Ithaca, N.Y.: Cornell University Press.
- (1996) 'Constructing Norms of Humanitarian Intervention', in Katzenstein, P. (1996), *The Culture of National Security,* 153–83.
Fischer, F. (1967) *Germany's Aims In The First World War*, New York: W.W. Norton.
Fisher, R. and Brown, S. (1988) *Getting Together: Building a Relationship that gets to YES,* Boston: Houghton Mifflin.
Fowler, M. and Bunck, J. M. (1996) 'What Constitutes the Sovereign State?' *Review of International Studies,* 22 (4): 381–404.
Frank, RH. (1985) *Choosing the Right Pond: Human Behavior and the Quest for Status,* New York: O. U. P.
Frank, R. H. (2001) *Luxury Fever: Money and Happiness in an Era of Excess*, New York: Simon & Schuster.
Frankel, B. and Cohen, A. (eds.) (1991) *Opaque Nuclear Proliferation: Methodological and Policy Implications,* London: Routledge.
Fraser, N. and Honneth, A. (2003) *Redistribution or Recognition? A Political-Philosophical Exchange,* London: Verso Books.
Frey, K. (2004) 'Elite Perception and Biased Strategic Policy-Making: The Case of India's Nuclear Build-up' Inaugural Dissertation, Ruprecht-Karls-Universität Heidelberg.
Frow, J. (2003) 'The Uses of Terror and the Limits of Cultural Studies', *Symploke*, 11(1–2): 69–76.
Fukuyama, F. (1992) *The End of the History and the Last Man*, London: Hamish Hamilton.
Gabbard, G. (1993) 'On Hate in Love Relationships: The Narcissism of Minor Differences Revisited', *Psychoanalytic Quarterly,* 62.
Gaddis, J.-L. (1986) 'The Long Peace: Elements of Stability in the Postwar International System', *International Security,* 10 (4).
- (1987) *The Long Peace; Inquiries into the history of the cold war*, New York: Oxford University Press.
- (1998) *We now know*, Oxford: Oxford University Press.
- (2004) *Surprise, Security and the American Experience*, Harvard: Harvard University Press.
Gaertner, S. (2000) *Reducing Intergroup Bias: The Common Ingroup Identity Model,* Philadelphia: Psychology Press.
Gallup Poll. 8th–10th February and 19th–21st August 2002; 13th–16th September and December 10–1, 2002, Accessed May 2006 www.gallup.com/home.aspx
Galtung, J. (1969) 'Violence, Peace and Peace Research', *Journal of Peace Research,* 6.
Ganguly, S. and Hagerty, D. (2006) *Fearful Symmetry: India-Pakistan Crises in the Shadow of Nuclear Weapons*, Seattle: University of Washington Press.
Ganser, D. 'Retour sur la crise des missiles à Cuba', *Le Monde Diplomatique*, Novembre 2002.
Garthoff, R. L. (1987) *Reflections on the Cuban Missile Crisis*, Washington DC: The Brooking Institution.
Garver, J. W. (2000) *Face Off: China, the United States, and Taiwan's Democratization*, Seattle: University of Washington Press.
Geertz, C. (1973) *The Interpretation of Cultures*, New York: Basic Books.
Geiss, I. (1967) *July 14: The Outbreak of the First World War*, New York: Scribner.
- (1990) *Der lange Weg in die Katastrophe. Die Vorgeschichte des Ersten Weltkrieges 1815–1914*, Munich: Piper.
Geller, D. S. and Singer, J. (1998) *Nations at War*, Cambridge: C. U. P.
Gellner, E. (1983) *Nations and Nationalism*, Ithaca: Cornell University Press.
Gelpi, C., Feaver, P. D. and Reifler, J. (2005) 'Success Matters; Casualty Sensitivity and the War in Iraq', *International Security,* 30 (3): 7–46
Gelpi, C. (1997) 'Democratic Diversions: Governmental Structure and the Externalization of Domestic Conflict', *Journal of Conflict Resolution*, 255–282.
- (2003) *The Power of Legitimacy; Assessing the Role of Norms in Crisis Bargaining,* Princeton: Princeton University Press,
George, A. (1979) 'Case Studies and Theory Development: The Method of Structured, Focused Comparison' in Lauren, P.-G. *Diplomacy; New Approaches in History, Theory, and Policy,* New York: The Free Press, pp. 43–68.
George, A. and Benett, A. (2005) *Case Studies and Theory Development in the Social Sciences,* Cambridge: The MIT Press.
George, A. and Smoke, R. (1974) *Deterrence in American Foreign Policy*, New York: Columbia

University Press.
George, A. L. and Bennett, A. (2005) *Case Studies and Theory Development in the Social Sciences*, Cambridge: The MIT Press.
Geva, N., and Sirin, C.V. (2008) 'Reactions to International Terror: Thematic Relevance of Negative Affect', paper prepared for presentation at the Annual Meeting of the *International Studies Association*, San Francisco, March 26–29, 2008.
Geva, N., and Skorick, M. J. (2006) 'The Emotional Calculus of Foreign Policy Decisions: Getting Emotions Out of the Closet' in Redlawsk, D. (2006) *Feeling Politics: Emotion in Political Information Processing*, New York: Palgrave Macmillan.
Ghaith, S. A. (2001) 'Al-Qa'ida Statement ' in Rubin, B. and Rubin, J. C. (eds.) (2002) *Anti-American Terrorism and the Middle East: A Documentary Reader*, New York: Oxford University Press.
Giddens, A. (1990) *The Consequences of Modernity*, Stanford: Stanford University Press.
Giesen, B. (1999) *Kollektive Identität. Die Intellektuellen und die Nation 2: 2, Kollektive Identität*, Frankfurt am Main: Suhrkamp.
Giesen, K.-G. (1992) *L'éthique des relations internationales*, Bruxelles: Bruylant.
Gilpin, R. (1981) *War and Change in World Politics*, Cambridge: C. U. P.; (1989) 'The Theory of Hegemonic War' in Rotberg, R. and Rabb, *The Origin and Prevention of Major Wars*, Cambridge: Cambridge University Press, pp. 15–37.
Girault, R. and Frank, R. (1998) *Turbulente Europe et nouveaux mondes 1914–1941*, Paris: Payot.
Glaser, C. (2004) 'When Are Arms Races Dangerous?: Rational Versus Suboptimal Arming' *International Security*, 28 (4).
Goebel, S. (2007)) *The Great War and Medieval Memory: War, Remembrance and Medievalism in Britain and Germany, 1914–1940*, Cambridge: Cambridge University Press.
Goffman, E. (1969) *Asiles*, Paris: Editions de Minuit.
– (1973) *La mise en scène de la vie quotidienne*, Paris: Les Editions de Minuit.
– (1974) *Les rites d'interaction*, Paris: Editions de Minuit.
– (1999) *The Presentation of Self in Every Day Life*, New York, Peter Smith Inc.
Golomstock, I. (1991) *L'Art totalitaire. Union soviétique, IIIe Reich, Italie fasciste, Chine*, Paris: Editions Carré.
Gould, R. V. (2003) *Collision of Wills: How Ambiguity about Social Rank Breeds Conflict*, Chicago: University of Chicago Press.
Greenhill, B. (2008) 'Recognition and Collective Identity Formation in International Politics', *European Journal of International Relations*, 14 (2).
Grosser, P. (1999) *Temps de la Guerre froide*, Editions Complexe, Paris.
– (2001) *Guerres et crises au 20e siècle*, Paris: Hachette.
Gudykunst, W. B. and Ting-Toomey, S. (1988) *Culture and Interpersonal Communication*. Newbury Park: Sage.
Guerdon, J. (1970) 'La guerre éclair d'Israël', *Historia*, 283.
Guibernau, M. (1999) *Nations without States: Political Communities in a Global Age*, Cambridge: Polity.
Gurr, T. (1970) *Why Men Rebel*, Princeton: Princeton University Press.
– (2000) *Peoples versus States: Minorities at Risk in the New Century*, Washington DC: US Institute of Peace.
Guzzini, S. (2005) 'Multilateralism and Power', Conference at the I.e.,P. of Bordeaux.
Guzzini, S. and Leander, A. (eds.) (2005) *Constructivism and International Relations. Alexander Wendt and his critics*, London: Routledge.
Gympel, J. and Nothias, J.-M. (2005) *Histoire de l'architecture; De l'antiquité à nos jours*, Paris: Palaces des Victoires.
Haacke, J. (2005) 'The Frankfurt School and International Relations: On the Centrality of Recognition.' *Review of International Studies*, 31 (1): 181–194.
Haddad, S. (2003) 'Le retour à la communauté des nations ou la stratégie américaine de la Libye', *L'Annuaire de l'Afrique du Nord*, 41: 173–88.
– (2004) 'La Libye et l'Occident depuis 1999; entre tropisme américain et ancrage euro-méditerranéen', *Afrique Contemporaine*, 209.
Haine, J.-Y. (2000) 'Débat, la crise des missiles de Cuba', in Haine, J.-Y. *Cultures et Conflits*, Paris: L'Harmattan.
Hamerow, S. (1966) *Restoration, Revolution, Reaction: Economics and Politics in Germany*,

*1815–1871*, Princeton: Princeton University Press.
Hamilton, F. and Herwig, H. (2004) *Decisions For War, 1914–1917*, New York: Cambridge University Press.
Haslam, S. A., Turner, C. and McGarty, C. 'Salient group memberships and persuasion: The role of social identity in the validation of beliefs' in Nye, J. and Brower, A. (1996) *What's Social about Social Cognition?: Research on Socially Shared Cognition in Small Groups*, London: Sage Publications, Inc.
Hassner, P. (1995) *La violence et la paix; De la bombe atomique au nettoyage ethnique*, Paris: Ed. Esprit.
– (1999) 'Le barbare et le bourgeois', *Politique internationale*, 84.
Hassner, P. and Vaïsse, J. (2003) *Washington et le reste du monde. Dilemmes d'une superpuissance*, Paris: Autrement.
– (2003) 'Ascension ou déclin de la puissance américaine', *Questions Internationales*, 3.
Hassrick, B. (1964) *Sioux: Life and Customs of a Warrior Society*, Norman: University of Oklahoma Press.
Hayne, M. B. (1993) *The French Foreign Office and the Origins of the First World War, 1898-1914*, Oxford: Clarendon Press.
Hazan, P. (1989) *La guerre de Six Jours: La victoire empoisonnée*, Bruxelles: Editions Complexe.
Hegel, G. W. F. (1973) *Phänomenologie des Geistes*, Paris: Frankfurt a.M.
– (1979) *Phenomenology of Spirit*. Oxford: Oxford University Press, USA; (1991) *Elements of the Philosophy of Right*, Cambridge: Cambridge University Press.
Heinemann, U. (1983) *Die verdrängte Niederlage*, Göttingen: Vandenhoeck & Ruprecht.
Heins, V. (2006) 'Internationale Hilfe: Umverteilung oder Anerkennung?', *WestEnd: Neue Zeitschrift für Sozialforschung*, 3 (2): 126–36.
Heins, V. (2008) *Nongovernmental Organizations in International Society; Struggles over recogniton*, London: Palgrave Macmillan.
Herberg Rothe, A. (2007) *Clausewitz's Puzzle; The Political Theory of War*, Cambridge: Cambridge University Press.
Herrmann, G. (1996) *The Arming of Europe and the Making of the First World War*, Princeton: Princeton University Press.
Herwig, H. (1987) 'Clio Deceived: Patriotic Self-Censorship in Germany after the Great War' *International Security*, 12 (2): 5–44.
– (1991) 'The German Reaction to the Dreadnought Revolution', *International History Review*, 13 (2): 221–283.
Herz, H. (1950) 'Idealist Internationalism and the Security Dilemma.' *World Politics*, 2 (2).
Hildebrand, K. (1976) 'Hitler's War Aims', The Journal of Modern History, 48 (3): 522–530.
Hipp, H. and Seidl, E. (1996) *Architektur als politische Kultur*, Berlin: Reimer Verlag.
Hobbes, T. (1996) *Leviathan*, Cambridge: Cambridge University Press.
– (1991) *Man and Citizen: De Homine and De Cive*, Indianapolis: Hackett Publishing Company.
Hobsbawm, E. (1992) *Introduction: Inventing Traditions*, in Hobsbawm, E. and Ranger, T. Cambridge: Cambridge University Press.
Holbo, P.-S. (1967) *Isolationism and Interventionism, 1932–1941*, Chicago: Rand McNally/Company.
Holborn, H. (1964) 'Origins and Political Character of Nazi Ideology', *Political Science Quarterly*, 79.
Holsti, K. J. (1991) *Peace and War; Armed Conflicts and International Order 1648–1989*, Cambridge: CUP.
Honneth, A. (1991) *The Critique of Power; Reflective Stages in a Critical Social Theory*, Cambridge, MA : The MIT Press
– (1992) *Kampf um Anerkennung*, Frankfurt a.M.: Surkamp.
– (1996) *The Struggle for Recognition*, London: The MIT Press.
– (1997) 'Recognition and Moral Obligation' *Social Research*, 64 (1): 16–34.
– (2006) *La société du mépris,* Paris: La découverte.
– (2010) 'Recognition between States: On the Moral Substrate of International Relations' , in Lindemann, T. and Ringmar, E. (eds.) *The International Politics of Recognition*, Boulder: Paradigm.
Hopf, T. (1996) 'Russian Identity and Russian Foreign Policy in Estonia and Uzbekistan' in

Wallander, C. A and Wildermuth, A. (eds.) *The Sources Of Russian Foreign Policy After The Cold War*, Boulder: Westview Press.
- (1998) 'The Promise of Constructivism in International Relations Theory', *International Security*, 23 (1).
- (1999), *Understandings of Russian Foreign Policy*, Pennsylvania State University Press.
- (2002) *Social Construction of International Politics; Identities and Foreign Policies, Moscow 1955 and 1999*, Ithaca: Cornell University Press.

Horowitz, L. (1985) *Ethnic Groups in Conflict*, Berkeley: University of California Press.
Howard, M. (2002) 'What's in a Name?: How to Fight Terrorism.' *Foreign Affairs*, 81 (1): 8–13.
Howard, M. and Hunter, R. (1967) *Israel and the Arab World. The Crisis of 1967*, London: Institute for Strategic Studies.
Hsu, A. (2007) 'U.S. Official's Comments on Taiwan's Status Cause Uproar.' *Taiwan Journal*, 6th September, 2007.
Huang, Z. (2006) *The ROC's 2006 Report on Foreign Policy*, Taipei: Ministry of Foreign Affairs.
Huddy, L., Feldman, S. and Cassese, E. (2007) 'On the Distinct Political Effects of Anxiety and Anger' in Neuman, R., Marcus, W., MacKuen, M. and Crigler, A. (eds.) *The Affect Effect: Dynamics of Emotion in Political Thinking and Behavior*, Chicago: University Of Chicago Press.
Huizinga, J. (1971) *Homo Ludens*, Boston: Beacon Press.
Hume, D. (1986) [1739] *A Treatise of Human Nature*, Harmondsworth: Penguin.
Huntington, S. P. (1996) *The Clash of Civilizations and the Remaking of World Order*, New York: Simon & Schuster.
Huth, P. and Russett, B. (1993) 'General Deterrence Between Enduring Rivals – Testing 3 Competing Models', *American Political Science Review*, 87: 61–73.
Hymans, JE. (2006) *The Psychology of Nuclear Proliferation: Identity, Emotions and Foreign Policy*, Cambridge: Cambridge University Press.
Iggers, G. (1968) *The German Conception of History*, Middletown: Wesleyan University Press.
Ignatieff, M. (2001) 'It's a War – But It Doesn't Have to be Dirty', *The Guardian*, October 1, 2001.
Ikenberry, G. J. (1981) *After Victory*, New Jersey: Princeton University Press.
- (2001) *After Victory; Institutions, Strategic Restraint, And the Rebuilding of Order After Major Wars*, New Jersey: Princeton University Press.
- (2002) 'America's Imperial Ambition', *Foreign Affairs*, 81.
- (2002) (ed.) *America Unrivalled: The Future of the Balance of Power*, Ithaca: Cornell University Press.

Isbell, L. M., Ottati, V. C. and Burns, K. (2006) 'Affect and Politics: Effects on Judgment, Processing, and Information Seeking' in Redlawsk, D. (ed.) *Feeling Politics: Emotion in Political Information Processing*, New York: Palgrave Macmillan.
ISS, *The Military Balance 2009*, London: Routledge.
Jackson, T. P. and Ringmar, E. (eds.) (2010) *The State as Person in International Relations*, Leiden: Brill.
Janieson, K. H (2007) 'Justifying the War in Iraq; What the Bush Administration's Uses of Evidence Reveal', *Rhetoric and Public Affairs*, 10 (2): 249–74.
Janis, I. L. (1972) *Victims of Groupthink*, Boston: Houghton Mifflin.
Jeannesson, S. (2002) *La Guerre froide*, Paris: La Découverte.
Jeffrey W. (1997) 'Which Norms Matter?: Revisiting the "Failure" of Internationalism', *International Organization*, 51 (1): 31–63.
Jennings, F. (ed.) (1985) *The History and Culture of Iroquois Diplomacy: An Interdisciplinary Guide to the Treatises of the Six Nations and their League*, Syracuse: Syracuse University Press.
Jentleson, B. (1992) 'The Pretty Prudent Public', *International Studies Quarterly*, 36 (1): 4974.
Jepperson, R. L., Wendt, A. and Katzenstein, P. J. (1996) 'Norms, Identity and Culture' in Katzenstein, P. (1996) (ed.)
Jervis, R. (1976) *Perception and Misperception in International Politics*, Princeton University Press.
- (1978) 'Cooperation Under the Security Dilemma' *World Politics*, 30 (2).
- (1989) *The Meaning of the Nuclear Revolution: Statecraft and the Prospect of Armageddon*, Ithaca: Cornell University Press.

- (1998) 'War and Misperception', *Journal of Interdisciplinary History*, 18 (4): 675–700.
Jettleson, B.W. and Whystock, C. (2006) 'Who Won Libya?' *International Security*, 30 (3): 47–87.
Johnson, D. D. and. Tierney, D. (2004) 'Essence of Victory; Winning or Losing International Crises', *Security Studies* 13: 330–81.
Johnston, A. (2008) *Social States: China in International Institutions, 1980–2000*, Princeton: Princeton University Press.
Jones, D.M , Bremer S.A and Singer, J. D. (1996) 'Militarized Interstate Disputes 1816–1992', *Conflict Management and Peace Science*, 15 (2).
Joxe, A. (1990) *Le Cycle de la dissuasion*, Paris: La Découverte.
Kagan, D. (1995) *On the Origins of War and the Preservation of Peace*, New York: Doubleday.
Kahl, H. C. (1998) 'Constructing a Separate Peace: Constructive Collective Liberal Identity and Democratic Peace', *Security Studies*, 8 (2/3): 94–144.
Kahneman, D. and Tversky, A. (1979) 'Prospect Theory; An Analysis of Decision Under Risk', *Econometrica*, 47: 263–29.
Kan, S. (2007) *Taiwan: Major U.S. Arms Sales Since 1990*, Report to Congress. Washington D.C.: Committee on Foreign Affairs, Defense and Trade.
Kant, I. (1991) 'Perpetual Peace: A Philosophical Sketch' in Reiss, H. (ed.) *Kant: Political Writings*, Cambridge: Cambridge University Press.
Kantorowicz, H. (1997) *The King's Two Bodies*, Princeton: Princeton University Press.
Kaplan, M. A. (2005) *Systems and Process in International Politics*, Essex: ECPR.
Kaspi, A. (1994) in Winock, M. (ed.) *Les temps de la guerre froide*, Paris: Seuil.
Katzenstein, P. (1996) (ed.) *The Culture of National Security*, Ithaca: Cornell University Press.
Kaufman, C. (2004) 'Threat Inflation and the Failure of the Marketplace of Ideas', *International Security*, 29 (1): 5–48.
Keal, P. (2003) *European Conquest and the Rights of Indigenous Peoples*, Cambridge: Cambridge University Press.
Kedourie, E. (1993) *Nationalism*, Wiley-Blackwell.
Kelman, H.C. (ed.) (1965) 'Social-Psychological Approaches to the Study of International Relations: The Question of Relevance' in *International Behavior: A Social-Psychological Analysis*, 565–607.
- (1977) 'The Conditions, Criteria, and Dialectics of Human Dignity: A Transnational Perspective', *International Studies Quarterly*, 21: 529–552.
- (1990) 'Applying a human needs perspective to the practice of conflict resolution. The Israeli-Palestinian case', in Burton, J. (ed.) *Conflict; Human needs theory*, New York: St. Martin's Press.
- (1997) 'Negotiating National Identity and Self-Determination in Ethnic Conflicts: The Choice Between Pluralism and Ethnic Cleansing' *Negotiation Journal*, 13.
- (1997) 'Nationalism, Patriotism, and National Identity: Social-Psychological Dimensions', in Bar-Tal, D. and Staub, E. (eds) *Patriotism in the Lives of Individuals and Nations*, Chicago: Wadsworth Publishing.
- (2008) 'A Social-Psychological Approach to Conflict Analysis and Resolution' in Sandole, D. Byrne,S., Sandole-Staroste, I. and Senehi, J. (eds.) *Handbook of Conflict Analysis and Resolution*, London: Routledge.
- (2007) 'Social-Psychological Dimensions of International Conflict' in Zartman, W. (ed.) *Peacemaking in International Conflict: Methods and Techniques*, Washington D.C.: United States Institute of Peace.
Kelsen, H. (1941) 'Recognition in International Law: Theoretical Observations', *The American Journal of International Law*, 35 (4): 605–617.
Kennedy, P. (1970) 'Tirpitz, England and the Second Navy Law of 1900: A Strategical Critique', *Militärgeschichtliche Mitteilunger*, 2.
- (1988) *The Rise and Fall of Great Powers*, New York: Random House.
Kennedy, R. (1999) *Thirteen Days*, New York: Norton.
Keohane, R. O. (ed.) (1984) *After Hegemony; Cooperation and Discord in the World Economy*, New York: Princeton University Press.
- (1986) (ed.) *Neorealism and its Critics*. New York: Columbia University Press.
Kershaw, I. (1983) *Popular Opinion and Political Dissent in the Third Reich: Bavaria 1933–1945*, Oxford: Oxford University Press.

- (1987) *The Hitler Myth: Image and Reality in the Third Reich*, New York: Oxford University Press.
Keynes, J. M. and Bainville, J. (2002) *Les conséquences économiques de la paix, les conséquences politiques de la paix*, Paris: Gallimard.
Khosrokhavar, F. (2007) *Quand Al-Qaïda parle*, Paris: Points.
Khrushchev, N. K. (1971) *Khrushchev Remembers*, London: Strobe Talbott.
King, G. and Keohane, R. O. and Sidney, V. (1994) *Designing Social Inquiry*, New York: Princeton University Press.
Kippenberg, G. (2004) 'Einleitung' in Kippenberg, G. and Seidensticker, T. (eds.) *Terror im Dienste Gottes: Die 'Geistliche Anleitung' der Attentäter des 11th September 2001*, Frankfurt: Campus Verlag.
Kissinger, H. (1973) *A World Restored; Metternich, Castlereagh and the Problems of Peace, 1812–1822*, Boston: Houghton Mifflin.
- (1994) *Diplomacy*, New York: Simon and Schuster.
Klavenas, J.-L., Gelpi, C. and Reifler, J. (2006) 'Correspondance; Casualties, Polls and the Iraq War', *International Security*, 31 (2): 186–98.
Kleef, van. Dijk, van., Steinel, W. Harinck, F. and Beest, I. van. (2008) 'Anger in Social Conflict: Cross-Situational Comparisons and Suggestions for the Future' *Group Decision and Negotiation*, 17 (1): 13–30.
Klein, C. (1968) *Weimar*, Paris: Flammarion; (1999) 'Vingt ans de négociations sur le désarmement et la maîtrise des armements', *Politique étrangère*, 64.
Kochi, T. (2009) *The Other's War: Recognition and the Violence of Ethics*, London: Taylor and Francis.
Kocka, J. (1988) 'German History before Hitler: The Debate about the German Sonderweg.' *Journal of Contemporary History*, 23 (1): 3–16.
Kojève, A. (1980) [1947] *Introduction to the Reading of Hegel: Lectures on the Phenomenology of Spirit*, Ithaca: Cornell University Press.
Konstan, D. (2006) *Emotions of the Ancient Greeks: Studies in Aristotle and Classical Lit*, Toronto: Toronto University Press.
Koskenniemi, M. (1994) 'National Self-Determination Today: Problems of Legal Theory and Practice', *The International and Comparative Law Quarterly*, 43 (2): 241–269.
Koslowski, R. and Kratochwil, F. (1994) 'Understanding Change in International Politics: The Soviet Empire's Demise and the International System', *International Organization*, 48: 215–47.
Krasner, S. (1999) *Sovereignty: Organized Hypocrisy*, Princeton: Princeton University Press.
Kratochwil, F. (1987)'Rules, Norms, Values and the Limits of 'Rationality', *Archiv für Rechts- und Sozialphilosophie* 73: 301–21.
- (1989/1991) *Rules, norms and decisions*, Cambridge: Cambridge University Press.
- (1991) 'Is the ship of culture at sea returning?' in Kratochwil, F. and Lapid, Y. (1995) *The Return of Culture and Identity in IR Theory*, New York: Lynne Rienner.
Krieger, P. (1996) 'Spiegelnde Curtain Wall als Projektionsflächen für politische Schlagbilder', in Hipp and Seidel (1996) *Architektur als politische Kultur*.
Krüger, P. (1994) *Deutschland und die Reparationen, 1918/19*, Stuttgart: Deutsche Verlags-Anstalt.
Kugler, J. and Zagare, F. (1990) 'The Long-Term Stability of Deterrence', *International Interactions*, 15.
Kukathas, C. (1992) 'Are There Any Cultural Rights?', *Political Theory*, 20:1.
Kull, S. (2003) *Misperceptions, The Media and the Iraq War*, The PIPA Knowledge Networks Poll. Accessed Sept. 2003 www.knowledgenetworks.com/gam.
Kupchan, C. A. and Kupchan, G. (1995) 'The Promise of Collective Security', *International Security*, 20 (1).
Kurtulus, E. (2002) 'Sovereign Rights in International Relations: A Futile Search for Regulated or Regular State Behaviour', *Review of International Studies*, 28 (4): 759–777.
Kymlicka, W. (1989) *Liberalism, Community and Culture*, Oxford: Oxford University Press.
- (1997) *Multicultural Citizenship; A Liberal Theory of Minority Rights*, Oxford: Oxford University Press.
Lahwej, Y.-A. (1998) *Ideology and Power in Libyan Foreign Policy*, Department of Politics, University of Reading, UK, (unpublished thesis).
Laroche, J. (2005) *Canal + et les majors américaines*, Paris: L'Harmattan.

Larson, E. (1996) *Casualties and Consensus. The Historical Role of Casualties in Domestic Support for U.S. Military Operations*, Santa Monica, California: RAND.
Lascoumes, P. (1991) 'Le protocole, ou comment s'épargner la politesse', in Dhoquois, R. (1991) *La politesse*, Paris: Editions Autrement, pp. 118–29.
Laurent, E. (2004) *La Guerre des Bush*, Paris: Plon.
Lauterpacht, H. (1944)'Recognition of States in International Law.' *The Yale Law Journal*, 53 (3): 385–458.
Lavoy, R. (1995) 'The Strategic Consequences of Nuclear Proliferation.' *Security Studies*, 4 (4): 695–753.
Layne, C. (1994) "Kant or Cant'. The Myth of the Democratic Peace', *International Security*, 19 (2): 5–49.
Lebow, R.N. (1981) *Between Peace and War*, Baltimore: Hopkins J. University Press ; (1984) 'Windows of Opportunity. Do states jump through', *International Security*, 9 (1); (1996)'Play it again Pericles', *European Journal of International Relations*.
- *(1996) The Art of Bargaining*, Baltimore: John Hopkins University Press.
- (2008) *A Cultural Theory of International Relations*, Cambridge: C. U. P.
Lebow, R. N. and Risse-Kappen, T. (eds.) (1995) *International Relations Theory and the End of the Cold War*, New York: Columbia University Press.
Lebow, R. N. and Stein, J. (1987) 'Beyond Deterrence', *Journal of Social Issues* 43 (4): 155–170.
- (1994) *We all lost the Cold War*, New Jersey, Princeton University Press.
- (1998), 'Nuclear lessons of the Cold War', in Booth, K. *Statecraft and Security*, Cambridge University Press, p. 71–86.
Lee, Teng-hui (1999) *Taiwan's Proposals*, Taipei: Yuanliu Publishing Housing.
- (1995) *What the People Want is Always in My Heart*, Taipei: Office of the President.
Lefebvre, R. and Sawicki, F. (2006) *La société des socialistes*, Bellecombe-en Bauges: Editions du Croquant, 2006.
Lefranc, S. (2002) *La politique du pardon*, Paris: PUF.
Lemann, N. 'Remember the Alamo', *New Yorker*, 18 October 2004.
Lentin, A. (2006) 'A Comment' in Boemeke, M., Feldman, G. and Elisabeth Glaser (eds.), *The Treaty of Versailles: A Reassessment After 75 Years*, Cambridge: Cambridge University Press.
Lerner, J. S., and Keltner, D. (2000) 'Beyond Valence: Toward a Model of Emotion-Specific Influences on Judgement and Choice', *Cognition & Emotion*, 14 (4): 473–493.
- (2001) 'Fear, Anger, and Risk.' *Journal of Personality and Social Psychology*, 81 (1): 146159.
Lesaffer, R. (ed.) (2004) *Peace Treaties and International Law in European History: From the Late Middle Ages to World War One*, New York: Cambridge University Press.
Levitt, M. (2006) *Hamas: Politics, Charity, and Terrorism in the Service of Jihad*. New Haven: Yale University Press.
Levy, J (1983) 'Misperception and the Causes of War: Theoretical Linkages and Analytical Problems', *World Politics*, 36 (1): 76–99.
(1989) 'Domestic Politics and War', in Rotberg, R. and Rabb, T. (eds.), *The Origin and Prevention of Majors Wars*, Cambridge: Cambridge University Press.
(1990) 'Preferences, Constraints, and Choices in July 1914' International Security, 15 (3).
(1996) 'Contending Theories of International Conflict', in Crocker, C. and Hampson, R. O. *Managing Global Chaos*, Washington: US Institute of Peace Press.
Levy, J. and Thompson W. S. (2005) 'Hegemonic Threats and Great Power Balancing in Europe, 1495–1999' *Security Studies*, 14: 1–33.
- (2010) *Causes of War*, London: Wiley-Blackwell.
Lewis, W. H. (2001) 'U.S.-Libya Relations: a new chapter?' *Bulletin, The Atlantic Council of the United States*, 12 (4).
Lieber, A. (2007) 'The New History of World War I and What It Means for International Relations Theory' *International Security*, 32 (2): 155–191.
Lindblom, E. (1997) *Politics and Markets: The World's Political Economic Systems*, New York: Basic Books.
Lindemann, T. (2001) *Les doctrines darwiniennes et la guerre de 14*, Paris: Economica.
- (2008) *Penser la guerre: L'apport constructiviste*, Paris: L'Harmattan.
- (2010) *War for Recognition*, Colchester: ECPR Press.

Lindemann, T. and Ringmar, E. (eds.) (2010) *The International Politics of Recognition*, New York: Paradigm.
Lindner, E. G., (2001) *Traumatology*, 7 (1).
Linklater, A. (1998) *The Transformation of Political Community: Ethical Foundations of the Post-Westphalian Community*, Cambridge: Polity.
Livy, T. (2002) *The Early History of Rome*, Harmondsworth: Penguin Classics.
Long, W. J. (2003) *War and Reconciliation*, London: MIT Press;
Longhorne, R. (1986) 'Reflections on the Significance of the Congress of Vienna', *Review of International Studies*, 12 (4): 314.
– Jervis, R. (1985) 'From Balance to Concert. A Study of International Security Cooperation', *World Politics*, 38 (1).
Lundestad, G. (2005) *The United States and Western Europe since 1945*, Oxford University Press, pp. 27–63.
Lynn-Jones, S. -M. and Miller, S. and Van Evera, S. (eds.) (1990) *Nuclear Diplomacy and Crisis Management*, Cambridge Massachusetts: MIT.
MacMillan, M. (2001) *Paris 1919: Six Months That Changed the World*, New York: Random House Trade.
Maier, C. (1988) 'Wargames: 1914–1919' *Journal of Interdisciplinary History*, 18 (4): 581–90.
Maier, C. E (2007) *Among Empires*, Harvard: Harvard University Press.
Maitland, W. (1900) 'Translator's Introduction' in *Political Theories of the Middle Age*, vii-xlv., Cambridge: Cambridge University Pres.
Mann, T. (1987) *Reflections of a Nonpolitical Man*, New York: Ungar.
Mansfield, E.D. and Snyder, J. (2007), *Electing to Fight. Why Emerging Democracies Go to War*, Cambridge, Mass.: The MIT Press.
Mansfield, S. (1982) *The Gestalts of War: An Inquiry into Its Origins and Meanings as a Social Institution*, New York: Dial Press.
Maoz, Z, and. Russett, B. (1993) 'Normative and Structural Causes of Democratic Peace, 1946–1986' *American Political Science Review*, 624–638.
Mapel, R., and Nardin, T. (eds.) (1999) *International Society: Diverse Ethical Perspectives*, Princeton: Princeton University Press.
Markell, P. (2003) *Bound by Recognition*, Princeton: Princeton University Press.
Markey, D. (1999) 'Prestige and the Origins of War', *Security Studies*, 8(4).
Marschall, M.G. (2005) 'Major Episodes of Political Violence 1946–2006'. Accessed http://members.aol.com/CSPmgm/warlist.htm
– (2005) Marshall, M.G. and T. R. Gurr, *Peace and Conflict*, Center for International Development and Conflict Management, University of Maryland, Accessed members.aol.com/cspmgm/Global Report 2007.pdf
Marshall, J. (1987) 'Worcester vs. the State of Georgia, 6 Peter 515 (U.S.S.C. 1832)' in *The Writings of John Marshall, Late Chief Justice of the United States, Upon the Federal Constitution*, Littleton: F.B. Rothman Press.
Martinez, L. (2006) 'Libya. The Conversion of a Terrorist State', *Mediterranean Politics*, 111 (2): 151–65.
Marx, K, and Engels, F. (1972) 'On the Jewish Question' in *Collected Works*, New York: International Publishers, 1972.
Maslow, A. (1973) *Dominance, Self-Esteem, Self-Actualization*, Monterey: Calif. Brooks
Mattingly, G. (1988) *Renaissance Diplomacy*, Mineola: Dover Publications.
Mauss, M. (1991) 'Essai sur le don', in Mauss, M. *Sociologie et Anthropologie*, Paris: PUF.
– (2007) *Essai sur le don*, Paris: PUF.
May, E. and Zelikov, P. (2000) *The Kennedy Tapes*, New York: Norton.
McNamara, R. 'The Miracle of October: Lessons from the Cuba Missile Crisis', Accessed June 2007 www.watsoninstitue.org/Cuba/OctMiracle.pdf
Mead, G. H. (1963) *L'esprit, le soi et la société,* Paris: PUF, (translation of *Mind, Self and Society*, 1934).
Mearsheimer, J. J. (2001) *The Tragedy of Great Powers*, New York: Norton.
Meinecke, F. (1997) *Machiavellism: The Doctrine of Raison D'Etat and its Place in Modern History*, New Brunswick: Transaction Publishers.
Melandri, P. (1994) in Winock, M. *L'Histoire, Le Temps de la guerre froide*, Paris: Seuil.
Melvin, J. (2002) *Comprendre l'architecture*, Paris: Editions de l'Organisation
Mercer, J. (1996) *Reputation and International Politics*. Ithaca, NY: Cornell University Press.

- (2009) *Reputation and International Politics,* Ithaca: Cornell University Press.
Midlarsky, I. (1975) *On War: Political Violence in the International System,* New York: Free Press.
Milbank, D. and Allen, M. 'Iraq flap shakes Rice's Image ', *Washington Post,* 27 July 2003.
Miller, D.T. (2001) 'Disrespect and the Experience of Injustice' *Annual Review of Psychology,* 52 (1): 527–553.
Millner, B. (2007), *States, Nations and the Great Powers. The Sources of Regional War and Peace,* Cambridge: CUP.
Milza, P. (1996) *Les relations internationales 1945–1973,* Paris: Hachette.
Miscamble, WD. (1978) 'Anthony Eden and the Truman-Molotov conversations, April 1945', *Diplomatic History,* 2 (2).
- (2007) *From Roosevelt to Truman Potsdam. Hiroshima, and the Cold War,* Cambridge: Cambridge University Press;
Mitzen, J. (2006) 'Ontological Security in World Politics', *European Journal of International Relations,* 12(3): 341–370.
Modelski, G. (1978) 'The Long Cycle of Global Politics and the Nation-State' *Comparative Studies in Society and History,* 20 (2): 214–235.
Mombauer, A. (2005) *Helmuth von Moltke and the Origins of the First World War,* Cambridge: Cambridge University Press.
Mommsen, H. (1996) *The Rise and Fall of Weimar Democracy,* Chapel Hill: University of North Carolina Press.
- (2006) 'Max Weber and the Peace Treaty of Versailles' in Boemeke, M., Feldman, G. and Glaser, E. (eds.) *The Treaty of Versailles: A Reassessment After 75 Years,* Cambridge: Cambridge University Press.
Monnet, S. (2000) *La Politique extérieure de la France depuis 1870,* Paris: Armand Colin.
Monnier, G. (2001) *Histoire de l'architecture,* Paris: PUF.
Montesquieu, Baron de (1777) *De l'Esprit des Lois,* Paris: Garnier.
Moravcsik, A. (1997) 'Taking Preferences Seriously: a Liberal Theory of International Politics', *International Organization,* 51.
Morelli, M. (2000) *Splendeur des palais royaux,* Paris: Gründ.
Morgenthau, H. (1948 /1978) *Politics Among Nations,* New York: Knopf.
Morgenthau, H. and Thompson, K. (1985) *Politics Among Nations,* New York: McGraw-Hill.
Mosse, G. L. (2003) 'interview', in Cabanes, B. and Husson, H. (2003) *Les Sociétés en guerre 1911–1946,* Paris: Armand Colin, pp. 269–273.
Mosse, L. (1975) *The Nationalization of the Masses: Political Symbolism and Mass Movements in Germany from the Napoleonic Wars Through the Third Reich,* New York: Columbia University Press, 1975.
Müller, H. (2005) 'A Treaty in Troubled Waters: Reflections on the failed NPT Review Conference' *International Spectator,* 40 (3).
Mueller, J. (1973) *War, Presidents and Public Opinion,* New York: Wiley and Sons.
- (1989) *Retreat from Doomsday; The obsolescence of major war,* New York: Basic Books.
Muller, P. (2000) *Les politiques publiques,* Paris: PUF.
Mumford, L. (1972) *The City in History,* New York: Penguin.
Münkler, H. (2002) *Über den Krieg. Stationen der Kriegsgeschichte im Spiegel ihrer theoretischen Reflexion,* Weilerwist: Velbrück.
Murray, M. (2008) 'The Struggle for Recognition in International Politics: Security, Identity and the Quest for Power' Ph.D. dissertation, University of Chicago.
Nancy, J. -L. (2000) *Being Singular Plural,* Stanford: Stanford University Press.
Nandy, A. (1992) *Traditions, Tyranny and Utopias: Essays in the Politics of Awareness.* New Delhi: Oxford University Press.
National Intelligence Estimate, *Key Judgements. Iraq's Continuing Programs for Weapons of Mass Destruction,* Washington D.C., Oct. 2002.
Neilson, K. (2006) *Britain, Soviet Russia and the Collapse of the Versailles Order, 1919–1939,* New York: Cambridge University Press, pp. 43–88.
Neumann, I.B. (1998) 'Identity and the outbreak of war: or why the Copenhagen School of Security Studies should include the idea of 'violation' in its framework of analysis', *The International Journal of Peace Studies,* 3 (1); (1999) *Uses of the Other: "The East" in European Identity Formation,* Minneapolis: University of Minnesota Press

Nicholson, H. G. (1970) *The Congress of Vienna: a study in allied unity, 1812–1822*, New York: Harcourt, Bruce and Company.
Nieburg, H. L. (1969) *Political Violence: The Behavioral Process*, New York: St. Martin's.
Nipperdey, T. (1969) 'Nationalidee und Nationaldenkmal in 19. Jahrhundert', *Historische Zeitschrift*, 106: 529–585.
Nye, J. (1988) 'Old Wars and Future Wars: Causation and Prevention', *Journal of Interdisciplinary History*, 18 (4); (2002) *The Paradox of American Power: Why the world's superpower can't go it alone*, Oxford University Press.
– (2007) 'Just Don't Mention the War on Terrorism' *International Herald Tribune*, February 8, 2007.
Offer, A. (1995)'Going to War in 1914: A Matter of Honor?' *Politics and Society*, 23 (2).
O'Neill, B. (2004) *Honor, Symbols and War*, Ann Arbor: Michigan University Press.
Oppenheim, L. (1912) *International Law, a Treatise*, Vol.1, London: Longmans.
Oren, M. (2002) *Six Days of War*, Oxford: Oxford University Press.
Organski, A. F. K. and Kugler J. (1980) *The War Ledger*, Chicago: Chicago University Press.
Orgel, S. (1995) *The Illusion of Power: Political Theater in the English Renaissance*, Berkeley: University of California Press.
Osgood, C. E. (1962) *An Alternative to War and Surrender*, Urbana: University of Illinois Press.
Osiander, A. (2001) 'Sovereignty, International Relations and the Westphalian Myth', *International Organization*, 55 (2): 251–287.
Owen, J. W. (1994) 'How Liberalism Produces Democratic Peace', *International Security*, 19 (2): 87–125.
Pagden, A. (1995) *Lords of All the World*, New Haven: Yale University Press.
Parekh, B. (2000) *Rethinking Multiculturalism: Cultural Diversity and Political Theory*, London: Macmillan.
Paul, T.V. (2000) *Power Versus Prudence: Why Nations Forgo Nuclear Weapons*, Montreal: McGill-Queen's University Press.
Paul, T.V., Wirtz, J. and Fortmann, M. (eds.) (2004) *Balance of Power: Theory and Practice in the twenty first century*, Stanford: Stanford University Press.
Peel, Q., Graham, R., Harding, J. and Dempsey, J. 'How the US set a Course for War with Iraq', *Financial Times*, 26 May 2003.
Perkovich, G. (1999) *India's Nuclear Bomb: The Impact on Global Proliferation*, Berkeley: University of California Press.
Perrin, D. (2004)'La politique juridique extérieure de la Libye', in Pliez, O. *La nouvelle Libye. Sociétés, espaces et géopolitique au lendemain de l'embargo*, Paris: Karthala, pp. 21–42.
Petsch, J. (1977) *Architektur und Gesellschaft. Zur der deutschen Architektur im 19. und 20, Jahrhundert*, Köln/Wien.
Phillips, A. (1991) *Engendering Democracy*, Philadelphia: University of Pennsylvania State Press.
Pious, R. (2001) 'The Cuban Missile Crisis and the Limits of Crisis Management', *Political Science Quarterly*, p. 85.
Pizzorno, A. (1986) 'Some Other Kind of Otherness' in Foxley, A. (ed.) *Development. Democracy and the Art of Trespassing: Essays in Honor of Albert Hirschman*, Notre Dame: University of Notre Dame Press.
– (1990) 'Considérations sur les théories des mouvements sociaux', *Politix*, 9.
– (2000) *Identité et action collective*. Interview in Cabin, P and Dortier, J.-F. *La sociologie. Histoire et idées*, Paris: Editions Sciences Humaines, pp. 135–146.
Plato (1962) *La République*, Book II, Paris, Gonthier.
Platow, M., Wenzel, J. and Nolan, M. (2003) 'The Importance of Social Identity and Self-Categorization Processes for Creating and Responding to Fairness' in Haslam, S., van Knippenberg, S, Platow, M. J. and Ellemers, N. (eds.) 'Social Identity at Work: Developing Theory for Organizational Practice', *Psychology Press*.
Plessner, H. (1959) *Die verspätete Nation*, Stuttgart: Kohlhammer.
Pocock, G. A. (2005) *The Discovery of Islands: Essay in British History*, Cambridge: Cambridge University Press.
Poirrier, P. (ed. (2006), *Art et pouvoir*, Paris: CNDP.
Polity IV Project 2005. Political Regime Characteristics and Transitions. College Park, University of Maryland. Accessed December 2008 www.bsos.umd.edu/cidcm/inscr/

polity/index.htm (www.cidcm.umd.edu/mar/assessment.asp?groupId=14501)
Pond, E. (2003) *Friendly Fire: The Near-Death of the Transatlantic Alliance*, Washington D.C.: Brookings Institution Press.
Posen, B. (1984) *The Sources of Military Doctrine*, Ithaca: Cornell University Press.
Pouliot V. (2010*)* *International Security in Practice; The Politics of NATO-Russia Diplomacy*, Cambridge: Cambridge University Press.
Powaski, R. E. (1991) *Toward an Entangling Alliance. American Isolationism, and Europe, 1901–1950*, New York: Greenwood Press, pp. 27–56.
Powell, C. (2001) 'Press Briefing on Route to Cairo, Egypt', Accessed 23 February 2001 www.state.gov/secretary/rm/2001/931.html
Price, R. (1997) *The Chemical Weapons Taboo*, Ithaca: Cornell University Press;
Prozorov, S. (2004) 'Three Theses on 'Governance' and the Political', *Journal of International Relations and Development*, 7 (3): 267–293.
– (2005) 'X/Xs: Towards a General Theory of the Exception', *Alternatives*, 30 (1): 81–112.
Puhle, H. -J. (1972) *Von der Agrarkrise zum Präfaschismus*, Zabern.
Qian, Q. (2003) *Ten Stories of a Diplomat*, Beijing: World Affairs Press.
Rawls, J. (1999) *The Law of Peoples*, Cambridge: Harvard University Press.
Razoux, P. (2003) *La guerre des 6 jours*, Paris: Economica.
Reichel, P. (1996) 'Berlin nach 1945 – eine Erinnerungslandschaft zwischen Gedächtnis-Verlust und Gedächtnis-Inzenierung', in Hipp and Seidl *Architektur und politische Kultur*, pp. 273–296.
Reiss, M. (1995) *Bridled Ambition: Why Countries Constrain Their Nuclear Capabilities*, Baltimore: Johns Hopkins University Press.
Remond, R. (2002) *Le XXe siècle de 1914 à nos jours*, Paris: Seuil.
Renault, E. (2004) *L'expérience de l'injustice. Reconnaissance et clinique de l'injustice*, Paris: La Découverte.
Renouvin, P. (1994) *Histoire des Relations internationales*, Paris: Hachette.
Rich, N. (1973) *Hitler's War Aims, Volume I: Ideology, the Nazi State, and the Course of Expansi*, New York: W. W. Norton.
Ringmar, E. (1996) *Identity, interest and action a cultural explanation of Sweden's intervention in the thirty years' war*, London: Cambridge University Press;.
– (1996) 'On the Ontological Status of the State' *European Journal of International Relations*, 2 (4): 439–466
– (2002) 'The Recognition Game: Soviet Russia Against the West', *Cooperation & Conflict*, 37 (2): 115–36
– (2006) 'Liberal Barbarism and the Oriental Sublime: The European Destruction of the Emperor's Summer Palace', *Millennium*, 34 (3): 917–33.
Risse, T. (2000) "Let's Argue'. Communicative Action in World Politics'*, International Organization*, 54 (1): 1–39.
Risse-Kappen, T. (1995) 'Democratic Peace; Warlike Democracies?', *European Journal of International Relations* 1 (4): 491–517.
Ritter, G. (1956 *The Schliefen Plan: Critique of a Myth*, New York: Praeger, 1956.
Ritter, S. (2002) *War on Iraq*, New York: Context Books.
Roberts, N. (2009) 'Recognition, Power, and Agency' *Political Theory* 37 (2): 296–309.
Robin, C. (2004) *Fear: The History of a Political Idea*, Oxford: Oxford University Press, 2004.
Roche, J. -J. (2005) *Relations Internationales*, Paris: L.G.D.J.
Rohl, J. (1973) *1914 Delusion Or Design?: The Testimony of Two German Diplomats*, London: St. Martin's/Marek.
Rolo, P. J. V. (1969) *Entente Cordiale: The Origins and Negotiation of the Anglo-French Agreements of 8 April 1904*, London: Macmillan.
Romberg, D. (2003) *Rein in at the Brink of the Precipice: American Policy Toward Taiwan and US-PRC Relations*, Washington D.C.: The Henry L. Stimson Center.
Rook,S. (2000) *Appeasement in International Relations*, The University Press of Kentucky.
Rosecrance, R. N. (1986) *The Rise of the Trading State*, New York: Basic Books.
Rosen, S. (2005) *War and Human Nature*, Princeton: Princeton University Press.
Rosenberg, M. (2003) *Nonviolent Communication*, New York: Puddle Dancer Press.
Rothe, A. H. (2007) *Clausewitz's Puzzle*, Cambridge University Press.

Rubin, D., Barry, F. and Rubin, J.-C. (eds.) (2002) *Anti-American Terrorism and the Middle East: A Documentary Reader*, New York: Oxford University Press.
Ruggie, J.-G. (1998) 'What makes the World hang together? Neo-utilitarianism and Social Constructivist Challenge', *International Organization*, 52 (4).
Ruloff, D. (2003) *Wie Kriege beginnen. Ursachen und Formen*, München: Becksche Reihe.
Ruskin, J. (1999) *The Lamp of beauty. Writings on art*, London: Phaidon.
Russett, M. (1993) *Grasping the Democratic Peace: Principles for a Post-Cold War World*, Princeton: Princeton University Press.
Sadler, A. L. (2009) *Japanese Architecture; A Short History*, New York: Tuttle Publishing.
Sagan, D. (1991) '1914 Revisited: Allies, Offense and Instability' in *Military Strategy and the Origins of the First World War*, Princeton: Princeton University Press.
Sagan, Scott D. (2004) 'Realist Perspectives on Ethical Norms and Weapons of Mass Destruction', in Hashmi, S. and Lee, P. (eds.) *Ethics and Weapons of Mass Destruction: Religious and Secular Perspectives*, Cambridge: Cambridge University Press.
– (2003) 'The Perils of Proliferation' in Waltz, K. and Sagan, S. (eds.) *The Spread of Nuclear Weapons: A Debate Renewed*, New York: W.W. Norton.
Saif Aleslam al Qadhafi, (2003) 'Libyan-American Relations', *Middle East Policy Council Journal*, 10 (1).
Satow, E. M. (1917) *A Guide to Diplomatic Practice*, London: Longmans, Green, & Co.
Sauer, T. (2006) 'The Nuclear Nonproliferation Regime in Crisis' *Peace Review*, 18 (3).
Saurel, L. (1968) *Hitler; L'Agonie et la chute*, Paris: Editions Rouff.
– (1968) *Hitler. La lutte pour le pouvoir*, Paris: L'Histoire.
Saurette, P. (2006) 'You Dissin Me? Humiliation and Post 9/11 Politics', *Review of International Studies*, 32(3): 495–522.
Scheff, J. (1994) *Bloody Revenge: Emotions, Nationalism, and War*, Boulder: Westview Press.
Schelling, T. (1960) *Strategy of Conflict*, Harvard: Harvard University Press.
Schimmelfennig, F. (2004) *The EU, NATO and the Integration of Europe: Rules and Rhetoric*, Cambridge: Cambridge University Press.
Schivelbusch, W. (2004) *The Culture of Defeat: On National Trauma, Mourning, and Recovery*, London: Picador.
Schmitt, E.-E. (2003), *La part de l'autre*, Paris: Le Livre de poche.
Schmitt, K. (1991) *Der Begriff des Politischen. Text von 1932 mit einem Vorwort und drei Corrolarien*, Berlin: Duncker & Humblot.
– (1995) *Theorie des Partisanen. Zwischenbemerkung zum Begriff des Politischen*, Berlin: Duncker & Humblot.
Schoenbaum, D. (1966) *Hitler's Social Revolution: Class and Status in Nazi Germany, 1933–1939*, Garden City: Doubleday.
Schroeder, P. (1992) 'Did the Vienna Settlement Rest on the Balance of Power?', American Political Science Review, 97 (3): 683–706.
– (1994) *The Transformation of European Politics 1763–1848*, New York: Oxford University Press.
– (1996) *The Transformation of European Politics 1763–1848*, Oxford University Press.
Schumacher, T. L. (1991) *Surface and Symbol; Giuseppe Terrangi and the Architecture of Italian Rationalism*, New York/London.
Schwabe, K. (2006) 'Germany's Peace Aims and the Domestic and International Constraints', in Boemeke, F., Feldman, G. and Glaser, E. (eds.) *The Treaty of Versailles: A Reassessment After 75 Years*, Cambridge: Cambridge University Press.
Schweigler, G. L. (1975) *National Consciousness in Divided Germany*, London: Beverly Hills, Calif: Sage Publications.
Schweller, L. (2008) *Unanswered Threats: Political Constraints on the Balance of Power*, Princeton: Princeton University Press.
Scott, L. and Smith, S. (1994) 'Lessons of October; Historians, Political Scientists, Policy-makers and the Cuban Missile Crisis', *International Affairs*, 70 (4): 2.
Seiler, B. (1966) "Dolchstoss' und 'Dolchstosslegende'.' *Zeitschrift für Deutsche Sprache*, 22: 1–20.
Seligman, B. (1995) *The Idea of Civil Society*. Princeton: Princeton University Press.
Serfaty, S. (1986) *La Politique étrangère des Etats-Unis de Truman à Reagan*, Paris: PUF.
Shakespeare, W. (2003) *As You Like It*, London: Chelsea House Publications.

Sheer, R. (2006) 'Now He Tells Us'. Accessed 4th April 2009, www.alternet.org/world/34861
Shepsle, K. A. and Bonchek, M. S.(1997) *Analyzing Politics, Rationality, Behaviour, and Institutions*, New York: W. W. Norton and Co.
Shotter, J. (1989) 'Social Accountability and the Social Construction of "You"' in Shotter, J. and Gergen, J. (eds.) *Texts of Identity*, Thousand Oaks: Sage Publications.
Simons, J. (2000) 'Modernist Misapprehensions of Foucault's Aesthetics', *Cultural Values*, 4 (1): 40–57.
Simpson, G. (2004) *Great Powers and Outlaw States. Unequal Sovereigns in the International Legal Order*, Cambridge: Cambridge University Press.
Sindjoun, L. and Vennesson, P. (2000) 'Unipolarité et integration régionale. L'Afrique du Sud et la 'renaissance africaine'', *Revue Française de Science Politique*, 50(6): 883–940.
SIPRI Yearbook 2004, Oxford University Press.
SIPRI Yearbook 2009, Oxford University Press 2009.
Skinner, Q. (1989) 'The State' in Ball, T., Farr, J. and Hanson, R. (eds.) *Political Innovation and Conceptual Change*, Cambridge: Cambridge University Press.
– (1996) *Reason and Rhetoric in the Philosophy of Hobbes*, Cambridge: Cambridge University Press.
Skocpol, T. (1979) *States and Social Revolution. A Comparative Analysis of France, Russia and China*, Cambridge: Cambridge University Press.
Small, R., and Singer, D. (1981) *Resort to arms*, Beverly Hills/London: Sage Publications;
Smith, B. (1989) *Hegel's Critique of Liberalism*, Chicago: The University of Chicago Press.
Smith, H. J., Tyler, T. R. and Huo, Y. (2003) 'Interpersonal Treatment, Social Identity and Organizational Behavior' in Haslam, S. L., Knippenberg, D. van, Platow, M. J. and Ellemers, N. (eds.) *Social Identity at Work: Developing Theory for Organizational Practice*, Psychology Press.
Smith, H. J., Tyler, T. R., Huo, Y. J., Dortiz, J. and Lind E. A. (1998) 'The Self-Relevant Implications of the Group-Value Model: Group Membership, Self-Worth, and Treatment Quality' *Journal of Experimental Social Psychology*, 34 (5): 470–493.
Snyder, J. (1984) *The Ideology of the Offensive: Military Decision Making and the Disasters of 1914*, Ithaca: Cornell University Press.
– (2000) *From Voting to Violence: Democratization and Nationalist Conflict*, New York: W. W. Norton & Co.
Snyder, J. and Jervis, R. (1999) 'Civil War and the Security Dilemma' in Walter, B. and Snyder, J. (eds.) *Civil Wars, Insecurity, and Intervention*, New York: Columbia University Press.
Sobek, D. (2009) *The Causes of War*, Cambridge: Polity.
Sofsky, W. (1996) *Traktat über die Gewalt*, Frankfurt: Fischer.
– (2002) *Zeiten des Schrecken*, Frankfurt: Fischer.
Sommier, I. (2000) *Le Terrorisme*, Paris: Flammarion.
Sorensen, T. (1966) *Kennedy*, Paris: Gallimard.
Sorokin, P. (1997) 'Social and Cultural Dynamics; Fluctuations of Social Relationships', in *War and Revolution*, New York and Boston: American Books.
Soutou, G.-H. (2001) *La Guerre de cinquante ans*, Paris: Fayard.
Speer, A. (1970) *Inside the Third Reich*, London: Macmillan.
Spengler, O. (1939) *The Decline of the West*, New York: A.A. Knopf.
Stadelmann, R. (1948) 'Die Epoche der deutsch-englischen Flottenrivalität' in *Deutschland und Westeuropa*, Wurttemberg: Lauphein.
Stahel, D. (2009) *Operation Barbarossa and Germany's Defeat in the East*, Cambridge: Cambridge University Press.
Staley, E. (1932) 'Mannesmann Mining Interests and the Franco-German Conflict over Morocco', *Journal of Political Economy*, 40 (1).
Stein, J. (1991) 'Arab-Israeli War of 1967; Inadvertent War through miscalculated escalation', in George, A. L. *Avoiding War; Problems of Crisis Management*, Boulder: Col: Westview Press, pp. 140–142;
– (1991) 'Reassurance in International Conflict Management', *Political Science Quarterly*, 106 (3): 431–51.
– (2008) 'Foreign Policy Decision-Making: Rational, Psychological, and Neurological Models' in Smith, S., Hadfield, A. and Dunne, T. (eds.) *Foreign Policy: Theories, Actors, Cases*, New York: Oxford University Press.

Steinberg, B. (1996) *Shame and Humiliation: Presidential Decision-Making on Vietnam*, Montreal: McGill-Queens.
Steinberg, J. (1966) 'The Copenhagen Complex' in Laqueur, W. and Mosse, G. L., *The Coming of the First World War*, New York: Harper & Row;
– (1965) *Yesterday's Deterrent: Tirpitz and the Birth of the German Battle Fleet*, London: Macdonald.
Stern, P. C. (1995) 'Why Do People Sacrifice for Their Nations?' *Political Psychology*, 16 (2) pp. 217–235.
Stern, Paul C. et al. (2000) (eds.) *International Conflict Resolution after the Cold War*. Washington: National Academy Press.
Stern, R. (1992) *The Failure of Illiberalism*. New York: Columbia University Press.
Stevenson, D. (1996) *Armaments and the Coming of War: Europe, 1904–1914*, Oxford: Oxford University Press
– (1997) 'Militarization and Diplomacy in Europe before 1914', *International Security*, 22 (1).
– (2006) 'French War Aims and Peace Planning' in Manfred F., Boemeke, F. and Glaser, E. (eds.) *The Treaty of Versailles: A Reassessment After 75 Years*, Cambridge: Cambridge University Press.
Stewart, D. B. (2003) *The Making of a Modern Japanese Architecture*, New York: Kodansha International.
Stoessinger, J. (2000) *Why Nations go to War*, Belmont, C. A: Wadsworth Publishing.
Stokesbury, L. (1981) *A Short History of World War I*, New York: Harper.
Stone, C. H. and Crisp, R. J. (2007) 'Superordinate and Subgroup Identification as Predictors of Intergroup Evaluation in Common In-group Contexts', *Group Processes & Intergroup Relations*, 10 (4).
Stöver, B. (1996) *Berichte über die Lage in Deutschland*, Bonn: Dietz Verlag J.H.W. Nachf.
Su, Chi. (2003) *Brinkmanship: From Two-States-Theory to One-Country-on-Each-Side*, Taipei: Bookzone.
Suskind, R. (2004) *The Price of Loyalty; George W. Bush, the White House, and the Education of Paul O'Neill*, Paris: Simon/Schuster.
Szabo, F. (2004) *Parting Ways: The Crisis in German-American Relations*, Washington D.C.: Brookings Institution Press.
Tabory, E. (1978) 'The Attribution of Peaceful Intentions to the Visit of Sadat to Jerusalem and Subsequent Implication for Peace', *Journal of Peace Research*, 15 (2):193–95.
Tabouis, G. (1958) *20 Ans de suspens diplomatique*, Paris: Albin Michel.
Tahfel, H. and Turner, J. (1978) 'An Integrative Theory of Intergroup Conflict' in Austin, W. and Worchel, S. (eds.) *Social Psychology of Intergroup Relations*, Monterey: Brooks/Cole.
– (1986) 'The Social Identity Theory of Intergroup Behaviour' in Worchel, S. and Austin, W. (eds.) *Psychology of Intergroup Relations*, Chicago: Nelson-Hall.
Tang, S. (2004) 'Reputation, Cult of Reputation, and International Conflict' *Security Studies*, 14 (1): 34–62.
Tannenwald, N. (1999) 'The Nuclear Taboo: The United States and the Normative Basis of Nuclear Non-Use', *International Organization*, 53 (3):433–68.
– (2005) 'Stigmatizing the Bomb; Origins of the Nuclear Taboo', *International Security*, 29 (4).
– (2008) *The United States and the Non-Use of Nuclear Weapons Since 1945*, Cambridge: Cambridge University Press.
Taylor, C. (1992) *Multiculturalisme*, Paris: Flammarion.
– (1994) 'Politics of Recognition' in Guttman, A. (ed.) *Multiculturalism: Examining the politics of recognition*, Princeton: Princeton University Press.
Taylor, J. (2000) *Generalissimo's Son: Chiang Ching-kuo and the Revolutions in China and Taiwan*, Cambridge: Harvard University Press.
Taylor, J. -P. (1946) *The Course of German History*, London: Hamilton.
Terray, E. (1999) *Clausewitz*, Paris: Fayard.
Tetlock, E. (1998) 'Social Psychology and World Politics' in Gilbert, D., Fiske, S. and Lindzey, G. (eds.) *The Handbook of Social Psychology*, New York: Oxford University Press.
Thies, J. (1982) *Architekt der Weltherrschaft. Die Endziele Hitlers*, Munich, DVA.
Thomas, H. (2006) *La Traite des noirs 1440–1870*, Paris: Robert Laffont.
Thomas, W. (2001) *The Ethics of Destruction*, Ithaca: Cornell University Press.

Thompson, W. (1988) *On Global War*, Columbia: University of South Carolina Press.
Thucydides (2000) *La guerre du Péloponnèse*, Paris: Folio, livre 5.
Tickner, A. (1996) 'Identity in International Relations Theory: Feminist Perspectives' in Lapid, Y. and Kratochwil, F. (eds.) *The Return of Culture and Identity in IR Theory*, Boulder: Lynne Rienner.
Tiffin, H., Griffiths, G. and Ashcroft, B. (2000) *Post-Colonial Studies: The Key Concepts*, London: Routledge.
Tilly, C. (2003) *The Politics of Collective Violence*, Cambridge: Cambridge University Press.
Ting-Tooney, S. (1990) *A Face Negotiation Perspective Communication for Peace*, London: Sage.
Tocqueville, A. de. (2002) *Democracy in America*, Chicago: University of Chicago Press.
Tod, E. (2002) *Après l'Empire. Essai sur la décomposition du système américain*, Paris: Gallimard.
Todorov, T. (1984) *The Conquest of America: The Question of Other*, New York: Harper.
Touvaal, S. (1996) 'Case Study: Lessons of Preventive diplomacy in Yugoslavia' in Crocker, C., Hampson, F. and All, P. (eds.) *Managing Global Chaos*, Washington, D.C: United States Institute of Peace Press, pp. 403–418.
Trachtenberg, M. (1990) 'The Meaning of Mobilization in 1914', *International Security*, 15 (3).
Tuck, R. (1999) *The Rights of War and Peace: Political Thought and International Order from Grotius to Kant*, Oxford: Oxford University Press.
Tully, J. (2004) 'Approaches to Recognition, Power, and Dialogue' *Political Theory*, 32: 855–862.
- (1955) *Strange Multiplicity: Constitutionalism in an Age of Diversity*, Cambridge: Cambridge University Press.
Turner, A. (1989) *Geißel des Jahrhunderts: Hitler und seine Hinterlassenschaft*, Berlin: Siedler Verlag.
Turner, C., Hogg, M.A., Oakes, P. J., Reicher, S. D. and Wetherell, M. S. (1987) *Rediscovering the Social Group: A Self-categorization Theory*, New York: Blackwell Publishers.
Tyler, T. R., and Blader, S. L. (2000) *Cooperation in Groups: Procedural Justice, Social Identity, and Behavioral Engagement*. Philadelphia: Psychology Press.
- (2001) 'Identity and Cooperative Behavior in Groups', *Group Processes & Intergroup Relations*, 4 (3).
Van Evera, S. (1985) 'Why Cooperation Failed in 1914', *World Politics*, 38 (1): 80–117.
- (1994) 'Hypotheses on Nationalism and War', *International Security*, 18 (4): 5–39.
- (1997) *Guide to Methods for Students in Political Science*, Ithaca, New Jersey: Cornell University Press.
- (1999) *Causes of War*, Ithaca: Cornell University Press.
Varian, H. R. (2005) *Intermediate Microeconomics*, Berkeley: University of California.
Vasquez, J. A. (1993), *The War Puzzle*, Cambridge: Cambridge University Press
Vattel, E. de. (2001) *Le droit des gens, ou Principes de la loi naturelle appliqués à la conduite et aux affaires des nations et des souverains*, Paris: Adamant Media Corporation.
Veblen, T. (1953) *The Theory of the Leisure Class*, New York: Mentor.
Venesson, P. (2000) 'Bombarder pour convaincre? Puissance aérienne, rationalité limitée et diplomatie coercitive au Kosovo', *Culture et Conflits*, 37: 23–59.
- (2006) 'Identité' in Smouts, M. -C., Battistella, D., Venesson, P., *Dictionnaire des relations internationales*, Paris: Dalloz.
- (2008) 'Case studies and process tracing: theories and practices' in Della Porta, D. and Keating, M. (eds.) *Approaches and Methodologies in the Social Sciences*, Cambridge: Cambridge University Press.
Vertzberger, Y. (1998) *Risk Taking and Decision Making: Foreign Military Intervention Decisions*, Stanford: Stanford University Press.
von Reikhoff, H. (1971) *German-Polish Relations, 1918–1933*, Baltimore: Johns Hopkins University Press.
Waever, O. (1995) 'Securization and Desecurization' in Lipschutz, R. (ed.) *On Security*, New York: Columbia University Press.
Walker, R. B. J. (1992) *Inside/Outside: International Relations as Political Theory*, Cambridge: Cambridge University Press.
Walter, F. (2001) *Committing to Peace: The Successful Settlement of Civil Wars*, Princeton: Princeton University Press.

Waltz, K. (1979) *Theory of International Politics*, Reading Mass: Addison-Wesley.
- (2003) 'The Spread of Nuclear Weapons: More May Be Better' in Waltz, K. and Sagan, S. (eds.) *The Spread of Nuclear Weapons: A Debate Renewed*, New York: W. W. Norton.
Walzel, F. (2007) *Die Anfänge deutscher Außenpolitik in der Weimarer Republik – Ulrich Graf von Brockdorff-Rantzau und der Streit um die deutsche Kriegsschuld in Versailles*, Berne: Lang.
Walzer, M. (1994) *Thick and Thin: Moral Argument at Home and Abroad*. Notre Dame: University of Notre Dame Press.
Weber, C. (1998) 'Performative States', *Millennium*, 27 (1): 77–95.
Weber, E. (1976) *Peasants into Frenchmen: The Modernization of Rural France, 1870–1914*. Stanford: Stanford University Press.
Weber, M. (1971) *Economie et société*, Paris: Plon.
- (2002) *Le Politique et le savant*, Paris: Plon.
Wedeen, L. (2002) 'Conceptualizing Culture: Possibilities for Political Science', *American Political Science Review*, 96 (4).
Wehler, H-U. (1977) *Deutsche Geschichte: Das Deutsche Kaiserreich 1871–1918*, Bk. 9, Göttingen: Vandenhoeck & Ruprecht.
Wei, Min. (1993) *The Bilateral Diplomacy of the ROC*. Taipei: Yeqiang Publishing House.
Weinberg, G. L. (1970) *The Foreign Policy of Hitler's Germany: Diplomatic Revolution in Europe 1933–36*, Chicago: University of Chicago Press.
Welch; D. A. (1995) *Justice and the Genesis of War*, Cambridge: Cambridge University Press
- (2001) *Propaganda and the German Cinema 1933–1945*, Oxford: Clarendon Press.
Wendt, A. (1994) 'Collective Identity Formation and the International State System', *American Political Science Review*, 88 (2).
- (1992) 'Anarchy is what states make of it', *International Organizations*, 46 (2).
- (1999) *Social Theory of International Politics*, Cambridge: Cambridge University Press.
- (2003) 'Why a World State is Inevitable', *European Journal of International Relations*, 9 (4).
- (2004) 'The State as Person in International Theory', *Review of International Studies*, 30 (2): 289–316.
Wendt, A. and Friedheim, D.V. (1995) 'Hierarchy under anarchy. Informal Empire and the East German State', *International Organization*, 49 (4): 689–721.
White, M. (2001) *The Kennedys and Cuba*, New York: Ivan R. Dee
White, R. (1991) *The Middle Ground: Indians, Empires, and Republics in the Great Lakes Region, 1650–1815*, New York : Cambridge University Press.
Wieseman, C. (2000) *Twentieth-Century American Architecture. The Buildings and their Makers*, New York: Norton and Company.
Wieviorka, M. (2005) *La Violence*, Paris: Hachette.
Wight, C. 'State Agency: Social Action Without Human Activity?' *Review of International Studies*, 30 (2): 269–280.
Wihaib, H. R. (2004) *Dans l'ombre de Saddam Hussein. Les révélations inimaginables de son chef du protocole*, Paris: Michel Lafon.
Williams, A. (1999) *Linking Arms Together. American Indian Treaty Visions of Law and Peace, 1600–1800*, London: Routledge.
Williamson, R., and May, E. (2007) 'An Identity of Opinion: Historians and July 1914.' *Journal of Modern History*, 79 (2): 335–387.
Winkler, H. (2000) *Der lange Weg nach Westen*, Munich: C. H. Beck.
- (2002) *The Long Shadow of the Reich: Weighing Up German History: the 2001 Annual Lecture*, London: German Historical Institute.
Wittgenstein, L. (2001) *On Certainty*, New York: Harper.
- (1991) *Philosophical Investigations*, Oxford: Blackwell.
Wohlforth, W. (1999) 'The Stability of a Unipolar World', *International Security*, 24 (1): 5–41.
Wolf, R. (2008) 'Respekt ein unterschätzter Faktor in den Internationalen Beziehungen', *Zeitschrift für Internationale Beziehungen*, 1: 5–42.
- (2009) 'Unipolarity, Status Competition, and Great Power War.' *World Politics*, 61 (1): 28–57.
- (2010) 'Prickly States?: Recognition and Disrespect between Persons and Peoples',

in Lindemann, T. and Ringmar, E. (eds.) *The International Politics of Recognition*, Boulder: Paradigm
Woodward, B. (2003) *Bush s'en va-t-en guerre,* Paris: Denoël.
– (2004) *Plan d'attaque*, Paris: Folio.
Worchel, S. (2003) 'Come One, Come All: Toward Understanding the Process of Collective Behavior' in Hogg, M. and Cooper, J. (eds) *The Sage Handbook of Social Psychology*, Sage Publications Ltd.
Wright, R. (1994) *The Moral Animal: Why We Are The Way We Are: The New Science of Evolutionary Psychology*, New York: Pantheon.
Yates, R. (2006) 'Song Empire: The World's First Superpower?' in Tetlock, P. and Lebow, R-N. and Parker, N (eds.) *Unmaking the West*, Ann Arbor: University of Michigan Press.
Yergin, D. (1977) *La Paix saccagée*, Paris: Complexe.
Yetiv, S. -A. (2004) *Explaining Foreign Policy,* Baltimore: John Hopkins University Press.
Yuen Foong Khong, (1992) *Analogies at War: Korea, Munich, Dien Bien Phu, and the Vietnam Decisions of 1965*, Princeton: Princeton University Press.
Zehfus, M., Guzzini, S. and Leander, A. (2006) 'Wendts constructivism: a relentless quest for synthesis' in *Constructivism and its critics,* New York: Routledge.
Zehfuss, M. (2002) *Constructivism in International Relation: The Politics of Reality*, Cambridge: Cambridge University Press.
Zizek, S. (2002) *Welcome to the Desert of the Real: Five Essays on 11th September and Related Dates*, London: Verso.
Zuber, T. (2002) *Inventing the Schlieffen Plan: German War Planning 1871–1914*, Oxford: Oxford University Press.
(1999) 'The Schlieffen Plan Reconsidered.' *War in History* 6 (3).
Zubok, V. and Pleshakov, C. (1996) *Inside the Kremin's cold war*, Harvard: Harvard University Press.
Zuo, Y. (2009) *Taiwan's Identity Evolution since the 1940s and its Impact on the Cross Taiwan Strait Relationship*. PhD dissertation, University of Bristol.

# index

Acheson, D. 78
Adler, E. 22, 35, 131 n.59
Afghanistan 30
  Taliban regime 30, 36, 42, 48, 61, 92, 94
  US involvement in 5 30, 34, 36
  USSR and 34
Ahmadinejad, M. 29, 33, 48, 85, 130
Aix-la-Chapelle (1818) 55
Al Qaeda 103, 130
Albin, C. 41
Alexander I 54
Allende, S. 61
Allison, G. 87, 116
Alsace-Lorraine 56
Algeria 4, 61, 106, 121
Allan, P. 24, 25, 38, 39
Alliance of the Three Emperors (1873) 55
anarchy 22
  Hobbesian 36
  Kantian 21
Anderson, B. 35
Annan, K, 110
Aoun, E. 9
architecture, governmental 3, 42, 50, 52–4, 58, 59, 81–2
  as indicator of self image 81, 82, 83
  classical 53, 67
  forms of 50
  hubristic identities and 50, 81
  messianic ideologies and 73–4
  state superiority and 32–3, 43
Arendt, H. 28
Armitage, R. 101
Aron, R. 15, 17, 33, 41, 47
Auriol, V. 59
Austria 27, 54–5, 57
  Congress of Vienna 80, 82
  Nazi invasion of 72 n.13
Austro-German War (1866) 52

Austro-Hungarian Empire 53, 54–5, 56, 57
authoritarian regimes 32, 48, 61
autonomy, confirmation of 92

Badie, B. 4
Bainville, J. 71
balance of power, theory of 5, 48
Baldwin, D. 87
Bar-Zohar, M. 99, 105, 106
Barnett, M. 35, 131 n.59
Barry, Sir C. 53
Bartelson, J. 38
Battistella, D. 5, 15 n.1, n.2, 23 n.18, 30, 55, 73, 74, 78
Bauhaus 59
Baumeister, R. F. 32
Beck, A. T. 16
Benett, A. 49 n.2, 96, 97
Berlin 35, 115
  architecture in 53
  Blockade (1948/49) 34, 50, 74, 81
  Congress of (1878) 57
  Cuban Missile Crisis and 60
  Nazi architecture in 65–6
Berstein, S. 54, 69
Bially Mattern, J. 22, 24, 27, 36, 88 n.2, 90
Biermann, V. 67
Biersteker, T. 40
Bigo, D. 23, 131 n.58, 132 n.63
Bin Laden, Osama 3, 5, 30, 122
Bismarck, O. van 54, 56, 57–8
Blainey, G. 1
Blair, T. 101
Blanchard, C. 115
Blättler, S. 42
Blix, H. 102, 109, 110, 111
Blore, E. 53
Bohlen, C. 77
Boltanski, L. 2, 13, 15

160 | causes of war

Bonaparte, N. 3, 33, 52
Borngässer, B. 67
Boudon, R. 21 n.14
Boulding, K. 18
Bourdieu, P. 2, 11
Bracher, K. D. 70
Braud, P. 2, 9, 12, 18, 24, 28 n.27, 36, 126, 134 n.64
Bremer, S. 50 n.3, 79, 80 n.20
Bretton Woods 60
Briand, A. 69, 70, 73
British Guinea 61
Brown, P. 91, 92
Buckingham Palace 53
Bukovansky, M. 34, 35
Bull, H. 36, 38, 40, 41, 52
Bundy, G. M. 119, 125
Burton, J. 24, 25, 26, 90
Bush, G. 102, 103, 108
Bush, G. W. 4, 9, 19, 20, 27, 47, 49, 61, 64, 84, 102, 103, 109, 111–12, 123–4, 131, 134
Bushman, B. J. 32
Buzan, B. 23

Cadier, D. 23
Caillé, A. 2, 14, 37
Canada 22
Carr, H. 47, 51, 52
Cashman, G. 103, 111, 112, 128
Castlereagh, Lord 54, 55
Castro, F. 113, 120
Ceausescu, N. 32
Chad 61
Chamberlain, N. 72
Chaumont, Treaty of (1814) 52, 55
Che Guevara, E. 120, 126
Cheney, D. 101, 110, 111
Chevallier-Bellet, B. 124
Chile 2, 61
China 81, 82, 83, 84, 85, 94, 95, 114, 134
  Libya and 115
  Mao's era 39, 40, 70, 74
    architectural styles of 74
  Taiwan Crises and 34, 78, 96
  United Nations and 78
Chirot, D. 33
Churchill, W. 63, 75, 77, 79

Clausewitz, C. Von 15–17, 29
Clemenceau, G. 63, 68, 69
Cleveland, G. 62
Clinton, B. 27, 49, 64
Cohen, A. 20 n.12
Cold War (1945–53) 5, 41, 52, 60, 61, 64, 73, 84, 85, 91, 102, 123
  armed conflicts during 81
  messianic ideologies of 73, 74, 76–7
  origins of 77, 78
Coleman, J. S. 21 n.14
collective security, system of 56, 71
Colonomos, A. 85
'commercial liberalism' 48
Congress of Berlin (1878) 57
Congress of Carlsbad (1819) 55
Congress of Troppa (1820) 55
Congress of Verona 55
Congress of Vienna (1815–1853) 5, 32, 35, 49, 52–3, 55, 56, 80, 82
  armed conflicts and 79–80
  collective security, system of and 56
  exclusion from 84
Copeland, D. 48
Cornette, J. 57
Correlates of War Project 29, 50, 80 n.20
Crimean War (1853–56) 52, 80 n.20
crisis, concept of 5, 88
Cuba 114
Cuban Missile Crisis (1962) 6, 20, 41, 60, 79, 87, 88, 92, 93, 95, 96, 98, 112, 117–20, 125, 126, 132
  role of deterrent factor in 92, 116
Cullon, S. 62
Czechoslovakia 27, 72, 81 n.21

Daalder, I. H. 101, 108, 109, 111
Danner, M. 110
Davis, J. W. 94
Dayan, M. 99
de Gaulle, C. 18, 107
De la justification; Les économies de la grandeur 13
Dean, J. 33
Dehio, L. 47
democracies, nature of 20–1, 58, 130
  leadership and 21
democratic peace theory 58, 60, 61,

62, 131
  alternative explanations to 61–4
  armed conflicts, number of 79–80
  deterrence, policy of 1, 39, 88–9, 92, 94, 95–7, 106, 119, 120 133
    effects of 95
    limits of 89
    psychological approaches 1–2
    'pure' 94, 95
    realist explanations of 1, 73
Devin, G. 36, 49
dictatorships 2, 20, 64, 122
dignity 37–8, 39, 40
  equal, recognition of 55, 126
  politics of 91
  war for 43, 87, 131
distinction, quest for 11
Dobrynin, A. 118, 120, 125
Doran, C. 9, 83, 131, 132 n..61
Drazen, A. 21 n.15

Eban, A. 107
Egypt 48, 63, 89, 92, 96, 97, 115, 126
  Israel, relations with 30, 36
    Six Days War (1967) 6, 19, 30, 87, 98–101, 104–7, 127
  Suez Crisis 36
Ehrman, J. 64
Einsel, W. 17 n.5
Einstein, A. 23
Eisenhower, D. D. 36, 79
El Baradei, M. 122
Elias, N. 13, 40
Elman, C. 49 n.2
emotions, politics and 12 n.1, 19–20
empathy 41–2, 87, 90
  recognition through 127
Enderlain, C. 98, 100
Eshkol, L. 98, 104, 104, 124
Essai sur le don 11
Ethridge, M. 77
European Union 50, 51, 58, 60, 63, 68
exclusion 13–14, 31, 40, 42, 43, 47, 49, 51, 60, 71, 73, 124
  International Order 84
  League of Nations and 84

Falkland War (1982) 29–30
Favre, P. 29

Fayazmanesh, S. 85
Fearon, J. D. 1, 128 n.49
Fendius, M. 49 n.2
Finland 61
Foch, Marshall 69
Fontaine, A. 77
France 37, 55, 57, 63, 80, 81, 82, 83, 107
  architectural styles 32, 53, 59, 67, 74
    Elysée Palace 59
    Versailles, Palace of 56
  Charles X 53
  Great Britain and 63
  Louis XVIII 53
  Louis XIV 3, 56, 57
  Napoleon Bonaparte 3, 33, 52, 56
  Napoleon III 56
  national identity of 18
  political leadership and 20 n. 12
  Ruhr crisis (1923) 62, 69
  Second Republic 56
  Treaty of Paris (1815) 55
  Weimar Republic, attitude to 68
  World War II 18
    Action Française 69
    interwar period 68, 69, 70, 71, 82
Franco-German war (1870/1) 18, 52
Frank, R. H. 68, 70, 71
Franks, T. 109
French Revolution 35, 41, 54
Freud, S. 12
Friedheim, D. V. 23
Fukuyama, F. 32

G7 85
Gabbard, G. O. 25
Gaddis, J.-L. 60, 63, 73, 79, 114
Galtung, J. 12
Garthoff, R. L. 114
GATT 60
Gautier, C. 36
Geiss, I. 55, 57, 62
Gelpi, C. 88 n.2, 103
George, A. 49 n.2, 96, 97
Georgia 4
  2008 conflict with Russia 4, 31, 96
German Confederation 57
Germany 29, 55, 56, 57, 80, 81, 82, 83
  architectural styles 58, 59

Nazi era 50, 65
Federal Republic 2, 29, 58, 59, 60
interwar period 64–70
Marshall Plan 60
National Socialism 2–3, 9–10, 23, 29, 30, 32, 33, 58, 64–6, 71–3, 88, 131–2
  state identity and 23, 31, 32, 42, 64, 70, 72, 92, 131–2
  World War II and 39, 43, 48, 63, 64–5, 67–70, 72, 73, 94
  see also Hitler, A.
Ruhr crisis (1923) 62, 69, 81 n.21
Weimar Republic 29, 39, 62, 63, 67, 73
Wilhelm II, Empire of 3, 33, 39, 62, 97
  see also Berlin; German Confederation; Prussia
Giddens, A. 24
Gilbert, C. 67
Gilpin, R. 1, 47
Girault, R. 68, 70, 71
Giscard d'Estaing, V. 58
globalisation 4, 92
Goffman, E. 2, 5, 9, 13–14, 24, 89
Golomstock, I. 74
Gorbachev, M. 24
Göring, H. 73
Great Britain 34, 47, 53, 55, 56, 62, 80, 81, 82, 83,
  architectural styles 53, 59, 67, 74
  British Guinea border dispute 61–2
  Egypt and Six-Day War (1967) 107
  France and 63, 68, 70
  interwar period 68, 70, 71
    Miner's Strike (1929) 71
  Iraq War (2003) 109
  19th Century hegemonic power of 56–7
    role identity in 57
  Russia and 63, 71
  Suez Crisis and 36
  US relations 34, 61–2
  World War II, events leading to 71, 73
    Poland and 73
Greece 55, 59, 74, 77, 77, 78, 80
Grosser, P. 71, 72, 76, 79, 114

Guerdon, J. 104, 105
Gurr, T. R. 36, 58
Gustavo Adolphus II 22
Guzzini, S. 2, 23 n..16, 34
Gympel, J. 53

Haas, R. N. 110
Hadaad, S. 121, 122, 123, 124,
Haine, J.-Y. 113, 114
Hamas 39
Harriman, A. 75 n.17, 77
Hassner, P. 12, 35, 64, 84
hatred 16, 43, 67
  recognition problematic and 16
Hazan, P. 100, 104, 105, 106, 107
Hegel, G. W. F. 33
hegemony 3, 5, 39, 51, 83, 84, 97, 133
  benevolent 47
  pacifying 47
  peace and 56, 57
  power and 47, 51–2, 55–6, 131
Heins, V. 17 n.8, n.9, 18 n.10
Herriot, E. 67, 71
Hildebrand, K. 64 n.11
Hipp, H. 53 n.5, 59 n.10
Hiroshima 48, 79, 80, 129 n.52
Hitler, A. 19, 32, 33, 34, 50, 64–5, 67–8, 69–70, 72–3, 94, 130
  architectural projects 65, 66
  Poland, attack on 50, 72–3
  racial ideology and 64–5, 71, 77, 94
  Reichskanzlei 50
  USSR and 67–8, 71
  World War II entry 72–3
Hobbes, T. 15, 61, 93
  Hobbesian anarchy 36
Holbo, P. S. 63
Holocaust 27, 93, 99, 104
Holsti, K. J. 3 n.10, 5
Holy Alliance 38, 54, 55
homo economicus 1, 87 127
homo politicus 1, 87, 127
homo symbolicus 1, 87, 127
Honneth, A. 2, 3, 5, 6, 9, 12–13, 17 n.8, 20 n. 13, 24, 25, 26, 30 n.28, 37, 49, 90
honour 2, 16, 30, 33, 37, 40, 47, 55, 56, 58, 65, 68, 87, 93, 120, 126, 128, 130, 131, 134

war for 15, 33, 34, 42, 43
World War II and 43, 65
Hopf, T. 49, 131 n.57
Hopkins, H. 75
humiliation 12, 17, 103, 106, 117, 128, 134
Hussein, King of Jordan 100, 104, 105
Hussein, S. 3, 4, 19, 26, 28, 29, 32, 33, 41, 42, 47, 95, 101–4, 108–112, 121, 122, 125, 126, 128, 130, 131, 132, 134

IAEA 4, 42, 101, 102, 110, 122, 127, 128, 131
identity dilemmas 50, 51
identity, national 22–4, 25–6, 27, 31, 40
  collective 12, 18, 20, 27, 31, 35, 54, 60
  'damaged' 24
  dignity and 9–10, 13, 27
  egalitarian 50
  'fragilisation' of 12
  hubristic 31, 32–3, 38, 48, 50, 52, 84, 131–2
  prestige and 18
  self-esteem and 25, 50
  shared 22, 35–6, 41, 43, 59, 64, 68, 127, 129, 131
  superiority, assertion of and 34
  violence and 12, 23, 27, 50
ideological heterogeneity 35, 67, 77
Ikenberry, G. 5, 49, 55, 56, 60
'imagined communities' 36
India, Pakistan and 36, 87
Indochina 61
Indonesia 48
institutional liberalism, theory of 49
interwar period (1919–1939) 52, 63, 64–71, 77
  architecture and 59
  armed conflicts within 81
Iran 3, 29, 33, 41, 47, 48, 74, 77, 85, 87, 115, 131, 134
  'Axis of Evil' 41, 131
  identity dilemma in 50
  Iraqi war 103
  nuclear weapons and 48
Iraq 29, 47, 49, 85, 97

'dignity' dynamics and 39–40
Kuwait annexation 36, 49, 93
1990 Crisis and War 87, 102
non-proliferation treaty, respect of and 41–2
September 11th reaction 96, 101, 102, 103, 108, 110, 125, 127
US relations 97, 101–4, 108–112, 124–5, 127
War (2003–) 4, 6, 19, 21, 27, 28, 29, 30, 34, 36, 37, 40, 42, 47, 88, 95, 98, 101–4, 108–112, 123
'hostility justification' and 101
WMD debate 101–2, 103, 109, 110–11, 127
see also Hussein, Saddam
Islamic terrorism 48
Israel
  Arab relations and 26, 34, 41, 74, 134
  deterrence policy 106
  Egypt, relations with 30, 89
  1967 Six-Day war 6, 19, 30, 87, 96, 97, 98–101, 104–7, 125, 126, 127
  identity recognition and 9, 27, 36, 94, 125, 126, 132
  Holocaust syndrome and 99, 126
  Palestinian relations 3, 26, 29 n.27, 40, 132 n.62
  2006 military operations 40
  US relations 123
Italy 55, 59
  architecture, Fascist period 66–7
  armed conflict and 80, 81, 82, 83
  interwar period 67, 70–1
  national identity of 64

Janieson, K. H. 103
Japan 58–9
  architectural styles 59, 66–7
  armed conflict and 80, 81, 82, 83
  interwar period 64, 66–7, 70
  Manchuria, invasion of 64
  national identity 64
  nuclear attacks on 78
  World War 11 78, 79, 117
Jeannesson, S. 74, 75, 77, 79, 80
Jentleson, B. 103

Jefferson, T. 59, 63, 74
Jervis, R. 52, 87, 88, 89, 94, 128
Jones, D. M. 50 n.3
Joxe, A. 48

Kabyle society 11
Kamel, H. 102
Kant, I. 12
  Kantian 'anarchy' 21, 35, 61
Kaplan, M. A. 58, 68 n.12
Kaspi, A. 77
Katzenstein, P. 22, 88
Kaufman, C, 103
Kay, D. 102, 109
Keitel, W. 73
Keller, A. 25, 38, 39
Kellogg-Briand Pact 70
Kelman, H. C. 25
Kennan, G. 77
Kennedy, J. F. 20, 60, 92, 93, 95, 113, 114, 116, 117, 118, 119, 120, 124, 125, 126, 127, 132
Kennedy, R. 20, 117, 118, 120, 125
Kenzo, T. 59
Keohane, R. O. 49, 50
Keynes, J. M. 71
Khrushchev, N. 20, 76, 92, 95, 112–14, 116, 117–20, 124, 125, 126
Kim Jong-Il 19, 41, 130
King, G. 50
Kissinger, H. 41, 52, 54, 55, 56, 57, 62, 102, 112
Klein, C. 69, 70
Kojève, A. 2
Korea, North 3, 22, 34, 40, 47, 48, 76, 78, 80, 123, 131, 134
Korea, South see South Korea
Korean War (1950) 74, 75, 77, 79
Koslowski, R. 23 n.17
Kosovo 4, 19, 87, 92
Kratochwil, F. 2, 23, 24, 49, 117 n.26
Kreiger, P. 59, 74
Kremlin, Great Palace of 53–4, 114
Kubizek, A. 64
Kugler, J. 1, 47
Kull, S. 103
Kupchan, C. A. 49
Kupchan, G. 49
Kuwait 4, 36, 93, 106

Kymlicka, W. 42
La Rochefoucauld 11
Labrouste, H. 53
Lahwej, Y. 116
Lapid, Y. 24
Laroche, J. 4, 48
Larson, E. 103
Lascoumes, P. 52
Latvia 77, 81 n.21
Layne, C. 62
Le Corbusier 59, 67, 74
League of Nations 69, 70, 72, 84
Leahy, W. D. 75, 77
Leander, A. 2, 23
Lebanon 40
Lebow, R. N. 9, 39, 69, 79 n.19, 87, 88 n.2, 90, 91, 98, 99, 101, 106, 113, 116, 119, 120, 124
Lefebvre, R. 11
LeFranc, S. 89
Lenin, V. L. 33, 66, 74
Leviathan 15
Levinson, S. 91, 92
Levy, J. 48, 89
Lewis, W. H. 115, 123
Libya 4, 6, 21
  Pan Am Flight 103 and 21, 121, 125
  September 11th reaction 96, 121, 127
  US relations 6, 21–2, 28, 95, 97, 121–4, 125
  1986–2004 crisis 87, 88, 96, 114–16, 125
  policy of 'reassurance' and appeasement 121–4
  recognition through empathy 127
Lindemann, T. 23, 39, 132
Lindner, E. G. 12 n.1
Lindsay, J.-M. 101, 108, 109, 111
Lloyd Wright, F. 59, 67
Locarno, Treaty of (1925) 69, 70
Lockerbie Pan Am crash see Libya, Pan Am Flight 103
Long, W. J. 89
Longhorne, R. 52
Louis XIV 56, 57, 130
Louis XVIII 53
Lundestad, G. 58, 60
Luxembourg 22, 51

Luxenburg, R. 28
Lynn-Jones, S.-M. 88 n.2

Mackintosh, C. R. 67
Maier, C. E. 60
Mao, T. 39, 74
Marshall Plan (1947) 60, 77
Marti, I. M. 28
Martinez, L. 123
Maslow, A. 24
Matthews, F. P. 79
Mauss, M. 2, 11
May, E. 114, 118
McNamara, R. 118, 119
Mead, G. H. 2, 25
Mearsheimer, J. J. 1
Mein Kampf 64, 66
Melandri, P. 60
Melvin, J. 53, 59, 66
Mercer, J. 21, 29, 127
Metternich, K.W. von 54
Millner, B. 47 n.1
Milosevic, S. 28, 29, 33, 47, 94, 95, 130
Milza, P. 54, 69, 100, 104
Miscamble, W. D. 78
Mitterrand, F. 59
Mitzen, J. 25–6, 27
Molotov, V. 75, 78
Monnet, S. 70
Monnier, G. 53 n.5
Monroe Doctrine (1823) 63
Morelli, M. 53, 54
Morgenthau, H. 17, 33, 41, 47, 72
Morocco 63, 106
Mosse, G. L. 65
Mumford, L. 53 n.5
Munich Agreements (1938) 19 n.11, 72, 81, 87, 95
Münkler, H. 16
Mussolini, B. 65
mutually assured destruction (MAD) 48

Nagasaki 48, 79, 80, 129 n.52
Naples-Sicily 55
Napoleon, B. 3, 33, 52, 56, 130
Napoleon III 56, 130
Nash, J. 53

Nasser, G. A. 92, 96, 100, 104, 126, 132
nationalism 9, 32, 34, 36, 54, 64, 69, 73, 104
  see also identity, national
NATO 35, 58, 60, 63, 85, 131
Neilson, K. 71
Neumann, I. B. 27, 131
Nicaragua 62
Nicholas I 54
Nicholson, H. 52, 54 n.7, 68
Nidal, A. 121
nuclear weapons, use of 3, 48, 78, 79, 80, 100, 129 n.51, 130
  Cold War era and 78
  balance of power theory and 48
  Libya and 115, 122, 126
  US and 49, 130
  see also Iraq, WMD debate
Nye, G. 63
Nye, J. 51

O'Neill, P. 9, 108
OECD 48, 129
oil, war and 4, 28, 29, 97, 101
On War 15–16
Oren, M. 103
Organski, A. F. K. 1, 47
Osgood, C. E. 89, 90, 91
Osiander, A. 38
Ottoman Empire 54, 57, 80 n.20

Pakistan 36, 87, 115
Palais de Tuileries 53
Palestinians 28 n.27, 40, 100, 105, 132
Palmerston, Lord 62
Panama 61
Paris, Treaty of (1815) 55
Partnership for Peace (PfP) 85
Pax Americana 47
Pax Britannica 47
Peace of Augsburg 40
peace treaties, punitive 84
Peloponnesian War 15, 98
Perrin, D. 114, 121, 124
Petsch, J. 58
Philippines 121
  US War (1899) 61
Pinochet, A. 2

Pious, R. 113, 114, 116, 120, 125
Pitt, W. 57
Pizzorno, A. 2, 13, 129 n. 51
Pleshakov, C. 76
Poincaré, R. 63, 69, 71
Poirrier, P. 53 n.5
Poland 34, 38, 50, 55, 81 n.21
　Cold War period and 74–5, 78, 80
　Hitler's invasion of 37, 50, 65, 72, 73, 95
　Soviet attack (1920) 70
Politics Among Nations 33
Polity IV 58 n.9
Pompidou, G. 59
Poncet, A.-F. 72
Portugal 55
Posen, B. 19
Postyshev, P. 76
potlach 11
Potsdam Conference 18, 53, 63
Powell, C. 41, 101, 103, 108, 109, 110, 111, 127
power, exercise of 1, 5, 51
　hegemonic 45, 51–2, 55–6, 131
prestige 2, 10, 11, 16, 17, 18, 20, 43, 105, 113, 114, 126
　architectural styles and 54
　loss of 100, 133
　national identity and 18, 35
　war for 19, 43, 87, 129
Price, R. 22, 48
Principi di una scienza nuova 15
Prussia 16, 17, 53, 54, 55, 56, 57, 80, 82, 83
　architecture in 53
Pugin, A. W. 53

Rapallo, Treaty of (1922) 71
rational choice theory 14, 21, 22, 24, 34, 133
Razoux, P. 98, 99, 100, 101, 104, 105, 106, 107
Rebel Without a Cause 33
Reagan, R. 61, 115
Realpolitik 63, 73, 79
reciprocity, norm of 38
recognition, concept of 10, 17, 80
　constructivist approach 22–4, 90
'recognition, politics of' 6, 39, 63, 88, 90–1, 94, 128, 129, 132, 133, 134
　autonomy, confirmation of and 92, 94
　definition of 91
　dilemmas of 18
　dissuasion theory and 97
　effects of 95
　identities, respect for 92–3, 94
　new identities, construction of 90
　non-recognition and war 3, 5, 9, 10, 27–43, 83, 84, 127, 134
　'psycho-logics' and 12–14
　self-esteem and 91–2, 94
Reichel, P. 58
Remond, R. 69, 70
Renault, E. 25 n.20
Renouvin, P. 54–5, 56
Rice, C. 101, 102, 109, 110, 111, 112
Riefenstahl, L. 65
Ringmar, E. 9, 22, 33, 39
Risse, T. 35, 127
Risse-Kappen, T. 79 n.19
Ritter, G. 102
Roche, J.-J. 17 n.7
Rome 4
Rook, S. 72 n.13, n.14, 73 n.15
Roosevelt, F. D. 63, 75, 77
Rosecrance, R. N. 48
Rosen, S. P. 12 n.1, 19 n.11, 20, 116
Rothe, A. H. 16, 17 n.6
Ruggie, J.-G. 31
Ruloff, D. 52 n.4, 101
Rumsfeld, D. 101, 109, 110
Rusk, D. 120
Ruskin, J. 53
Russia 40, 47, 54, 55, 63, 85, 97, 134
　architectural styles in 53–4
　armed conflict and 80, 81, 82 83
　Austro-Hungarian Empire and 53–4, 57
　Chechen Wars 19
　Georgian War (2008) 4, 32, 96
　Ottoman Empire and 57
　Soviet transition 23, 85
　see also Soviet Union
Rwanda 12, 35–6

Sadat, A. 89, 100
Sadler, A. L. 67

Sartre, J.-P. 13
Saudi Arabia 28, 105, 106
Saurel, L. 69, 73
Saurette, P. 9, 19, 24, 103, 134 n.64
Sawicki, F. 11
Schelling, T. 21, 127
Schinkel, K. F. 53
Schmidt, H. 58
Schmitt, E.-E. 64
Schönbrunn Palace 53
Schroeder, P. 39, 40, 52, 56 n.8
Schumacher, T. L. 67
Schwippert, H. 58
security community 35
Seidl, E. 53 n.5, 59 n.10
self-esteem 2, 12, 13, 15, 16, 17, 19, 24, 25, 26, 50, 51, 78, 89, 90, 91, 128
  politics of recognition and 91–2
Serafty, S. 62, 63
Serbia 19, 29, 40, 132
Shapira, M. H. 99
Shirer, W. L. 65, 68
Sidney, V. 50
Sierra Leone 30
Singer, J. D. 29, 50 n.3
Small, R. 29, 50 n.3
Snyder, J. 20
social conflict, framework of 5
  recognition, quest for and 10, 13
  resolution of 13
  'symbolic interests', role of 14
Sorel, G. 13
Sorensen, T. 116, 117, 118
Sorokin, P. 52 n.4
South Korea 76, 78, 80
  see also Korean War (1950)
Soutou, G.-H. 60, 74 n.16
sovereignty, principle of 4, 37, 41, 94, 132
Soviet Union 23, 24, 29, 36, 39, 85
  Afghanistan and 35
  architecture 66, 74
  Cold War period 73, 74–5, 77, 114, 117–18
    messianic ideology and 74, 75–6
  détente of 1970's 48
  Eastern Europe and 31, 60, 77, 78
  interwar period 67, 70

  alliance against Bolshevism 70–1
  Marxist-Leninist ideology and 51
  cult of personality and 74
  nuclear weapons, use of 78
  US relations and 34, 63, 98
    see also Cold War period; Cuban Missile Crisis
  World War II and 31, 65
Spain 32, 55, 80
Speer, A. 50, 65–6, 67
Sprenger, P. W. 53
stability, international 5–6, 42, 47, 49, 51, 52, 54, 80–1, 85
Stahel, D. 72
Stalin, J. 32, 33, 34, 63, 66, 71, 74, 75, 77, 79, 80
  personality of 75–6
  cult surrounding 66, 74
Stein, J. 90, 91, 98, 113, 116, 119, 120, 124, 126
Steinberg, B. 33
Stewart, D. B. 67
stigmatisation 84, 90, 91, 123–4
  see also exclusion
Stoessinger, J. 65, 68, 72, 104
Strachan, H. 16
Streseman, G. 69, 70, 73
Suez Crisis (1956) 36, 74
Sweden 22
  Thirty Years War (1630) and 9, 22, 33
Switzerland 22

Tabory, E. 89
Tabouis, G. 67, 68
Taiwan 34, 78, 81, 94, 95, 96
Tajfel, H. 25
Taliban 2, 5, 36, 41, 48, 61, 85, 92, 109, 121
  see also Afghanistan
Tannenwald, N. 23, 48, 97, 129, 130
Taylor, A.-J. 73
Taylor, C. 6, 25 n.23
Taylor, J. -P. 64
Tenet, G. 101, 102, 110
Terray, E. 16
Theory of the Leisure Class 10
Thévenot, L. 2, 13, 15
Thies, J. 66

Thomas, H. 49
Thompson, T. 119
Thucydides 15, 98
Ting-Tooney, S. 125
Titanic, The 14
Tito, J. B. 76
Ton, A. 53
Touvaal, S. 26 n.24
trade 34, 48, 133
  free 68, 80, 85
  interdependency and war 48
Trafalgar Square 53
Triumph of Will, The 65
Troyanowki, O. 113
Truman, H. S. 59, 63, 74, 75, 77, 78
  Truman Doctrine (1947) 59, 73
Turkey 20, 59, 74, 76, 80, 81 n.22, 113, 114, 118, 120, 126
Turner, J. C. 24

United Kingdom see Great Britain
United Nations 74, 75, 78
  Iraq WMD and 101, 102
  Security Council 47, 84
United States
  Afghanistan and 30, 36
  architectural styles 59, 67, 74
  Berlin Crises (1948, 1961) 35
  CIA 101, 102, 110, 115
  Cold War and 60, 74, 79, 92, 93, 112, 117–20, 132, 196
  Cuban Missile Crisis 20, 60, 92, 98, 112, 119–20
  hegemonic power of 39, 47, 60, 129
  identity and 31, 35, 62–3
  interwar period 70
  Iraq War 4, 6, 19, 21, 27, 28, 36, 38, 40, 42, 97, 101–4, 108, 112, 124–5, 127
    see also Iraq, War (2003-)
  Libya and 6, 21–2, 28, 88, 95, 97, 114–16, 121–4
    Pam Am Lockerbie attack 124, 125
  Marshall Plan and 60
  military capability of 3, 79
  nuclear weapons, use and attitude to 49, 78, 79
  presidential autonomy 20

USSR, relations with 24, 63, 98
Vietnam War 4, 21, 74, 76
  see also Cold War Period; Cuban Missile Crisis; World Trade Centre, September 11th 2001
UNMOVIC 109
UNSCOM 101
USSR see Soviet Union

Vaïsse, J. 64, 84
van Crevald, M. 15
van der Rohe, M. 59, 73
van Evera, S. 50, 88, 97, 98
Veblen, T. 10–11
Venesson, P. 24 n.19, 72
Venezuela 62
Versailles, Palace of 53, 56, 65, 67
Versailles Treaty and system (1919–39) 5, 18, 28, 49, 64, 68, 69–70, 84, 131
Vico, G. 15
Vietnam 4, 21
Vietnam War 73, 75
violence 12, 14, 48, 50, 61, 131
  symbolic aspects of 128–9
vulnerability 88–90, 94, 95
  pacific states and 112–14

Waever, O. 22, 23
Waltz, K. 1, 47
war, theories of 97, 128–9
  liberal approaches to, 1, 2, 128, 130, 133
  rationalist 1, 2, 90
  realist 1, 2, 128, 129, 133
  utilitarian 87
  see also dignity; honour; identity, national; prestige; recognition, politics of
Weber, C. 2, 40, 68
Weber, M. 14, 68, 129 n.53
Weinberg, G. 72
Weinberger, C. 115
Welch, D. A. 37
Wellington, Duke of 54
Wendt, A. 2, 21, 23, 25, 26, 27, 31, 33, 36, 40, 49, 91, 93, 127, 131
Westminster, Palace of 53
'Westphalian Myth' 38

White House 59
Whystock, C. 89, 90
Wieseman, C. 67
Wieviorka, M. 2, 12, 36, 131
Wilhelm II 4
Wilson, W. 62, 72, 75, 85
  Wilsonianism 75
Winnicott, D. W. 25
Wohlforth, W. 49
Wolf, R. 9, 89, 134 n.64
Wolfowitz, P. 101, 109
Woodward, B. 112
World Trade Centre
  September 11th 2001 2, 3, 5, 18, 19,
    22, 23, 29 n.27, 30, 42, 93, 102,
    103
    Iraq/Libya reactions to 96, 103,
      108, 122, 125, 127, 128
World War I 28, 34, 62, 68, 97
  1918 armistice 68–9
  Sarajevo 1914 93, 96, 132
  US intervention 63
World War II 43, 47
  balance of power and 48
  Eastern Europe and 31, 34, 38
  Massada 126
  nuclear weapons, use of 48
  origins of 64, 71–2
  US response 60
    Bretton Woods 60
    identity and 31, 60
    Marshall Plan (1947) 60, 77
  see also interwar period (1919–
    1939)
Wright, F. L. 59, 67

Yalta Conference (1945) 18, 75
Yergin, D. 75, 76, 77, 78
Yetiv, S.-A. 87, 101, 111, 118
Young Plan (1929) 70
Yuen Foong Khong 87
Yugoslavia 26 n.24, 27, 65, 76

Zagare, F. 47
Zehfuss, M. 23
Zelikov, P. 87, 114, 116, 118
Zhdanov Doctrine 74
Zubok, V. 76

www.ingramcontent.com/pod-product-compliance
Lightning Source LLC
Chambersburg PA
CBHW061450300426
44114CB00014B/1914